S0-BXK-803

The Evolution of Presidential Polling

The Evolution of Presidential Polling is a book about presidential power and autonomy. Since FDR, virtually all presidents have employed private polls in some capacity. This book attempts to explain how presidential polling evolved from a rarely conducted secretive enterprise to a commonplace event that is now considered an integral part of the presidency. Professor Eisinger contends that because presidents do not trust institutions such as Congress, the media, and political parties – all of which also gauge public opinion – presidents opt to gain autonomy from these institutions by conducting private polls to be read and interpreted solely for themselves.

Robert M. Eisinger is Associate Professor of Political Science at Lewis & Clark College in Portland, Oregon. He is also the Political Analyst for KPAM (AM 860) in Portland.

The Evolution of Presidential Polling

ROBERT M. EISINGER
Lewis & Clark College

CAMBRIDGE
UNIVERSITY PRESS

JK
516
.E37
2003

.i 12348028

49225693

PUBLISHED BY THE PRESS SYNDICATE OF THE UNIVERSITY OF CAMBRIDGE
The Pitt Building, Trumpington Street, Cambridge, United Kingdom

CAMBRIDGE UNIVERSITY PRESS
The Edinburgh Building, Cambridge CB2 2RU, UK
40 West 20th Street, New York, NY 10011-4211, USA
477 Williamstown Road, Port Melbourne, VIC 3207, Australia
Ruiz de Alarcón 13, 28014 Madrid, Spain
Dock House, The Waterfront, Cape Town 8001, South Africa

http://www.cambridge.org

© Robert M. Eisinger 2003

This book is in copyright. Subject to statutory exception
and to the provisions of relevant collective licensing agreements,
no reproduction of any part may take place without
the written permission of Cambridge University Press.

First published 2003

Printed in the United States of America

Typeface Sabon 10/12 pt.   *System* LATEX [TB]

A catalog record for this book is available from the British Library.

Library of Congress Cataloging in Publication Data

Eisinger, Robert M. (Robert Martin), 1965–
The evolution of presidential polling / Robert M. Eisinger.
    p.   cm.
Includes bibliographical references and index.
ISBN 0-521-81680-7 – ISBN 0-521-01700-9 (pbk.)
1. Presidents – United States.   2. Executive power – United States.   3. Public
opinion – United States.   4. Public opinion polls.   I. Title.

JK516 .E37   2002
324–dc21   2002022283

ISBN 0 521 81680 7 hardback
ISBN 0 521 01700 9 paperback

Contents

List of Illustrations   *page* vi

Acknowledgments   vii

1   Seeking Autonomy: The Origins and Growth of Presidential
    Polling   1

2   Planting the Seeds of Presidential Polling   21

3   Checks and Imbalances: Congress and Presidential Polling   35

4   Dodging the Hill: Presidential Polling in the Post-Eisenhower
    Years   52

5   Take the Money and Poll: Parties and the Public Opinion
    Presidency   74

6   The Media Are Not the Messengers   105

7   Counting the People: The Evolution of Quantification and Its
    Effects on Presidential Polling   136

8   White House Polling in the Post-Watergate Era
    coauthored with Andrew Zahler   147

9   Presidential Polling in the Post-Reagan Era: Consequences and
    Implications of Presidential Polling   173

Bibliography   191

Index   209

List of Illustrations

Presidents Herbert Hoover and Franklin Delano Roosevelt *page* 44
Senator Hubert H. Humphrey and President John F. Kennedy 54
Harry O'Neill 70
Emil Hurja on the cover of *Time* magazine 82
President Lyndon B. Johnson and Oliver Quayle 91
President Richard Nixon and advisers 128
President Gerald Ford and advisers 149
President Jimmy Carter and Pat Caddell 158
President Ronald Reagan and Richard Wirthlin 165
President Bill Clinton and Stan Greenberg 180

Acknowledgments

In May of 1991, I had the privilege of eating breakfast with Hans Zeisel. Despite our difference in age, Zeisel and I had a few mutual friends, and after learning of my interest in writing about presidents and their private polls, he invited me over to his Hyde Park, Chicago, apartment, and listened to my ideas. When I told him that I had reservations about the accessibility of relevant data, Zeisel got angry. He upbraided me for my tentative nature and confidently said, "This is an important topic. Just do it." In many ways, this book is a culmination of Zeisel's "Just Do It" campaign. Having passed away in 1992, Zeisel cannot read this, but I hope that he and his friend Paul Lazarsfeld would have appreciated my attempt to study the evolution of presidents' private public opinion polls.

This book could not have been completed without many a friend and colleague, including Chris Achen, Scott Althaus, Don Balmer, Henry Brady, Jim Gimpel, Stan Greenberg, Mark Hansen, Mark O. Hatfield, Jeff Hayes, Diane Heith, Peter Jackson, Elaine Kamarck, Scott Keeter, Dan Kelley, Roger Larocca, David Moore, Chris Newkirk, Jim Norman, Elisabeth Noelle-Neumann, Harry O'Neill, Robert Shapiro, Robert Teeter, Kathryn Dunn Tenpas, Richard Wirthlin, Steve Wishod, and Dave Yaden. Lew Bateman at Cambridge University Press is a model editor; his candor and encouragement wonderfully complement each other. Anonymous reviewers provided outstanding advice and suggestions. All of these people have provided thoughtful criticisms and comments about some aspect of this work. I am especially indebted to Jeremy Brown, Andy Holder, and Andrew Zahler who served as tireless research assistants and editors, and to Susan Herbst for persistently encouraging me to pursue a historical analysis of presidential polling. The late David Greenstone served as an inspiration to me as well. His wit, passion for history, and love of teaching have made me appreciate doing political science in innumerable and immeasurable ways. Professors at Haverford College and the University of Chicago deserve special thanks for helping me think critically and write clearly. Archivists and librarians have aided me in ways too numerous to mention, and grants from Lewis & Clark College, the Arthur Vining Davis Foundation, the Goldsmith Grant from the John F. Kennedy School of Government at Harvard University, Zonis and Associates, the Rockefeller Archives Center, the George Bush, Gerald R. Ford, Dwight D. Eisenhower, Herbert Hoover, and Franklin D. Roosevelt presidential libraries further advanced completion of this project. I am grateful for all who assisted me and I apologize to those persons I mistakenly did not name.

Finally, I especially want to thank Norman Bradburn for his advice when I began this project. Norman sensed that I was easily distracted by current events, and so he suggested to me that I should try to minimize my digressions by writing down the theme of this project in one sentence; he then implored me to place the small sheet of paper in my wallet. Eventually, the question will become a part of you, he said, and you will never lose sight of the question you are trying to answer. This advice sounded too corny to do, but I did it anyway. As a graduate student, I frequently looked in my wallet, and saw nothing but that sentence. (I surely didn't see a lot of cash in there!) Bradburn's advice about focusing and writing clearly has made me a better scholar and teacher.

It is common to dedicate one's first book to one's family. I will proudly continue this tradition. My love and appreciation are extended to my father, mother, and sister. My father, who miraculously escaped Vienna in 1940, instilled in me a sense of direction and discipline. My mother fostered in me a sense of humor and compassion and a love of learning and teaching. My sister's insights and wit are unparalleled; she too possesses a sense of humor that keeps all troubles in perspective.

Presidential polling is a growing phenomenon in U.S. politics that deserves systematic analysis. With few exceptions, public opinion and presidency scholars have avoided attempting to explain how and why presidents use private polls. This reluctance to pursue such an endeavor is partly warranted; after all, studying the evolution of presidential polling requires an understanding of the qualitative and quantitative arenas of political science, a time commitment to accumulate and interpret historical documents, and an appreciation for weaving multiple interpretations about political institutions into a cohesive, theoretically engaging text. The room for error is great; some of the materials are not readily available, and many politicians are reluctant to discuss how they use polls. Yet the challenge to study the relationship between public opinion and democratic rule outweighs the possibility of criticisms (constructive or otherwise) by scholars, politicians, and journalists.

What role does public opinion play in democratic regimes? This question overwhelms us, for the answers tell us much about the politics in which we live, and the politics we seek to attain. Presidential polling, and political polling more generally, is now an endemic part of American politics, so much so that political scientists, journalists, and citizens take it for granted. How has presidential polling evolved and why? The answers to these questions lie in understanding and explaining the roots of how gauging public opinion has become a vital function of the presidency. Archival data are frequently messy and incomplete, and so what is presented here is not a crystal-clear photograph, but rather a colorful, carefully crafted sketch. In this regard, I hope that this book further stimulates a lively and spirited debate. As discussions continue to pervade the airwaves and newspapers about presidents and their polls, it is time that we begin to understand the courtship and eventual marriage between them.

Robert M. Eisinger
Portland, Oregon
May 2002

Seeking Autonomy

The Origins and Growth of Presidential Polling

> We have practically no systematic information about what goes on in the minds
> of public men as they ruminate about the weight to be given to public opinion
> in governmental decision.[1]

Since Franklin Delano Roosevelt, all presidents with the exception of Harry
Truman have privately polled citizens. Yet presidential polling remains a
puzzle. How have presidents used polls? What are the implications of presidential polling? How have polls become the predominant means by which
presidents gauge public opinion? This book attempts to answer these questions by conducting a comprehensive study of presidential polling from the
Hoover years to the present. I argue that the emergence and proliferation of
presidential polling stem from the tenuous relationships between the presidency and other institutions – specifically Congress, political parties, and
the media – that formally served as conduits of public opinion. Simply put,
presidents do not trust these institutions, and opt to poll privately rather than
rely on them as links to the American people.

President Nixon best exemplifies a president who distrusted these institutions and used polls to gain autonomy and power. According to one of
Nixon's advisers, President Nixon believed that "in order to reduce *federal*
power, it was first necessary to increase *presidential* power."[2] Nixon ad-
mits that he was determined to "knock heads together in order to get things

---

[1] V.O. Key, Jr., "Public Opinion and the Decay of Democracy," *Virginia Quarterly Review* 37
(Autumn 1961): 490.
[2] Joan Hoff, *Nixon Reconsidered*. New York: Basic Books, 1994, p. 67. Italics in original.
Nixon continued this line of thought, saying that "Bringing power to the White House [was
necessary] in order to dish it out." Ibid. For more on President Nixon's attempts to reorganize the executive branch, see Richard P. Nathan, *The Plot that Failed: Nixon and the
Administrative Presidency*. New York: Wiley, 1975.

done" in Congress. He recognized early in his presidency that resistance from Congress would be the norm rather than the exception.[3]

How did Nixon generate presidential power? In part, by using polls. He appointed his chief of staff, H.R. Haldeman, to "get in touch" with the average American.[4] Haldeman shared Nixon's view that the Democrat-controlled Congress was "an awkward and obnoxious obstacle, a hostile foreign power."[5] And so Haldeman read polls – voraciously – and denied others access to the poll data he was perusing. When Nixon aide Charles Colson asked to see an April 1971 poll about veterans, Haldeman denied the request, stating that "the President has ordered that no one is to see it."[6] Events inevitably shaped opinions about the president. Public opinion helped determine which events to highlight or downplay in the media and therefore public opinion had to be monitored.

Haldeman believed that poll data could be used as a means to advance the administration's legislative agenda. "The President was concerned as a result of the meeting with the Senators yesterday afternoon that we hadn't gotten the favorable poll data to them," Haldeman wrote.[7] Local polls showing support for President Nixon's policies were to be disseminated to enhance the president's popularity in order to ward off presidential challengers. Why? Because Haldeman and Nixon understood that poll data affected legislators' decisions.

Nixon's advisers did not want Congress to question how they were paying for polls and feared receiving negative attention if Congress learned about the president's extensive polling operation. The polls were his; they were none of Congress' business. Moreover, the polls had political overtones, and as a result, could not be paid for with governmental funds. So the White House resorted to outside funding, namely, the Republican National Committee (RNC) and private (sometimes secret) persons. When asked at one point if he could raise money to pay for some polls, Colson responded, "I would rather not because it is a drain from a more important use later and is a little bit dangerous."[8] In another instance, Haldeman informed Colson that he could not see a poll, adding that the paying for polls was aided by a secret

[3] Richard M. Nixon, *RN: The Memoirs of Richard Nixon, Vol. I*. New York: Warner Books, 1979, p. 414.

[4] H.R. Haldeman, *Haldeman Diaries*. CD-ROM (New York: Sony, 1994, January 29, 1969). Also see Lawrence R. Jacobs and Robert Y. Shapiro, "The Rise of Presidential Polling: The Nixon White House in Historical Perspective," *Public Opinion Quarterly* 59 (1995): 165.

[5] Rowland Evans, Jr., and Robert D. Novak, *Nixon in the White House: The Frustration of Power*. New York: Random House, 1971, p. 109.

[6] Richard Milhous Nixon Project at the National Archives [RMNP@NA], "ORC 4-28-30/71 Veterans Survey," Memorandum from Larry Higby to H.R. Haldeman (about Colson's request), May 4, 1971, Haldeman Files, Box 349.

[7] Ibid., Memorandum from Larry Higby to H.R. Haldeman, April 23, 1971, Box 334.

[8] Charles Colson, in Lawrence R. Jacobs and Robert Y. Shapiro, "The Rise of Presidential Polling: The Nixon White House in Historical Perspective," *Public Opinion Quarterly* 59

source. "And we can pay for it," reads a handwritten note by Haldeman, "the front man was in case we released it."[9]

Nixon's polls asked about a wide range of topics – the Vietnam War, whether J. Edgar Hoover should retire, and even if Nixon were responsible for the Watergate break-in. President Nixon read some of these polls and their accompanying analyses. In one memorandum, Nixon even criticized the question wording, claiming that alternative response options were more valuable. Haldeman's tight reins over access to poll data, and the secrecy, breadth, and depth of these polls all indicate how Nixon's polling operation was a critical part of his strategy to deal with Congress, the media, and both the Republican and Democratic parties.

THE EVOLUTION OF PRESIDENTIAL POLLING

Private presidential polling began during the Franklin Delano Roosevelt (FDR) administration, when Hadley Cantril, a Princeton University psychology professor and colleague of one of the founders of polling, secretly worked as an unpaid, unofficial public opinion advisor for the FDR White House. The polls that FDR received differ from the private polls of modern presidents in that FDR never hired Cantril or another public opinion expert as a private White House pollster. FDR welcomed the public opinion information offered by Cantril and expressed interest in receiving more. By utilizing private poll data, FDR did not abandon other forms of gauging public opinion, such as tabulating incoming White House mail, but Cantril's surveys for and advice to the FDR administration legitimized polls as viable political instruments for presidents to gauge public opinion.[10]

While President Truman did not employ polls, the Eisenhower administration did, albeit sparingly. Some of these polls, however, exacerbated tensions between the executive and legislative branches when Congress learned that the Eisenhower administration's State Department had secretly commissioned polls. A House Administration Committee investigation ensued, and hearings revealed that the two branches distrusted each other's interpretations of public opinion. One State Department official testified that opinions assessed by members of Congress did not comprise public opinion, but rather constituted "congressional opinion."[11] The House committee report

(1995): 171–172, citing RMNP@NA, Memorandum from Colson to Jack Gleason, April 18, 1970, Charles Colson Files, Box 100.

[9] RMNP@NA, "ORC 4-28-30/71 Veterans Survey," Memorandum from Larry Higby to H.R. Haldeman (about Colson's request), May 4, 1971, Haldeman Files, Box 349.

[10] Hadley Cantril, *The Human Dimension: Experiences in Policy Research.* New Brunswick, NJ: Rutgers University Press, 1967, p. 40; Gerard Lambert, *All Out of Step.* New York: Doubleday, 1956, pp. 266–279; Leila A. Sussman, "FDR and the White House Mail," *Public Opinion Quarterly* 20 (1956): 5–15.

[11] State Department Hearings, 85th Congress, H1612-1, June 21–July 11, 1957, 206–208.

concluded that the State Department's polling was illegal, and it served as a warning to the executive branch that Congress considered itself, not the executive branch, to be the official stethoscope of the nation's opinions. Additionally, the House report sent the executive branch a stern message about financing polls – do not use public monies for polling. The executive branch listened to Congress' covetous warning not to usurp its role as an interpreter of public opinion, but it did not quell presidents' yen for polling. What emerged was a process in which political parties, not the executive branch, paid for the president's private polls.

John F. Kennedy's use of polls began in late 1958, when Senator Kennedy was contemplating running for president. New Haven, Connecticut Mayor Dick Lee introduced Kennedy confidant Ted Sorensen to the pollster Lou Harris and Harris soon was hired as the senator's campaign pollster. Candidate and President Kennedy employed polls as a means to assess citizens' attitudes about character, personality, religion, and image. Kennedy's secretly funded polls served as indispensable tools to learn about what would sway the electorate, especially when other candidates did not have the financial resources to conduct polls.

With funding from the Democratic Party, President Johnson employed the polls of Oliver Quayle, a former assistant of Lou Harris. Like Harris' polls for JFK, President Johnson's polls were frequently comprised of local samples (that is, residents of a particular state, county, or congressional district, as compared to a national sample). In keeping with his predecessors Cantril and Harris, Quayle secretly sent his poll reports to senior White House officials, who attentively interpreted public opinion, both about the president's popularity and about particular policies. Johnson was an avid pollreader; when public opinion was measured, Johnson eagerly awaited poll analyses.

President Richard Nixon's polling operation was far more organized and comprehensive than his predecessors'. So concerned was Nixon that others not obtain some public opinion poll data, that he sanitized certain poll reports so the chairman of the Republican National Committee could not see certain poll questions and answers. Poll questions were also asked about the media and Vice President Spiro Agnew, without their knowledge. By this time, presidential polls had developed into an integral and independent function of the executive. Chief White House advisers believed that advancing the president's agenda required knowing the speed and direction of public opinion, without the assistance of one's party, Congress, or the media.

Foster Chanock, the assistant to President Ford's chief of staff, Richard Cheney, served as the official poll collector and interpreter for the Ford White House. Ford's poll data, like Nixon's, covered an array of policy and political arenas, and although Ford's term in office was brief, his use of polls was both extensive and well organized. President Carter's defeat of Gerald Ford catapulted Patrick Caddell to guru status as a surveyor of the public's mood, as Caddell became both a pollster and a de facto policy adviser. Caddell's successor, Richard Wirthlin, served as a key adviser and confidante to President Reagan. The business of presidential polling had become an accepted and legitimate institution in American politics. Presidents Bush and Clinton learned a lesson from the Reagan White House, and according to scholars, journalists, and former White House employees, private polls were also an integral part of their White House modus operandi.

This cursory synopsis underscores the extensive but understudied history of presidential polling. Although presidents' interest in public opinion is commonly perceived to stem from their wanting to know how popular they are, archival data show that presidential polling has often included a variety of questions about public attitudes, preferences, personalities, priorities, and policies, both foreign and domestic. This book explains how presidential polling evolved from a small and secretive enterprise to a large and secretive institution.

Presidential polls fulfill the desire by presidents to gauge public opinion autonomously and scientifically. Private polling begins with the premise that White House advisers value accurate, public opinion–related information. These advisers recognize that various political actors will disseminate public opinion information that does not necessarily advance presidents' electoral or legislative agendas. Members of Congress, interest groups, and media elites all have views that sometimes conflict with the presidents' agendas. As such, White House advisers do not trust these actors to provide them with public opinion data. Independent assessments of public opinion provide: 1) autonomy from various political institutions such as Congress, political parties, and the media; 2) a means to ensure that one's own gauges of public opinion are accurate; 3) a vehicle to execute electoral and legislative strategies; and 4) power that is derived from implementing these strategies. Presidents do not ask if polls reflect public opinion, or if polls positively affect their reelection campaigns or their passing of legislation. They believe that the answer is yes to both questions. Rather, given their belief that scientifically derived poll data are invaluable resources in these efforts, they ask, what poll data should they obtain?

CONGRESSIONAL INDIFFERENCE TOWARD POLLS
AND THE GROWTH OF THE PRESIDENCY

In *Congress: The Electoral Connection*, David Mayhew described congressional behavior to be largely oriented toward gaining reelection.[12] While presidents are constitutionally constrained by the 22nd Amendment to serve only two terms, Mayhew's logic also applies to presidents. Presidents' private

[12] David R. Mayhew, *Congress: The Electoral Connection*. New Haven, CT: Yale University Press, 1974.

polls are employed to advance the president's election strategies, despite federal laws prohibiting presidents from using White House resources for official campaign purposes. Today, the president receives valuable poll data that are paid for by his party; occasionally, he shares some of his data with party and congressional leaders.

Why don't presidents share all of their data and why don't members of Congress complain that the executive branch is exploiting them by using valuable party resources for secret polls? The answer may be found by recognizing how the rise of presidential polling is but one facet of the growth and power of presidential politics.[13] For example, presidents largely control who will become the chair of their party. John F. Kennedy, for example, chose his senate colleague Henry "Scoop" Jackson (D-WA) to be the Democratic National Committee (DNC) chair. Today, despite the recommendations by party leaders, the party chair remains by-and-large handpicked by the president, not congressional leaders.

The growth of the executive branch has also manifested itself in sheer numbers. The burgeoning presidency has made it difficult for members of Congress, regardless of party, to complain about the rise of the executive branch, in part because the legislative branch largely has condoned and sometimes even voted for it. With regard to polling, members of Congress now poll their constituents. Through their party caucuses, polling has burgeoned on the other end of Pennsylvania Avenue, as members of Congress receive poll-related information, some of which is similar to, albeit not identical to, the data that the president receives. If it is okay for us (members of Congress), then it must be okay for White House advisers. Congressional leaders recognize some degree of tension between the executive and legislative branches to be inevitable and, therefore, expect their president to horde sensitive, poll-related information, some of which may concern wooing or placating members of Congress. Today, perhaps more than ever, members of Congress think of these inherent tensions as normal, and therefore do not expect the White House advisers to share information obtained from presidential polls. By polling like presidents do, Congress has tacitly approved of presidential polling as a viable and necessary function of the executive branch.

It is worth noting that members of Congress were initially reluctant to use polls, and that their reluctance fortified the executive branch's view that Congress did not want or need to see private polls. Both Susan Herbst and Carl Hawver have confirmed the dearth of congressional polling in the 1930s, 40s, and 50s.[14] Interviews with U.S. senators and their chiefs of staff indicate

[13] See, for example, Arthur Schlesinger, *The Imperial Presidency*. Boston: Houghton Mifflin, 1989; and Stephen J. Wayne, *The Legislative Presidency*. New York: Harper & Row, 1978.

[14] Susan Herbst, *Numbered Voices: How Opinion Polling Has Shaped American Politics*. Chicago: University of Chicago Press, 1993; Carl Hawver, "The Congressman and His Public Opinion Poll," *Public Opinion Quarterly* 18 (1954): 123–129.

that tabulations of incoming phone calls, unsolicited mail, and conversations at town meetings continue to serve as an important means by which members of Congress evaluate and interpret constituents' opinions.[15] Herbst suggests that congressional reluctance toward using polls partly stems from the then popular belief, fostered by Walter Lippmann, that citizens' opinions were fickle, untrustworthy, and therefore not to be taken into account when making policy decisions. This view, combined with the fear that polls created a bandwagon effect, helps explain Congress' initial aversion to polls.[16]

While Congress dismissed polls as illegitimate and unnecessary, presidents gained access to poll-related resources and technology and made private polling part of their job. Financial and personnel resources helped presidents pay for and interpret polls. Money was frequently (and sometimes secretly) raised by presidents exclusively for private polling purposes and White House staffers were soon interpreting private surveys. Congress began to recognize that its function as the voice of the people was being replaced by opinion polling in 1957, when a House investigation about the financing of executive branch polling revealed that the executive branch attempted to pay for polls without congressional consent. This discovery of secret State Department polls reveals how the executive branch sought to measure public opinion independently of Congress, and it also signifies the degree to which the executive branch had been willing to use finances that were not originally intended for polling.

Now, members of Congress have armed themselves with their own polling apparatuses, and grievances about private presidential polling have been virtually eliminated. So long as presidents are not using congressionally appropriated monies to measure public opinion, and so long as the media, Congress, and political parties can also poll, objections to presidential private polling have disappeared. This cessation of complaining demonstrates that the issue at hand is not about which institution is the intended conduit for public opinion, but rather about power and autonomy. Presidents seek power and autonomy and use polls to acquire them.

Congress has condoned presidential polling, to an extent. Congress does not pay for White House polls and never has. Presidents such as Roosevelt benefited from polling information that was brought to their attention and financed by private funds. The public opinion research that Hadley Cantril

[15] Interview with Senator Charles Grassley (R-IA), August 2, 1994. Interview with Robert McDonald, Administrative Assistant to Senator John Danforth (R-MO), August 2, 1994. Conversation with Steven Solarz, former member of Congress (D-NY), November 15, 1994. Conversations with Jim Gimpel, former aide to Senator Dan Coats (R-IN), 1994–1998.
[16] Herbst, *Numbered Voices*, pp. 92–93. Also see Walter Lippmann, *Public Opinion*. New York: Free Press, 1965. See, for example, William Pierce, *Congressional Record*, 77th Congress, 1st session, 1941, Vol. 87; *The New York Times*, September 5, 1936, 14; *The New York Times*, November 6, 1936, 24, and November 11, 1936, IV, 8; and Herbst, ibid.

offered for FDR's perusal was conducted at Princeton University through the Office of Public Opinion Research (OPOR). OPOR had been funded by the Rockefeller Foundation to develop and refine the burgeoning field of survey research methods. Subsequently, much of Cantril's work was financed by retired businessman Gerard Lambert, including that which interested FDR. In 1957, an investigation of secret State Department polls initiated congressional concern about who paid for presidential polls, but after the investigation, many presidential polls were still paid for without full disclosure of their source. To this day, there are no memoranda detailing how President Kennedy's polls were financed; one memorandum from the Nixon Archives speaks of a "front man" to pay for polls. Secret funds from private individuals and political party resources available to the executive branch have enabled presidents to poll privately and in abundance. Despite laws prohibiting White House money from being spent on presidential polls, private polling continues to rise and party resources for presidential polling remain bountiful. While taxpayers do not pay for the polls, they do subsidize the salaries of the presidential advisers who interpret private poll data. This news is troubling to those who disdain polls. To historians and political scientists, however, such facts are puzzling, not because of any possible legal loopholes, but because the evolution of presidential polling has gone largely unexplained.

THE DECLINE OF POLITICAL PARTIES

According to James Caesar, the declining importance of political parties and the corresponding rise of presidential primaries have made presidential candidates' telegenic and communication skills essential components of the modern presidency.[17] Candidates without party leadership endorsements can become independent entrepreneurs who marshal interest groups to organize volunteers and raise money. "In the past," Thomas Patterson wrote in his book *Out of Order*, "the parties buffered the relationship between candidates and groups. Today, it is very difficult for candidates to ignore the demands of interest groups or to confine them to their proper place."[18] In his book, *The Party's Over*, David Broder shares this sentiment, arguing that the decline of parties as organizing devices for people and politics helps explain

[17] James Caesar, *Presidential Selection: Theory and Development*. Princeton, NJ: Princeton University Press, 1979, p. 310. Examples of works that discuss the decline in political parties include James I. Lengle, *Representation and Presidential Primaries: The Democratic Party in the Post-Reform Era*. Westport, CT: Greenwood Press, 1981; Nelson W. Polsby, *Consequences of Party Reform*. New York: Oxford University Press, 1983; Byron E. Shafer, *Bifurcated Politics: Evolution and Reform in the National Party Convention*. Cambridge, MA: Harvard University Press, 1988; and Martin P. Wattenberg, *The Decline of Political Parties 1952–1992*. Cambridge, MA: Harvard University Press, 1994.

[18] Thomas E. Patterson, *Out of Order*. New York: Vintage, 1994, p. 47.

a "systemic fragmentation" of American politics.[19] Marvin Kalb concurs by arguing that as parties no longer serve to distance presidential candidates from interest groups, the press has assumed the parties' former role as an "arbiter of American presidential politics – a position for which it is not prepared, emotionally, professionally, or constitutionally."[20]

Although much of the prevailing party decline literature alleges that changes in the presidential selection process in the late 1960s and early 1970s have affected the burgeoning of candidate entrepreneurship, the groundwork for presidential polling precedes the presidential selection and campaign finance reforms of this era. The presidential primary system enervated the role of political parties as the vehicles for political advertising, fund raising, and campaign strategizing. Presidential primaries and changes in campaign finance laws have diminished the influence of party bosses in choosing candidates and have encouraged presidential candidates and their campaigns to measure public opinion independently via private polls. The hiring of presidential pollsters, however, occurred before the McGovern-Fraser Commission ever met to discuss reforming the presidential selection process. Pollster Lou Harris, for example, played a prominent role in the 1960 presidential campaign of John Kennedy. A memorandum from the Kennedy archives reveals how the DNC asked to see Lou Harris' extensive polling for Senator (and presidential candidate) John F. Kennedy, suggesting that Harris' polls were commissioned without the Democratic Party's assistance. According to Larry Sabato, whereas party leaders once informed presidential candidates about voters' opinions and attitudes, pollsters now dispense the same information with a scientific legitimacy that party leaders never had.[21]

Here, another puzzle emerges. The McGovern-Fraser reforms exacerbated political polling by creating primaries that forced candidates to market themselves using various media, and to determine voter preferences quickly and accurately. However, the evolution of presidential polls precedes these reforms, suggesting once again that presidents' desire to seek autonomy from the media and political parties helps explain how pollsters have become key political advisers.

As presidential candidates use private polling as the primary source for measuring public opinion during their campaigns, they also adopt similar methods and organizations to interpret White House polls once they are elected. For example, after serving as the pollster for the Kennedy campaign, Lou Harris continued to poll for President Kennedy in a similar manner

---

[19] David S. Broder, *The Party's Over: The Failure of Politics in America*. New York: Harper & Row, 1972.
[20] Marvin Kalb, "Too Much Talk and Not Enough Action," *Washington Journalism Review* 14 (September 1992): 33.
[21] Larry J. Sabato, *The Rise of Political Consultants: New Ways of Winning Elections*. New York: Basic Books, 1981.

(that is, with minimal interference from JFK's advisers). A campaign strategist, Pat Caddell, becomes a key presidential adviser and pollster once Carter is elected. Party reforms, then, institutionalize the role of the presidential campaign pollster, as the pollster for the winning presidential candidate assumes the role as the chief interpreter of public opinion data in the White House. Presidents' pollsters have a great deal of autonomy; they largely determine what to ask, to whom, and how. By concentrating the flow of public opinion–related information in the hands of one person, alternative sources of public opinion information are discounted.

INTEREST GROUP PROPAGANDA IS NOT PUBLIC OPINION

Why don't presidents rely on interest groups to assess public opinion? While it is advantageous for interest groups to boast that the views they espouse are popular with a large public, no one believes that the tobacco lobby, for example, speaks for all citizens, smokers, and nonsmokers alike. Politicians know that interest groups advertise their views to be popular, because to do otherwise would be politically foolish. As a result, today's presidents know better than to rely on interest groups' assessments of public opinion as accurate and reliable. Rather, they realize that these appraisals are disseminated only if they benefit the interest group that provided the information.

In his seminal work on interest groups entitled *The Governmental Process: Political Interests and Public Opinion*, David Truman argued that interest groups seek to ascertain what public opinion is in order to control it:

Being almost inevitably minorities in the total population, organized interest groups must find some means of allying themselves with other groups and of mobilizing their 'fellow-travelers' if they hope to compete successfully for the attention and indulgence of other groups and of government institutions. The state of public opinion affects the limits to which such alliances can extend, and propaganda is a major means of mobilizing support and securing allies.[22]

To Truman, pressure groups gauge public opinion in order to build coalitions for gaining access to government officials. They seek to guide and control public opinion not by falsely claiming that they speak on behalf of all of the mass public, but rather by using propagandistic techniques to suggest that they speak on behalf of an influential group.[23]

[22] David B. Truman, *The Governmental Process: Political Interests and Public Opinion.* New York: Knopf, pp. 213–214.
[23] Additional readings about the functions of interest groups include V.O. Key, Jr., *Politics, Parties and Pressure Groups, Fourth Edition.* New York: Crowell, 1958; Harmon Zeigler, *Interest Groups in American Society.* Englewood Cliffs, NJ: Prentice-Hall, 1964; and James Q. Wilson, *Political Organizations.* New York: Basic Books, 1973.

Many politicians envision interest groups as Truman did – as vehicles for promulgating propaganda. New York State former Governor Herbert Lehman expressed the idea that interest groups inaccurately measured public opinion in a 1938 issue of *Public Opinion Quarterly*, then a new journal devoted to the study of public opinion research. To Governor Lehman, the power of pressure groups had to be fought vigilantly by informed citizens:

We must be vigilant lest we accept as public opinion that which is only propaganda of well-organized pressure groups. The power of pressure groups is very great. They are frequently actuated by selfish interests. Their power can be curbed only through the force of the informed opinion of the public. Failure of public opinion to assert itself against pressure groups is due largely to public indifference, to the partisan attitude of political parties, and to the apparent unwillingness or inability of our agencies of news-dissemination to place before the public as a whole the information on which sound judgments can be reached. These agencies frequently are unwilling to accept the unpopularity that comes through opposition to pressure groups.[24]

For Lehman, it is the duty of an informed public to fight the insidious partisan forces of interest groups. The demands of pressure groups on legislators are so intense that when citizens fail to counter pressure groups' propaganda, "bad government and legislation" ensues that is "in no way representative of the wishes of the people as a whole."[25]

Not surprisingly, political pollsters have served as articulate spokespeople for their profession, claiming that their surveys have been an antidote against pressure group propaganda. In one of the first issues of *Public Opinion Quarterly*, Archibald Crossley defended political polls as the only vehicle that could battle the pressure groups' campaign to shape and define public opinion:

If the polls are legislated out of existence, it will be chiefly because an open revelation of public opinion is not desired. *The New York Times* fears that legislators will be swayed by polls because they desire to be reelected. 'The American form of Government is not really built to function successfully on this pattern. It is properly assumed that our representative will think for themselves.' In other words, it might be dangerous if our lawmakers know the desires of their constituents . . . The desire for reelection being what it is, the argument may have some weight. But the choice is not between *vox populi* and silence. The real choice is between reliable information and unreliable information supplied by pressure groups.[26]

If legislators do not use polls, they will continue to measure public opinion inaccurately by relying on pressure groups' distorted assessments of

---

[24] Herbert H. Lehman, "A Public Opinion Sustaining Democracy," *Public Opinion Quarterly*, Special Supplement, Public Opinion in a Democracy (January 1938): 6.
[25] Ibid., 7.
[26] Archibald Crossley, "Straw Polls in 1936," *Public Opinion Quarterly* 1 (1937): 34.

constituents' opinions. Scientifically designed polls are apolitical, presumably, and therefore aid legislators in accurately assessing citizens' attitudes. As will be shown in forthcoming chapters, Crossley's notion of the apolitical poll has been replaced by a highly politicized enterprise. Pollsters are now routinely divided into partisan camps; poll questions often ask about political adversaries.

Two years after Crossley wrote his article in the *Public Opinion Quarterly*, George Gallup and Saul Forbes Rae enriched and advanced his arguments in *The Pulse of Democracy: The Public-Opinion Poll and How It Works*. Political polling, they claimed, would not only restore and enhance representative democracy, but was necessary for representative democracy to flourish. Dismissing interest groups' stated positions and citizens' vocal expressions as cacophony, Gallup and Rae claimed that legislators needed polls to locate public opinion. "[I]n this day of pressure groups, telegram barrages, and other forms of protest," Gallup and Rae said, "the worried legislator must cope with such techniques and therefore may mistakenly identify all the noise and clamor with public opinion."[27] They concluded with an elegant testimony for political polling:

That is why public-opinion polls are important today. Instead of being attempts to sabotage representative government, kidnap the members of Congress, and substitute the taxi driver for the expert in politics, as some critics insist, public-opinion research is a necessary and valuable aid to truly representative government. The continuous studies of public opinion will merely *supplement*, not destroy, the work of representatives. What is evident here is that representatives will be better able to represent if they have an accurate measure of the wishes, aspirations, and needs of different groups within the general public, rather than the kind of distorted picture sent them by telegram enthusiasts and overzealous pressure groups who claim to speak for all the people, but actually speak only for themselves. Public-opinion surveys will provide legislators with a new instrument for estimating trends of opinion, and minimize the chances of their being fooled by clamoring minorities. For the alternative to these surveys, it must be remembered, is not a perfect and still silence in which the Ideal Legislators and the Perfect Expert can commune on desirable policies. It is the real world of competing pressures, vociferous demonstrations, and the stale cries of party politics.[28]

---

[27] George Gallup and Saul Forbes Rae, *The Pulse of Democracy: The Public-Opinion Poll and How It Works*. New York: Simon and Schuster, 1940, p. 25.

[28] Ibid., 266–267. Over a decade after Lehman, Crossley, and Gallup and Rae's warnings about the dangers of pressure groups as inaccurate reflectors of the public mood, William Albig admonished scholars who ignored the role of pressure groups as representing the public at large. "Large publics preserve the sentiments of the culture in which they live, and frequently exhibit the ability to choose with reasonable accuracy among the proposals which come from leaders and from that stratum of the general public which is more broadly knowledgeable. The contribution of sentiment and of restraint on the excesses of special interest groups must not be underestimated." William Albig, "Two Decades of Opinion Study: 1936–1956," *Public Opinion Quarterly* 21 (1956): 22.

To Gallup and Rae, polls were the most viable antidote to the biased portrait of American opinions presented by pressure groups that misrepresent the direction and intensity of public opinion. Presidents have accepted and extended Gallup and Rae's claims; private polls are more accurate than alternative assessments of public opinion, and have provided autonomy from those political institutions wishing to derail presidential objectives.

PRIVATE SECTOR MARKET RESEARCH, THE *LITERARY DIGEST* DEBACLE AND THE "SCIENCE" OF POLLING

Government did not take the lead in creating modern surveys. Rather, polls were already developed somewhat in the private sector. Market researchers in the 1920s played a key role in advancing methods of assessing citizens' attitudes. The pioneers of polling began their careers as market researchers. Elmo Roper and Archibald Crossley both note how the private sector initiated the use of market research.[29] In what reads like an oral history of his trade, Crossley recalls touring New York City advertising agencies, and finding both Batten, Barton, Durstine, and Osborn (later known as BBD&O), and the Curtis Publishing Company, as having active "research" departments. These and other research departments primarily, but not entirely, dealt with monitoring media usage for their clients. Who, for example, listened to the radio? What advertisements might appeal to these listeners, and what commercials were broadcast on certain radio stations? The modern public opinion poll's roots lie in the private sector's attempts to market products for consumers.

Eventually and not surprisingly, primitive polling methods were sometimes deemed inaccurate. Straw polls, man-in-the-street polls, and mail-in polls were replaced by advances made by George Gallup, who used randomization and quota sampling to discern opinions from a large public without asking questions to each member of that public. If, for example, Gallup knew that sixty percent of a given region was comprised of Catholics, Gallup sought to approximate the proportion of Catholics in the sample of that region. When other pollsters used alternative methods, Gallup was quick to denounce them as unscientific and inaccurate.

Arguably the most infamous inaccuracies emanated from the 1936 *Literary Digest* poll, which used lists of telephone and car owners and its own magazine subscribers as instruments from which to generate a poll sample. The *Digest* poll showed Republican Alf Landon defeating President Roosevelt. Gallup proclaimed the *Literary Digest* poll a disaster before the election as he simultaneously promoted his more scientific polling methods.

[29] Archibald M. Crossley, "Early Days of Public Opinion Research," *Public Opinion Quarterly* 21 (1957): 159–164; and Elmo Roper, "The Client over the Years," *Public Opinion Quarterly* 21 (1957): 28–32.

Although George Gallup is widely regarded as the first person to discredit the unscientific methods of the *Literary Digest* poll, detailed criticisms of the *Digest* poll were published in 1933 by Robert C. Brooks in a book entitled *Political Parties and Electoral Problems*. Brooks, then a professor of political science at Swarthmore College, noted how the volume of responses to the *Digest*'s straw polls miserably failed in predicting the voting outcomes at the state level.

[I]ndeed the Digest poll gave Hoover these states [Massachusetts and Rhode Island] by a two to one vote whereas Smith carried both of them by scant margins. Examination of the forecasts for both 1924 and 1928 shows that in each of these years the Digest overestimated the Republican and underestimated the Democratic percentage of the vote actually cast in the November elections... Of course it is easy to explain away minor errors in forecasting as due to a last minute shift on the part of voters but the discrepancies just noted are much too large to be airily disposed of in that manner.[30]

Brooks and Gallup's objections to the *Digest* polls were based on their faulty sampling and poor predictive powers – in short, they thought the *Digest* was using poor social scientific methods. Gallup recalled that criticisms of his poll methods prevailed long after he correctly predicted FDR's 1936 victory over Landon:

Some claimed we were not measuring public opinion; public opinion could not be measured, at least not by the procedures we were using. Others said we were not scientific. Still others thought we were an evil force which might lead the country straight to Hell – or to direct democracy, which they regarded as equally terrifying. An Oregon congressman introduced a bill to curb polls. The fight was on.[31]

Gallup astutely recognized that criticism of polls was based on the belief that their samples and questions were more an art than a science, in part because some of his public opinion colleagues thought of their work as part art and part science. The title of Stanley Payne's seminal work, *The Art of Asking Questions*, written in 1951, exemplified how questionnaire design was considered, in part, a nonscientific enterprise. Political legitimacy therefore demanded that science be the backbone of survey research. But failures endured, especially after Gallup's 1948 polls incorrectly predicted that Thomas Dewey would defeat President Harry Truman. Nonetheless, Gallup informed the public not only that his polls were viable and reliable, but that they were scientifically rigorous.

I would like to bring up another long-standing complaint of those of us who conduct polls. This is the use of quotation marks around the word 'scientific' when applied to

---

[30] Robert C. Brooks, *Political Parties and Electoral Problems, Third Edition*. New York: Harper & Brothers, 1933, p. 352.
[31] George Gallup, "The Changing Climate for Public Opinion Research," *Public Opinion Quarterly* 21 (1957): 24.

polls. If our work is not scientific, then no one in the field of social science, and few of those in the natural sciences, have a right to use the word. Even under the most rigid interpretation of the word I venture to say that our work fully qualifies.[32]

Gallup insisted that polls were beneficial to democracy in part because of their scientific nature. Whether or not polling enhanced democracy was part of the political and intellectual discourse. In 1946, John C. Ranney questioned if polling methods improved democracy simply because polls were ostensibly more accurate than alternative methods. He argued that politicians need not concern themselves with the public's opinions, but rather the opinions of "specific organizations and individuals inside his constituency, especially the political machines and the organized pressure groups." Unless polls targeted these groups as respondents, polls were asking questions to the wrong people.[33]

After the debacle of 1948, the publication of Lindsay Rogers' *The Pollsters* further magnified public criticisms of opinion polls. Rogers criticized pollsters' pollyannaish views of the merits of polling. Perhaps there are times, he said, when the government should ignore polls and not listen to the pulse of the public. If this were so, then pollsters and their supporters should address the normative question of when democratic leaders should ignore public opinion. Additionally, Rogers argued that the amorphous, multidimensional nature of public opinion prevented it from being measured by polls with accuracy. He cited Carroll Mason Sparrow, who argued that "frantic efforts to imitate physics" in the social sciences were doomed to fail. "Instead of being willing to take their subject-matter for what it is, these mensurationists try to deck it out in misfit garments."[34]

Despite the scientific underpinnings of public opinion research advanced by Gallup, Roper, Crossley, and others, some studies of public opinion in the 1940s retained a qualitative flavor. Only in the 1950s, Bernard Berelson argued, did the field of public opinion become "a part of science," that was "technical and quantitative, atheoretical, segmented, and particularized, specialized and institutionalized, 'modernized' and 'group-ized' – in short, as a characteristic behavioral science, Americanized."[35] As polls gained scientific

---

[32] Ibid., 26.

[33] John C. Ranney, "Do Polls Serve Democracy?," *Public Opinion Quarterly* 10 (1946): 352.

[34] Carroll Mason Sparrow, "Measurement and Social Science." In *Voyages and Cargoes, University of Virginia Studies, Vol. III*. Richmond: Dietz Press, Charlottesville, University of Virginia, 1947, p. 176.

[35] Bernard Berelson, "The Study of Public Opinion." In *The State of the Social Sciences*, edited by Leonard D. White. Chicago: University of Chicago Press, 1956, pp. 304–305. Berelson continues his discussion by delineating the development of public opinion as a scientific field. "For if there was one factor that influenced the shift from 1930 to 1955 more than any other, it was surely the 'invention' and development of a method – the sample survey" (ibid., 309). He concludes on a less sanguine note by noting that although the methods of measuring and sampling have improved, it was in the theoretical vein that the scientific field of public

and academic legitimacy, their usage increased – by presidents and others. Presidents' pollsters today serve as unofficial public relations consultants, and do so with scientific techniques that fortify their roles as technical gurus who have the secrets of politics at their fingertips. Senior White House advisers entrust these presidential pollsters to interpret the data for the president, largely because they command a more thorough understanding of the statistical techniques and polling technology that are being used. In this regard, the evolution of presidential polling is explained by the rise of social science methods. Forthcoming chapters will delineate how presidential pollsters use these methods, and in doing so, serve key roles in guiding and interpreting presidential agendas.

THE SIMULTANEOUS INSTITUTIONALIZATION OF PRESIDENTIAL PRESS RELATIONS AND PROPAGANDA

Techniques of advancing presidential public relations complement the birth of modern polling methods. Political scientist Elmer Cornwell contends that the presidential press conference served as an important bridge between the chief executive and the citizenry by popularizing the presidency. President Wilson introduced biweekly press conferences, and after President Harding's unexpected death, President Calvin Coolidge used press conferences to connect with an American public that had not elected him. According to Cornwell, Coolidge realized how the press, especially the radio medium, could be used to create personalized news:

The usual and ordinary man is not the source of very much news. But the [press] boys have been very kind and considerate to me, and where there has been any discrepancy, they have filled it in and glossed it over, and they have manufactured some.[36]

Coolidge constantly met with the members of the media because he knew that they would fill in media vacuums with stories about his presidency. Coolidge rarely declined an opportunity to pose for pictures or to chat with the press, allowing them to join him on his vacations away from Washington, D.C. On April 14, 1917, President Wilson transformed this relationship by establishing the Committee on Public Information (CPI). Chaired by George Creel, a loyal Wilson supporter and former journalist, the Creel Committee as it later became known, was "a major factor underlying this growing tendency to see the Federal Government personified in Presidential terms."[37] The Creel Committee's function was to educate the citizenry about World

opinion research yearned for improvement. Also see Harold D. Lasswell, "The Impact of Public Opinion Research On Our Society," *Public Opinion Quarterly* 21 (1957): 33–38.
[36] Elmer E. Cornwell, Jr., "Coolidge and Presidential Leadership," *Public Opinion Quarterly* 21 (1957): 271.
[37] Elmer E. Cornwell, Jr., "Wilson, Creel, and the Presidency," *Public Opinion Quarterly* 23 (1959): 189.

War I, but ultimately it became an institutional vehicle through which government policies were propagandized and identified as stemming from the presidency. "[N]ever before had the Presidency been so consistently held up as prime focus of public attention, and never before had a course of national policy been so completely identified with a President."[38]

A consequence of the CPI was a constant focus and attention on the president. "It is certainly true that neither Creel nor Wilson himself planned to use the publicity machinery which was elaborated under the Committee for Wilson's personal aggrandizement," writes Cornwell. "[I]t is equally certain that Creel himself, worshipful follower of Wilson that he was, did visualize the President as personifying the war and its meaning... Clearly Creel was the President's unconscious publicity agent (if such a thing is possible), if not his conscious propagandist."[39] Creel and President Wilson were hardly oblivious to the potential consequences of the CPI. By promoting the president as a font of leadership and policy direction, Wilson and Creel began the process of institutionalizing managed press relations and presidential propaganda. As Presidents Coolidge and Wilson mastered how to promote themselves, so too the private sector developed ways to champion their products. The public relations industry blossomed soon after the turn of the century, and did so in part by explicitly employing strategies in which politics and marketing cleverly intersected.

Edward Bernays envisioned propaganda as a positive weapon in shaping and leading public opinion. "The function of a statesman is to express the will of the people in the way of a scientist," wrote Bernays (citing George Bernard Shaw) in his now famous 1928 book entitled *Propaganda*.[40] For Bernays, the failure to promote oneself foolishly disadvantaged the politician or corporation because they could be conquered by more articulate, vocal opponents who advanced their self-interest. Bernays believed that mass communication emanated from leaders who successfully manipulated public opinion until their views were regurgitated or resonated by the public:

No serious sociologist any longer believes that the voice of the people expresses any divine or specially wise and lofty idea. The voice of the people expresses the mind of the people, and that mind is made up for it by the group leaders in whom it believes and by those persons who understand the manipulation of public opinion. It is composed of inherited prejudices and symbols and clichés and verbal formulas supplied to them by leaders.[41]

Party leaders who sought to discredit opposing views appreciated Bernays' view that politicians should manipulate public opinion. During the 1920s,

---

[38] Ibid., 196–197.
[39] Ibid., 197.
[40] Edward L. Bernays, *Propaganda*. New York: Liveright, 1928, p. 112.
[41] Ibid., 92.

both the Republican National Committee (RNC) and the Democratic National Committee (DNC) established propaganda outfits that largely consisted of writing canned newspaper editorials.[42] The Democrats, having lost the presidency in 1928 to Herbert Hoover, hired Charles Michelson, a former Washington bureau chief of the *New York World*, to discredit Hoover and simultaneously exalt Democratic party ideas.

It has been his [Michelson's] pleasant task to minimize every Hoover asset and magnify his liabilities. He takes his little mistakes and makes them big. He is out to obscure every Hoover virtue and achievement and turn an exaggerated light upon all his personal-political shortcomings, missteps, and mishaps... If there is a way to widen the breach between Mr. Hoover and leaders of his party in the House and Senate, the gimlet-eyed Michelson will find the way and do as fine a piece of widening as any one can. To sum up, the whole aim and idea of Mr. Michelson's employment is to put Mr. Hoover 'in bad' with the American people.[43]

As the first professional party spin doctor, Michelson disseminated problems about President Hoover in order to manipulate public opinion to look favorably on the Democratic party. By finding and distributing negative information about Hoover, Michelson succeeded in annoying President Hoover and the Republican Party. In the process, Michelson altered the role of the party promoter; in order to combat future Michelsons, the presidency now demanded a professional who could successfully sway public opinion.

Although Hoover found Michelson to be a nuisance, Hoover appreciated Bernays' views about propaganda and public opinion. Hoover invited Bernays to the White House, and perhaps more importantly, took solace in believing that mobilized public opinion could and should rectify wrongs. Mankind's proclivity to legislate needed to be tempered by public opinion, which could respond to society's ills only if a reasoned public were armed with the "facts" to attain the right answer and a well-equipped leader who would marshal that information.

The most dangerous animal in the United States is the man with an emotion and a desire to pass a new law. He is prolific with drama and the headlines... The greatest antidote for him is to set him upon a committee with a dozen people whose appetite is for facts. The greatest catastrophe that could come to our country is that administration policies or legislation or voluntary movements shall be encouraged or enacted upon the basis of emotion, not upon facts or reason.[44]

In October of 1929, Hoover had already begun to create a massive ad hoc committee designed specifically to gather facts about American society. President Hoover wanted to ascertain "all possible practicable means by which the Government might inspire, promote, or guide both public

---

[42] Frank R. Kent, "Charley Michelson," *Scribners* 88 (1930): 291.
[43] Ibid., 293.
[44] Ibid., 189–190.

and private thought," and considered a comprehensive, scholarly study of American society to be "of the highest public as well as scientific value."[45] On December 19, 1929, President Hoover formally announced the Research Committee on Social Trends (known as the President's Research Committee [PRC]), which was designed to "direct an extensive survey into the significant social changes in our national life over recent years."[46] Hoover's decision to commission social scientists to conduct a survey of recent social trends was manifested by his belief that temporary commissions were "one of the sound processes for the search, production, and distribution of truth."[47] The PRC perfectly suited Hoover's faith in empiricism and reasoned public opinion as key factors in solving social problems.

Hoover's advisers trusted science and "facts." Before the PRC had been formally charged, an October 21, 1929 Report on the President's Committee (unsigned, but probably written by University of Chicago Sociology Professor William Ogburn, who corresponded frequently with Hoover's Administrative Assistant, E. French Strother) described the project as yielding "fruition in scientific papers, in committee and governmental action, or in other books."[48] The purpose of the committee was not just to assess societal trends, but also to "render government more scientific" by serving as a vehicle for Hoover's future domestic policy agenda.[49] Ogburn argued about the scientific nature of the PRC report, so much so that he wrote a "Prefatory Note" of the report's introduction stating that "if any contributor had departed from scientific method in their [sic] chapter, they were giving their own opinions, not presenting facts."[50]

To Hoover, systematically amassing facts to solve social problems constituted strong presidential leadership.[51] The PRC ultimately created *The Recent Social Trends in the United States*, a 1,536-page treatise that contained

[45] 22 October 1929, Box 3, Herbert C. Hoover Archives [HCHA].

[46] Herbert Hoover, *The State Papers and Other Public Writings of Herbert Hoover*, edited by William Starr Myers. Garden City, NY: Doubleday, Duran & Co., 1934, p. 193.

[47] Hoover, to Dr. William O. Thompson, January 12, 1930, *Public Papers of the Presidents of the United States, Herbert Hoover*. Washington, DC, 1976, p. 17.

[48] "Committee on Recent Social Trends – Correspondence 1929," Strother Papers, Box 3, HCHA.

[49] Martin Bulmer, "The Methodology of Early Social Indicator Research: William Fielding Ogburn and 'Recent Social Trends', 1933," *Social Indicators Research* 13 (1983): 110; Barry D. Karl, "Presidential Planning and Social Science Research: Mr. Hoover's Experts," *Perspectives in American History* 3 (1969): 364–371; Gene M. Lyons, *The Uneasy Partnership: Social Science and the Federal Government in the Twentieth Century*. New York: Russell Sage, 1969, pp. 46–49.

[50] President's Research Committee on Social Trends, *Recent Social Trends in the United States*. New York, McGraw Hill, 1933, pp. xciii–xcv.

[51] Martin L. Fausold, *The Presidency of Herbert C. Hoover*. Lawrence: University of Kansas Press, 1985, p. 60; Clyde P. Weed, *The Nemesis of Reform: The Republican Party during the New Deal*. New York: Columbia University Press, 1994, pp. 16–17.

unprecedented quantities of data about American society and legitimized
social science methods as a means for presidents to gauge public opinion.
Hoover's loss to FDR, however, effectively killed the project's implementation and neither the Hoover nor FDR administration employed the *Recent Social Trends* data. Nonetheless, presidential public relations had been
meshed with surveying the American social landscape; social science research
techniques had gained a rightful foothold in the White House.

CONCLUSION

Jean Converse notes that as early as 1908, the United States Department of
Agriculture (USDA) had accumulated questionnaires concerning farm families, but during Woodrow Wilson's presidential tenure, the surveys were
burned as useless.[52] By 1939, Rensis Likert had left New York University and
a job directing research for a life insurance institute to work for the USDA,
where he coordinated research about sampling and attitude measurement
for what later became the Division of Program Surveys. The development
of survey research at the USDA, however, does not appear to have aided the
emergence of polling in the presidential arena, as evidenced by the absence
of memoranda from Likert or others at the Division of Program Surveys to
White House advisers, or even to Hadley Cantril, the man who eventually
became Franklin Roosevelt's de facto White House public opinion adviser.

The evolution of presidential polling is an interesting puzzle precisely because it cannot be explained simply by the advent of statistical innovations or
the emergence of questionnaire use in the executive branch. Rather, this book
attempts to argue that the trajectory of presidential polling has been shaped
because presidents have sought autonomy – from Congress, from political
parties, and from the media. The dynamic and oftentimes strained relations
with Congress, the declining importance of political parties, the initial use of
polls as tools for private sector market research, the *Literary Digest* debacle,
the response in 1948 by academicians to thwart future errors in polling, and
the explosion of presidential press relations collectively created a political
environment in which presidential polling could eventually prosper beyond
anyone's expectations. Chapter 2 proceeds to discuss the theories underlying
presidential polling and why so many scholars, journalists, and students of
American politics are so interested in this topic.

---

[52] Jean M. Converse, *Survey Research in the United States: Roots and Emergence 1890–1960*.
Berkeley: University of California Press, 1987, p. 27, citing Clayton S. Ellsworth, "Theodore
Roosevelt's Country Life Commission," *Agricultural History* 34 (1960): 155–172.

2

Planting the Seeds of Presidential Polling

> Of all the heresies afloat in modern democracy, none is greater, more steeped
> in intellectual confusion, and potentially more destructive of proper govern-
> mental function than that which declares the legitimacy of government to be
> directly proportional to its roots in public opinion or, more accurately, in what
> the daily polls and surveys assure us is public opinion.[1]

PRESIDENTIAL POLLING AND ITS IMPLICATIONS
FOR DEMOCRATIC RULE

Presidential polling has shaped and transformed American politics in ways
unthinkable a century ago. Today, citizens and politicians alike routinely
criticize polls, even as they regularly read them. Our fascination with public
opinion is evidenced by the ubiquity of polls in politics, yet it remains unclear
whether or not democracy has been enhanced because of the proliferation
of polls. The view that public opinion is vital for democratic rule is all the
more revealing as one studies public opinion since the advent of the modern
public opinion poll. Public opinion has retained a prominent role in American
politics, in part because polls – the instruments most commonly used to
assess the public's opinions – have become an essential part of the politician's
tool kit. The interplay between politics and public opinion is so intertwined
into the fabric of governmental decision making, that one cannot imagine
a politician who dismisses or ignores citizens' views. American politicians,
whether they be elected or appointed, legislators or executives, assume that
the people's voice will be heard, and as such, they listen attentively.

Before the nineteenth century, mass opinion was not identified via polls,
but instead was measured by a variety of nonscientific measures, including
reading newspapers and their editorials, and listening to constituents who

[1] Robert Nisbet, "Public Opinion Versus Popular Opinion," *The Public Interest* 41 (1975):
166.

attended town meetings and wrote letters.[2] American founding fathers feared public opinion and created institutional obstacles, such as indirect elections of senators and the electoral college, to prevent it from exercising too much political power. Alexander Hamilton wrote, "The voice of the people has been said to be the voice of God. And however generally this maxim has been quoted and believed, it is not true in fact. The people are turbulent and changing; they seldom judge or determine right."[3] James Bryce cited an unnamed writer as describing the founders' conception of public opinion as "aggressive, revolutionary, unreasoning, passionate, futile, and a breeder of mob violence."[4]

Alexis de Tocqueville also had a less than sanguine view of how public opinion shaped the American psyche. He feared that if the government were too responsive to public opinion, the citizenry would become complacent and not question the state, even when it had overextended its authority.[5] The pioneer of the modern poll, George Gallup, envisioned polls as integral instruments for democracy by their ability to open windows that previously were either tinted or completely closed shut by the biases of pressure groups.[6] Similarly, Harwood Childs thought polls would, "bring public opinion into the open and thereby make governmental bodies more responsive to that opinion."[7] Whereas decisionmakers once relied on crude instruments to assess citizens' views, polls provide politicians with frequent and scientifically assessed barometers of public opinion.

More recently, Benjamin Ginsberg has argued that political elites employ polls to anticipate disruptive or threatening conduct by the masses. He claims that public opinion polling has stunted democratic development because it has controlled and constrained political discourse. By employing polls, political elites ascertain who is unhappy and simultaneously domesticate and pacify citizens who otherwise would express their opinions via spontaneous, voluntary means such as rioting or protesting.[8] By reading public opinion poll data, citizens are pacified because "polls elicit, organize, and publicize

---

[2] For a detailed analysis of nonpolling methods that have been used to measure public opinion in America, see Susan Herbst, *Numbered Voices*, and, also by Herbst, *Politics at the Margins*. New York: Cambridge University Press, 1994.

[3] Alexander Hamilton, June 18, 1787 speech. In *Selected Writings and Speeches of Alexander Hamilton*, edited by Morton J. Frisch. Washington, DC: American Enterprise Institute, 1985, p. 108.

[4] James Bryce, *The American Commonwealth, Volume II*. London: Macmillan, 1981, p. 229.

[5] Alexis de Tocqueville, *Democracy in America*, edited by J.P. Mayer. New York: Perennial Library, 1988, pp. 435–436.

[6] George Gallup and Saul Forbes Rae, *The Pulse of Democracy: The Public-Opinion Poll and How It Works*. New York: Simon and Schuster, 1940.

[7] Harwood Childs, *Public Opinion: Nature, Formation, and Role*. Princeton, NJ: Van Nostrand, 1965, 84.

[8] Benjamin Ginsberg, *The Captive Public: How Mass Opinion Promotes State Power*. New York: Basic Books, 1986.

opinion without requiring any action on the part of the opinion-holder."[9] A similar argument is advanced by Christopher Hitchens, who in 1992 wrote an article that rebuked politicians for using polls. Hitchens contends that polls create false choices for respondents and enable politicians to allege that they are responding to citizens' concerns. "Polls are developed only when they might prove *useful* – that is, helpful to the powers that be in their quest to maintain their position and influence."[10]

Archival data show that Ginsberg and Hitchens are wrong. Polls, particularly presidential polls, are political tools that enhance presidential power. They are not, however, employed to suppress citizens, but rather are used because alternative means of gauging public opinion are not politically feasible. White House polling now predominates American politics because of presidents' desire to assess public opinion independent of parties, media, and Congress. Tensions between presidents and the press, Congress and party leaders (that is, those political institutions that also measure public opinion) endure, so much so that presidential polling remains largely a private and secret enterprise, indicating that the inner circle of presidential advisers who interpret poll data consider poll-related information to be a valuable commodity not to be shared with others. Ginsberg's thesis, while provocative, is not supported by the archival data.

The presidential polls that are the focus of this book are confidentially administered, suggesting that many polls may not be the democratizing agents that Childs and Gallup thought they would be. While private polls make presidents more responsive to public opinion in the sense that they are evaluating it, polls do not engender full disclosure and openness as to what is being asked and why. Archival data show that presidents' polls are conducted secretly, often including a variety of questions about policies and issue priorities, including some policies not yet defined or codified. The poll questions themselves raise a number of queries (addressed in several insightful articles by Lawrence Jacobs and Robert Shapiro) about how polls may be used to shape and implement presidential legislative and electoral agendas.[11]

This book attempts to shed light on a presidential polling literature that is often descriptive but incomplete, in part because presidents and their polls are frequently studied in isolation of one another, as if the presidency were to shut down and reopen after a quadrennial November election.[12] There is

---

[9] Ibid., 278–279, 284.

[10] Christopher Hitchens, "Voting in the Passive Voice: What Polling Has Done to American Democracy," *Harper's* (April 1992): 39. Italics in original. Additional criticisms suggesting that public opinion polls debilitate democracy can be found in John S. Dryzek, "The Mismeasure of Political Man," *Journal of Politics* 50 (1988): 705–725.

[11] See Bibliography.

[12] See, for example, Elmer E. Cornwell, Jr., *Presidential Leadership of Public Opinion*. Bloomington: Indiana University Press, 1965; Charles W. Roll and Albert H. Cantril,

little analysis of how presidential polling affects the functions of the presidency or the executive branch's relationship with other political institutions. The failure to connect presidential polling to contemporary theories about the presidency, public opinion, representation, leadership, elections, or mass communications has created a disjointed literature, in which one learns about a particular administration's polls, but little about how it relates either in a theoretical or practical sense to changes in the American political system or representative democracy.

One exception can be found in works by Lawrence Jacobs. Jacobs' 1992 article, "The Recoil Effect," posited that the evolution of polling by the executive branch resulted in both a responsiveness and a manipulation of public opinion.[13] In short, rather than describe the presidency as functioning as a follower or a leader, Jacobs astutely noted that it has done both. This book advances this thesis further by documenting how the evolution of presidential polling occurred. By identifying the origins and development of these polls, I will attempt to show that presidential polling does not occur in a political vacuum. Rather, presidents seek to measure public opinion because of political constraints imposed on them by other institutions that also assess the views of the public.

This book seeks to complement scholarship written by Steven Shull, Sidney Milkis, George Edwards, Jeffrey Cohen, Ken Collier, Stephen Wayne, and Jeffery Tulis. Their works discuss how various elements of the presidency have grown and have become institutionalized.[14] Cohen and Collier in particular analyze how presidents seek to gain direct, unmediated access to public opinion. Similarly, this book substantiates Tulis' work on the rhetorical presidency. Tulis argues that modern presidents (post-Wilson) have sought to gain power by appealing to the public. Tulis contends that demagoguery has become part of the modern presidency. Tulis adds that changes in the mass

Polls: Their Use and Misuse in Politics. New York: Basic Books, 1972; Richard W. Steele, "The Pulse of the People: Franklin D. Roosevelt and the Gauging of American Public Opinion," *Journal of Contemporary History* 9 (1974): 195–216; David Gergen and William Schambra, "Pollsters and Polling," *Wilson Quarterly* 3 (1979): 61–72; Michael Barone, "The Power of the Presidents' Pollsters," *Public Opinion* 11 (September/October 1988): 2–5; Seymour Sudman, "The Presidents and the Polls," *Public Opinion Quarterly* 46 (1982): 301–310; Richard S. Beal and Ronald H. Hinckley, "Presidential Decision Making and Opinion Polls," *Annals of the American Academy of the Political and Social Sciences* 472 (1984): 72–84; Bruce E. Altschuler, *LBJ and the Polls.* Gainesville: University of Florida Press, 1990; and Charles C. Euchner, "Public Support and Opinion," *The Presidents and the Public.* Washington, DC: CQ Press, 1990, 75–90.

13 Lawrence R. Jacobs, "The Recoil Effect: Public Opinion and Policymaking in the United States and Britain," *Comparative Politics* 24 (January 1992): 199–217.

14 Steven A. Shull, ed., *Presidential Policymaking: An End-of-Century Assessment.* Armonk, NY: M.E. Sharpe, 1999; Stephen J. Wayne, *The Legislative Presidency.* New York: Harper & Row, 1978.

media and the decline of political parties do not fully explain the plebiscitary evolution of the presidency:

> [Nineteenth-century] presidents could have made speeches that looked very similar to those made today, but they did not. They spoke and acted very differently than they could have done within the limits of available technology. The differences between nineteenth- and twentieth-century political rhetoric do not depend upon the development of the modern mass media, though contemporary presidential rhetoric is certainly reinforced by requirements of modern television. Rather, the differences depend essentially upon the very phenomena that they reveal – the changing conceptions of leadership and the place of these conceptions in our political order.[15]

Tulis' argument is compelling, for it suggests that modern presidents envision leadership as the ability to address and appeal to a public audience. There is ample evidence that presidents realize that engaging the American people is no easy task; it requires actively seeking the views of the people. As will be shown in forthcoming chapters, presidents satisfy their yen for public opinion by conducting polls.

TENSIONS BETWEEN AND AMONG POLITICAL INSTITUTIONS

Presidential polls – both their evolution and consequences – arise from and are shaped by tensions (institutional, personal, and theoretical) between the presidency and Congress, political parties and the media. Presidents do not trust these institutions to provide them with unbiased versions of public opinion, and it is advantageous for the president to gauge public opinion independently of these institutions. As tensions with Congress, parties, and the media pushed presidents to poll, the vast array of intellectual and financial resources available to chief executives pulled them to perform this function that previously had been performed by these institutions.

Congress

Not surprisingly, a significant portion of the presidency literature discusses how the functions of the presidency relate to Congress, for the Constitution inhibits presidents from executing many of their duties without congressional approval. Richard Neustadt, author of the classic *Presidential Power*, argues that the president is constitutionally and institutionally constrained from excessively exerting its powers over the legislature and the judiciary. "The Constitutional Convention of 1787 is supposed to have created a government of 'separated powers,'" writes Neustadt. "It did nothing of the sort.

---

[15] Jeffrey K. Tulis, *The Rhetorical Presidency*. Princeton, NJ: Princeton University Press, 1987, p. 16.

Rather, it created a government of separated institutions *sharing* powers."[16]
Presidential effectiveness is a by-product of the president's ability to persuade
others that he has power over other groups and institutions. This process
requires that presidents constantly assess their power in order to determine
how and when to use it.

Theodore Lowi and James McGregor Burns claim that presidential power
may generate an antagonistic relationship between the president and other
political institutions. "Since the president's only real power was 'the power
to persuade,'" Lowi writes, "he [the president] had to manipulate each of
his constituencies in order to use each for the manipulation of the other."[17]
Burns articulates a similar theme, contending that the president must employ "transactional leadership," which Burns defines as "the ability to use
resources available to him in order to overcome systemic or institutional
obstacles in his way."[18]

If power is defined as a power to persuade, then one should expect presidents to seek information about public opinion in order to ascertain how to
persuade others and to learn if their persuasion techniques are effective. Perhaps the most elegant theory that connects public opinion, the presidency,
and Congress is advanced in Samuel Kernell's 1986 work *Going Public*.
Kernell asserts that modern presidents attempt to achieve their legislative
objectives by "going public." The going public strategy entails presenting
issues and policies directly to the American people so they will contact their
congressional representatives and encourage them to support the president's
policies. This strategy of taking one's case directly to the people, according
to Kernell, has replaced the traditional method of forging winning coalitions
in Congress.[19]

According to the going public thesis, embedded in presidential attempts to
shape and move public opinion is the belief that presidential popularity will
entice and allure citizens who will then sway members of Congress to support particular presidential programs. As Jon Hurwitz notes, "The desired
outcome of going public, from the executive's perspective, is that individuals can be mobilized to contact their representatives and encourage them

[16] Richard E. Neustadt, *Presidential Power and the Modern Presidents: The Politics of Leadership from Roosevelt to Reagan*. New York: The Free Press, 1990, p. 29. Italics in original.
Charles Jones tweaks this thesis, stating that such a relationship may better be described as
separated institutions competing for shared power. See Charles O. Jones, *The Presidency in
a Separated System*. Washington, DC: Brookings Institution, 1994, p. 16.

[17] Theodore J. Lowi, *The Personal President: Power Invested, Promise Unfulfilled*. Ithaca, NY:
Cornell University Press, 1985, p. 10.

[18] James MacGregor Burns, *Leadership*. New York: Harper & Row, 1978, pp. 19–20.

[19] Samuel Kernell, *Going Public: New Strategies of Presidential Leadership*. Washington, DC:
CQ Press, 1986. Also see Jon Hurwitz, "Presidential Leadership and Public Followership." In
Manipulating Public Opinion: Essays on Public Opinion as a Dependent Variable, edited by
Michael Margolis and Gary A. Mauser. Pacific Grove, CA: Brooks/Cole, 1989, pp. 222–249.

to support the administration's position."[20] The going public theory further advances why presidents have a reason to assess public opinion without any assistance from members of Congress. As public opinion analyses by members of Congress may reflect the biases of that member or her constituents, presidential polls empower presidents to seek public support without relying on members of Congress who may wish to derail presidential initiatives.

Presidential advisers' perception that going public is an effective strategy suggests that the relationship between Congress and the presidency can be episodically strained if not contentious. Mark Peterson notes that these theories are rooted in the notion that the executive and legislative branches are "inherently confrontational, driven by contradictory and often irreconcilable interests, perspectives, and goals . . ."[21] Charles Jones disagrees, arguing that the "separated system" among branches of government is not confrontational or antagonistic by definition, but he concedes that going public has debilitated presidential-congressional relations by increasing presidential masquerading and by decreasing traditional bargaining arrangements by large political institutions. Jones describes below how going public detrimentally affects the possibility for friendship between the branches:

What is of particular interest here is Kernell's argument that 'going public violates' and threatens 'to displace' bargaining. Instead of 'benefits for compliance,' the strategy of going public 'imposes costs for noncompliance.' It also involves 'public posturing' and may undermine 'the legitimacy of other politicians.' Kernell seems not to like this development, and yet he acknowledges that the president has a strong incentive to go public because of important changes that have occurred in Washington politics. 'Individualized pluralism' (a sort of atomized politics) has replaced 'institutionalized pluralism' (characterized by bargaining among large coalitions). As Washington comes to depend on looser, more individualistic political relations, presidents searching for strategies that work will increasingly go public.[22]

The politics of institutions have been replaced by the politics of individuals. Whereas in the past, presidents sought to work together with congressional leaders, today's presidents obviate traditional strategies, and instead opt to

---

[20] Hurwitz, "Presidential Leadership and Public Followership," p. 225.
[21] Mark A. Peterson, *Legislating Together: The White House and Capitol Hill from Eisenhower to Reagan*. Cambridge, MA: Harvard University Press, 1990, pp. 3–4. Additional works that analyze the contentious relationships between the presidency and the legislative branch include James MacGregor Burns, *The Deadlock of Democracy: Four-Party Politics in America*. Englewood Cliffs, NJ: Prentice Hall, 1963; Edward S. Corwin, *The President: Office and Powers, Fourth Edition*. New York: New York University Press, 1957; Thomas E. Cronin, *The State of the Presidency, Second Edition*. Boston: Little Brown, 1980; Stephen A. Shull, *Presidential-Congressional Relations: Policy and Time Approaches*. Ann Arbor: University of Michigan Press, 1997; James A. Thurber, ed., *Rivals for Power: Presidential-Congressional Relations*. Washington, DC: CQ Press, 1996; and Steven A. Shull and Thomas C. Shaw, *Explaining Congressional-Presidential Relations*. Albany, NY: SUNY Press, 1999.
[22] Jones, *The Presidency in a Separated System*, p. 122, citing Kernell, *Going Public*, pp. 1, 98.

market themselves with less help from parties or Congress. Boosting popularity (and implicitly, assessing what their popularity is), they think, will win legislative votes.

Presidential advisers think going public works, but going public can be costly, especially if members of Congress respond to presidents' going public by entrenching their positions, fostering more conflict between the branches. "If...going public solidifies positions and reduces the flexibility required for effective bargaining at the margins," writes Peterson, "then specialized public strategies may well generate more coalitional conflict."[23] Peterson also claims that going public enervates presidential power because it does not necessarily win votes in Congress, but instead results in a constant focus on the presidency – "put[ting] the president – and presidential weakness and failures – in a continual spotlight, on a national stage."[24]

Neustadt, Jones, and Peterson all agree that there is some degree of tension between the presidency and Congress. This friction with Congress, I argue, not only affects how presidential power is amassed and fortified, but it provides a reason why presidents opt to use private polls. While presidents sometimes "legislate together" in tandem with Congress, to use Peterson's phrase, presidents frequently envision themselves as competing with Congress, the media, and sometimes their own party. In this sense, presidents' private polls provide a direct, unmediated relationship between the president and the public – a relationship that presidents consider vitally important for advancing their respective agendas.[25]

The evolution of presidential polling reveals that Kernell probably understated his original argument. The executive branch is not content envisioning itself as a coequal partner with the legislative branch, but rather attempts to usurp the function of monitoring public opinion that previously has been administered by Congress, the media, and political parties. Rather than rely on Congress for these assessments of public opinion, presidents' private polls serve as the instruments through which presidents receive information about citizens' attitudes and opinions.

Political Parties

The evolution of presidential polling can also be traced to tensions between presidents and their political party. A. Lawrence Lowell noted in his 1913 classic *Public Opinion and Popular Government* that government's

---

[23] Peterson, *Legislating Together*, p. 279.

[24] Ibid., 139. For criticisms of going public's effectiveness, see Peterson, *Legislating Together*, and Jon R. Bond and Richard Fleisher, *The President in the Legislative Arena*. Chicago, University of Chicago Press, 1990.

[25] Lowi, *The Personal President*, pp. 115–117. For further analysis of the tandems institutions perspective, see Charles M. Cameron, *Veto Bargaining: Presidents and the Politics of Negative Power*. New York: Cambridge University Press, 2000.

expansion, technological improvements, and the modernization of society created demands for information about public attitudes in a democracy.[26] Ascertaining public opinion could be a daunting task, but Lowell thought that political parties were a natural conduit between the citizenry and the elected officials because they acted as "agencies whereby public attention is brought to a focus on certain questions that must be decided. They have become instruments for carrying on popular government by concentrating opinion . . . In short, their service in politics is largely advertisement and brokerage."[27]

Parties bridged public opinion and politicians, but Lowell believed that parties "falsified" public opinion by subduing extreme points of view so as not to alienate their centrist core supporters.[28] Rather than broadcast extreme positions that are frequently vocalized by activists, Lowell believed that parties tempered ideological immoderation and discounted extremists' vocalizations of the public mood.[29]

Lowell's thesis doesn't jibe with today's post-Watergate political parties. Presidential primaries bring out ideological extremists, not centrists. A preponderance of party volunteers, activists, and individual financial contributors lean toward the ideological extremes.[30] However Lowell rightly suggests that parties are not unbiased filters of the public mood. They are partisan organizations that make political decisions. Rather than think of parties as a natural conduit between the people and politics, it is possible that presidents envision them as political institutions that have an agenda of their own.

In *The President and the Parties,* Sidney Milkis posits that the growth of the executive branch largely stems from FDR's strategy to circumvent the Democratic Party.[31] Rather than rely on the sometimes hostile media and his own Democratic Party, FDR used independent, social scientific assessments of public opinion to bypass parties and the media. Beginning in 1940, Hadley Cantril offered polling-based insights to the president. It is

---

[26] A. Lawrence Lowell, *Public Opinion and Popular Government.* New York: Longmans Green, 1926, p. 49.

[27] Ibid., 66.

[28] Ibid., 88. Additional discussion about the role of parties as distorters of representativeness can be found in Marjan Brezovšek, "Changing Attitudes Towards Political Representation," *Javnost, The Public* 4 (1997): 105–118. For a discussion about the multiple functions of parties, see Maurice Duverger, *Political Parties: Their Organization and Activity in the Modern State.* Translated by Barbara and Robert North. London: Meuthen & Co., 1961; Samuel J. Eldersfeld, *Political Parties: A Behavioral Analysis.* Chicago: Rand McNally, 1964; and Robert Michels, *Political Parties: A Sociological Study of the Oligarchical Tendencies of Modern Democracy,* translated by Eden and Cedar Paul. New York: Free Press, 1968.

[29] Ibid., 94.

[30] See, for example, Paul S. Herrnson, *Playing Hardball: Campaigning for the U.S. Congress.* Upper Saddle River, NJ: Prentice Hall, 2001, p. 50.

[31] Sidney M. Milkis, *The President and the Parties: The Transformation of the American Party System Since the New Deal.* New York: Oxford University Press, 1993.

possible that FDR intentionally expanded the role of government in order to usurp functions (for example, shaping public opinion, job creation) previously administered by the Democratic Party and by the media, some of whose publishers thought of FDR as a socialist dictator. By appropriating the functions of the party and the press, FDR's analysis of poll data helped him to exercise this circumvention as it simultaneously aided him in marketing his policies. The evolution of presidential polling, therefore, additionally stems from the desire by presidents to seek autonomy from political parties.

The Media

The interconnected histories of political parties and the media as conduits of public opinion are best summarized in Michael Schudson's *Discovering the News: A Social History of American Newspapers*. Schudson documents how many newspapers were once arms of state and local political parties. The party-newspaper connection meant that many citizens did not read newspapers for independent assessments of public opinion, but rather as texts with political undertones. The notion of media objectivity, argues Schudson, is a post–New Deal phenomenon.[32] Newspapers proudly wore their partisan stripes, and it was considered the legitimate function of a partisan newspaper to criticize politicians on ideological grounds. Political scientist James David Barber, for example, cites numerous examples of political attacks in newspapers against FDR; readers were not outraged by the anti-FDR comments in large part because the readers were partisans who chose to read partisan, anti-FDR tracts in their favorite newspaper.[33]

The advent of the modern social survey precipitated new functions of the executive branch, including its ability to gauge public opinion independent of the media. Although private presidential polling began with Franklin Delano Roosevelt, FDR was not the first president who thought of the media as an inaccurate and untrustworthy barometer of public opinion. Woodrow Wilson, who was a political scientist before becoming governor of New Jersey and later president of the United States, wrote in *Constitutional Government in the United States* that newspapers were inaccurate reflectors of the public will because "the chief newspapers were . . . owned by special interests" and

---

[32] Michael Schudson, *Discovering the News: A Social History of American Newspapers*. New York: Basic Books, 1978. Also see Richard Hofstadter, *The Idea of the Party System*. Berkeley: University of California Press, 1969; Frederic Hudson, *Journalism in the United States*. New York: Harper & Brothers, 1972; and Thomas C. Leonard, *News For All: America's Coming-of-Age with the Press*. New York: Oxford University Press, 1995.

[33] James David Barber, *The Pulse of Politics: Electing Presidents in the Media Age*. New Brunswick, NJ: Transaction Publishers, 1992.

did not represent the "general opinion of the communities in which they are printed."[34]

In *The American Commonwealth*, James Bryce believed that although the print media contained "more domestic political intelligence" than most of their European counterparts, American newspaper readers did not follow blindly what their favorite newspapers wrote.[35] Bryce surmised that one of the reasons why American citizens may not believe all of what they read in the newspaper is because newspapers used crude measures to identify public opinion. If, for example, it was printed that a prominent judge or doctor were to have voted for a party or candidate, he became a de facto gauge of public opinion. Bryce sensed that some political elites, therefore, sought the media attention they were receiving:

[T]he leading citizen himself, when he has a fact on which to comment, or a set of views to communicate, sends for the reporter, who is only too glad to attend...All these devices serve to help the men of eminence to impress their ideas on the public, while they show that there is a part of the public which desires such guidance.[36]

For Bryce, newspapers were the primary means by which people determined what public opinion was, even though newspapers' methods of measuring public opinion were erratically and dubiously constructed by media-savvy, politically interested elites. If it were possible to assess accurately the public attitudes at all times, Bryce believed that "the sway of public opinion would have become more complete, more continuous, than it is in those European countries which, like France, Italy, and England, look chiefly to parliaments as exponents of national sentiment... 'Rule of public opinion,' might be most properly applied, for public opinion would not only reign but govern."[37] Instead, citizens and politicians relied on newspapers as inaccurate gauges of opinion because there were no polls to serve as an impartial alternative. Presidential polls make Bryce sound prophetic. Rather than rely on the media's distorted views of the people, presidents could gauge public opinion autonomously; it is now the norm for presidents to govern with the aid of private polling.

CONCLUSION

With the advent of polls, presidents have found the political instrument that provides them with autonomy, accuracy, and power. As will be shown in subsequent chapters, archival data demonstrate that presidents' repeated use of private polls has been a means to gauge public opinion independently and

[34] Woodrow Wilson, *Constitutional Government in the United States*. New York: Columbia University Press, 1908, p. 102.
[35] Bryce, *The American Commonwealth*. pp. 233, 234.
[36] Ibid., 236–237.
[37] Ibid., 220–221.

autonomously. Although there is no "smoking gun" memorandum explicitly stating that surveys are a scientifically derived political panacea to combat the untrustworthy alternative sources of public opinion data, White House advisers think of polls – especially their secret polls – as scientific, trustworthy, and as public opinion. Chapters 3 through 6 will show in great detail the institutionalization of presidential polling as evidenced by the existence of, increased sophistication of, and greater belief in private polling as the most accurate and valid means of assessing public opinion.

The remainder of this book proceeds as follows:

Chapters 3 through 6 look at various institutions that can and have attempted to gauge public opinion. Chapters 3 and 4 examine presidents' reluctance to employ members of Congress as a means to gauge public opinion. I will show that the antagonistic relationship between the executive and legislative branches as it specifically relates to measuring public opinion explains why presidents employ private polls. Quarrels between the two branches about public opinion reached their zenith in congressional hearings about private polls conducted for the State Department. In short, tensions between presidents and Congress helped cultivate presidential opinion polling.

Chapter 5 investigates the relationship between presidential polls and political parties. Even before the advent of modern polling, presidents' relationships with party leaders were periodically tense, so much so that presidents desired to seek public opinion–related information that was independent of party leaders. President Hoover preferred to rely on newspaper editorials than commentary from party bosses, and toward the end of his term, attempted to use academics to survey the political landscape using the latest methods employed in the universities. Journal articles, archival data from presidential libraries, and interviews with various elected officials and scholars will be used to explain how and why presidents poll independently of parties.

Chapter 6 evaluates the problems that presidents encounter when using the media to amass and interpret the opinions of the electorate. Presidents, I argue, do not trust the media as a public opinion conduit between themselves and the public in large part because many segments of the media were and are highly politicized. Given the option of using confidential, tailor-made, scientific polls, or comments in letters to the editor, or commentary by partisan editors and columnists, presidents have chosen to employ the former choice, in large part because the latter method is wrought with political biases.

Chapter 7 provides a brief history of how quantification of public opinion has been employed in the public sector. I argue that alternative explanations for the rise in presidential polling – namely, how availability of resources and technology by presidents – did not drive their decision to use polls. Rather, by showing how quantification of public opinion precedes the modern presidency, I attempt to show that autonomy, not technology, better explains the evolution of presidential polling. Chapter 8 looks at presidential polls of the post-Watergate era, particularly the polling conducted by Robert Teeter, Pat Caddell, and Richard Wirthlin for Presidents Ford, Carter, and Reagan. These polls indicate that the post-Watergate presidency continued to gauge public opinion largely independent of Congress, the media, and political parties, and that private polls were vehicles to secure more autonomy for the presidency. By the end of the 1980s, the White House pollster became more than a trusted adviser to presidents and their senior advisers; they became a critical part of the presidency.

Chapter 9 looks at the polling of Presidents Bush and Clinton and concludes with an eye to the future. While the archival data are limited or nonexistent, limited information suggests that the Clinton presidency in particular managed to intertwine public opinion analysis with advancing their communication strategies. The current trajectory of presidential polling, I conclude, is not likely to wane, but rather continue to proliferate.[38] Chief executives' private polling has empowered them to act like quasi-representatives. As polls (and focus groups) replace parties as conduits of public opinion information, parties have become financial subsidizers of presidential polls, mitigating the concern that presidential polling is an illegitimate enterprise, and in this regard, party decline has aided in institutionalizing the role of the president's pollster as the White House's chief interpreter of public opinion data. White House advisers entrust the president's pollster to interpret the poll data, legitimizing the president's pollster as an integral player in shaping the president's image and marketing his policies and campaign.

Presidential polling is inextricably stitched into today's political fabric. Some people think that presidents who follow poll results will be more likely to promote popular programs instead of unpopular policies that may better serve the national interest. Perhaps presidents should eschew polls and instead represent the national interest as Edmund Burke suggested by minimizing the role of public opinion in decision making.[39] An alternative argument posits that more assessing of public opinion is needed to strengthen the bonds between the public and their elected leaders. Citizens' dissatisfaction with government, it is argued, stems partly from government's failure to provide policies that the people want, and that faith in government can only rise if citizens are empowered with more legislative influence.[40] Debates abound as to the merits and demerits of these arguments, but the mere suggestion that presidential polls may foster or inhibit leadership and representation

---

[38] See Larry J. Sabato, *The Rise of Political Consultants: New Ways of Winning Elections.* New York: Basic Books, 1981.

[39] See, for example, George F. Will, *Restoration: Congress, Term Limits, and the Recovery of Deliberative Democracy.* New York: Free Press, 1992.

[40] This argument is raised in F. Christopher Arterton, *Teledemocracy: Can Technology Protect Democracy?* Washington, DC: Sage Publications, 1987; and Thomas E. Cronin, *Direct Democracy: The Politics of Initiative, Referendum, and Recall.* Cambridge, MA: Harvard University Press, 1989.

underscores their importance. Discussions about the advantages and disadvantages of presidential polling will continue to generate more heat than light unless they are placed in an understandable historical and theoretical context. Calls for electronic town hall meetings, deliberative opinion polls, and Burkean-style representation suggest that the public is still digesting what role public opinion polls should play in representative democracy, even as it has yet to learn how, why, and when presidents use polls, how this process has changed, and why. Chapter 3 begins to make sense of this debate by concentrating on the strained relations presidents have had with the legislative branch.

3

Checks and Imbalances

Congress and Presidential Polling

> If the polls are more accurate than other sources of reporting on opinion, they
> should be required reading for men in public life.[1]

This chapter discusses how the presidency and Congress do not trust one another. By looking at the relations between Congress and Presidents Hoover
through Eisenhower, I will show that presidential polling occurs because
of the chief executive's strained relations with the legislative branch. At
one point, Congress took exception to polls conducted for the executive
branch, claiming that Congress is the appropriate institution for assessing
citizens' views. State Department officials dismissed such claims, responding
that Congress measures congressional opinion, not public opinion. By the
end of the Eisenhower era, public opinion polling by the executive branch
may not have been universally accepted by Congress and the American
people, but the practice had become part of the presidential landscape.

Political scientist Wilfred Binkley contends that President Andrew Jackson
was responsible for rallying the mass electorate around the president by
openly "rescuing the presidency from the hegemony of the congressional
caucus and making it peculiarly the people's office." By the time the Whigs
nominated General Zachary Taylor for the presidency in 1848, the American
people were "convinced that the Executive had become the supremely important organ of the federal government."[2] After the Civil War, the status
of the presidency with respect to Congress declined, but that would change
with President Theodore Roosevelt's election to office, only to be tempered
by his successor, William Howard Taft.[3] Presently, historians generally agree

---

[1] William Albig, *Public Opinion.* New York: McGraw-Hill, 1939, p. 232.
[2] Wilfred E. Binkley, *American Political Parties: Their Natural History.* New York: Knopf,
1947, p. 68.
[3] See Arthur M. Schlesinger, Jr. and Alfred de Grazia, *Congress and the Presidency: Their Role
in Modern Times.* Washington, DC: American Enterprise Institute, 1974. Schlesinger cites

that the power of the presidency has prevailed, in part because of a trend toward greater assessment of public opinion on the part of the presidency. This trend does not discount other explanations of presidential ascendency, such as the proliferation of administrative agencies in FDR's New Deal and the growth of the mass media. Yet perceptions about the presidency and its relations with Congress today still center on questions about power and autonomy. This chapter focuses on one aspect of presidential autonomy – assessing public opinion independently of Congress.

Every president has some degree of tension with Congress, and from those pressures has arisen the desire for independent assessments of public opinion as a means of circumventing Congress, achieving greater autonomy, and acquiring leverage over it. As noted in Chapter 2, promoting positive public relations was an important function of the executive branch before modern polls were invented. Before Woodrow Wilson's Creel Committee, President McKinley was known to have used his office for advancing a positive image of his duties and himself.[4] This chapter begins with the Hoover presidency because Hoover was the last president not to gauge citizens' views via polls, and because Hoover, in the tradition of Binkley's assessment of the Jackson presidency, exhibits tendencies in his relationship with Congress that are apparent in subsequent presidents. From the tensions between Hoover and Congress emerge a variety of models for gauging public opinion that serve a loose pattern for later presidents in their use of polls. As a result, the Hoover presidency marks a significant turning point in how presidents gauge public opinion. This chapter continues chronologically, revealing how presidential polling has evolved and proliferated because of presidents' desires to seek autonomy from Congress.

HOOVER

President Hoover repeatedly failed in getting members of Congress to advance his agenda. Although *The New York Times* wrote that "harmony will be the rule" when President Hoover convened a special session of Congress in 1929, Hoover's inability to work with legislators resulted in legislative stagnation in the first session of the 71st Congress.[5] The second session brought Congress and Hoover again at loggerheads, in part because President Hoover

---

Republican Senator George F. Hoar of Massachusetts who served from 1877 to 1904, saying that "the most eminent senators would have received as a personal affront a private message from the White House expressing a desire that they should adopt any course in the discharge of their legislative duties that they did not approve. If they visited the White House, it was to give, not to receive, advice." Schlesinger and de Grazia, *Congress and the Presidency*, p. 11.
[4] See Jacobs, "The Recoil Effect."
[5] Jordan A. Schwarz, *The Interregnum of Despair: Hoover, Congress, and the Depression.* Urbana: University of Illinois Press, 1970, pp. 6–7; *The New York Times*, April 7, 1929.

stated that he would veto any bill that did not contain a flexible provision to change tariff rates. Congressional leaders balked, claiming that the provision usurped the power of the purse from Congress.

When the Hawley-Smoot Tariff Bill eventually was passed and signed, Hoover unofficially declared a truce with the Congress that successfully challenged him, but it did not take long for Hoover's relations with Congress to worsen. Hoover nominated to the Supreme Court John J. Parker, an enemy of organized labor and the National Association for the Advancement of Colored People (NAACP). The NAACP led a fight against his nomination in light of a pejorative remark made by Parker in 1922. When Majority Leader James E. Watson suggested to Hoover that he withdraw Parker's name, Hoover ignored the advice, partially because he and Watson never trusted each other.[6] On May 7, 1930, the Senate rejected the Parker nomination by a forty-one to thirty-nine vote, with seventeen Republicans opposing Hoover's choice for a Supreme Court justice.

An economic depression, combined with Hoover's passive executive style, generously described at the time as his "reluctance to intervene publicly," contributed to his troubles.[7] Hoover repeatedly disengaged from congressional leaders, and his relations with his own party stalwarts weakened when he publicly suggested that the Republicans should allow the Democrats to lead the Senate in the 72nd Congress, even though the Republicans had a one vote majority. The GOP interpreted abdication of majority powers as a disastrous move from a political neophyte who misunderstood the negative consequences of relinquishing congressional committee chairmanships. Not surprisingly, the Senate rejected Hoover's idea; years after leaving office, Hoover retained his disdain for the congressional GOP, saying that they "liked to hold committee chairmanships and the nicer offices in the capitol."[8] Hoover's fervent belief in natural economic cycles also angered members of Congress who thought President Hoover's assessment of them as wasteful spenders was both offensive and unnecessarily combative. Senators from agricultural states, for example, continued to fight for appropriations despite Hoover's sermonizing on the virtues of limited government. When Democrats attacked Hoover on the House and Senate floors, Republicans did not always respond, distancing themselves from the President's perceived ineptitude. Hoover knew he was disliked on the Hill, remarking that when Democratic Senate Leader Joe Robinson criticized him on the floor of the Senate, "Republicans

[6] After leaving office, Hoover described Watson as having "spasmodic loyalties and abilities." Watson, in return, wrote in his diary that Hoover dreadfully mismanaged his relations with Congress. See Herbert Hoover, *Memoirs, Vol. III: The Great Depression*. New York: Macmillan, 1952, p. 103; and James E. Watson, *As I Knew Them: Memoirs of James Watson, Former United States Senator from Indiana*. Indianapolis: Bobbs-Merrill, 1936, pp. 259–260.
[7] Arthur W. Macmahon, "Second Session of the Seventy-first Congress," *American Political Science Review* 24 (1930): 930.
[8] Hoover, *Memoirs*, p. 101.

went over and shook hands with him."[9] When Hoover responded by criticizing Congress for politicizing economic bad times, Hoover aide and former member of Congress James MacLafferty relayed to Hoover that one Republican ally approved of the move, saying that "Hoover has been sitting there . . . like a lump of putty, but now, thank God, he is beginning to fight."[10]

Given the hostile relations with Congress, Hoover was encouraged by his press secretary Ted Joslin to go public, that is, to appeal directly to the American people in the hopes that public support would translate into congressional approval for his policies. According to Joslin, Hoover objected to going public, as "[h]e felt that to be making continued appeals to the country over the head of Congress would, even if successful, only result in discredit of the legislative branch."[11] Hoover preferred instead to gather what he thought were objective facts, and make policy decisions based on those facts, rather than compromise with ideological opponents. To Hoover, engaging in arguments with Congress was undignified and unprofessional.[12]

Hoover's strained relations with Congress endured throughout his presidency. Still, he actively sought assistance from Republican allies in Congress through James MacLafferty, who served in Congress for three years. Excerpts from MacLafferty's unpublished diary exemplify how he appraised congressional sentiment for Hoover and how he interpreted these impressions as indicators of public opinion.

I believe that in the North Eastern states the people are for you . . . From my conversations with returning congressmen from the western states and from a long talk I had with the Vice President I fear that the people in the west are inclined to be cold toward you. The Vice President told me that his audiences were scant with their applause when he mentioned you to others. He says we are terribly short on our publicity all throughout the west; and Chief, I added we <u>should</u> have publicity stuff going to thousands of the country papers just as was done several years ago.[13]

MacLafferty believed that cordial relations with members of Congress were a key factor in generating public approval for Hoover and support for his policies, so he frequently visited his former colleagues in the House to assess their views toward Hoover and his agenda. He subscribed to the view that

---

[9] Herbert C. Hoover Archives [HCHA], MacLafferty Diary, December 11, 1930.

[10] Ibid.

[11] Theodore G. Joslin, *Hoover Off the Record*. New York: Doubleday, 1934, p. 66.

[12] Hoover's disinclination to bargain with members of Congress was shared by his predecessor Woodrow Wilson, who wrote that negotiating with members over appointments or using patronage to assist members, was "deeply immoral" and "destructive of the fundamental understandings of constitutional government itself. They are sure, moreover, in a country of free public opinion, to bring their own punishment, to destroy both the fame and the power of the man who dares to practice them." See Woodrow Wilson, *The Papers of Woodrow Wilson, Vol. 18: 1908–1909*, edited by Arthur S. Link. Princeton, NJ: Princeton University Press, 1974, p. 116.

[13] HCHA, MacLafferty Diary, November 14, 1930. Underline in original.

public relations and congressional support were integrally related. "There is just one reason why this [Hoover's lack of public support] is possibly so," he wrote, "and the reason is because we have fallen down on our publicity."[14] Given the negative sentiment he detected, MacLafferty provided sober assessments of what members of Congress thought of Hoover and his administration. He wrote that President Hoover's aide George Akerson was "driving his [Hoover's] friends away from him" and that some Republican members were so hostile toward Akerson that they would not visit the White House unless Hoover sent for them.[15]

In 1931, MacLafferty told Hoover that his relations with members of Congress were dangerously deteriorating:

[E]very day and almost every evening I have been in the company of congressmen and I have been preaching administration gospel... I have found many of them criticizing you, the [Republican] National Committee, Senator Fess its chairman, and saying about everything they should not be saying... These men would have more confidence in your winning if they knew you the way your pals know you ...[16]

MacLafferty then suggested that Hoover meet informally with members of Congress – "have a few open boxes of cigars around and in an exaggerated sense run a republican [sic] club." But Hoover would not succumb to changing his style of dealing with Congress. "MacLafferty," he replied, "I can't do that, it is impossible... I ask these men to dinner in groups and I will eventually have them all in. It [is] really a great physical strain, too."[17]

Conversations between MacLafferty and Hoover were secret. Hoover cautioned MacLafferty to be "very careful in your work on legislation on the hill. If certain congressmen find that the National Committee and the White House are trying to influence legislation it will make an awful row."[18] In return, MacLafferty maintained a low profile, intentionally failing to inform a reporter friend of his job for fear that "if the White House correspondents begin writing me up as a 'mystery man' it will mean my visits there may cease... I have so far eluded the eagle-eyed correspondents."[19]

To President Hoover, then, receiving congressional opinion was to be done discreetly. Charming members of Congress in order to sway their opinion toward him was minimized if not abandoned. Hoover refused to win over congressional friends with his personality or the personal perks of the presidency; public and personal interactions with Congress – the institutional voice of the people – were to be avoided altogether.[20] By deferring to MacLafferty the

---

[14] Ibid.
[15] Ibid. November 18, 1930.
[16] Ibid. December 19, 1931.
[17] Ibid.
[18] Ibid. November 18, 1930.
[19] Ibid. June 2, 1932.
[20] Only after losing to FDR in 1933 did Hoover regret his tactics with members of Congress, and in doing so, revealed anger toward the electorate that his attempts to work on their behalf

role of assessing and manipulating congressional opinion, Hoover deper-
sonalized presidential-congressional relations and instead forged ties with
the relatively inexperienced MacLafferty, who once suggested that he, not
Hoover, make as many as fifty speeches in the western United States in order
to garner support for the president. In this sense, MacLafferty envisioned
himself not just as an interpreter and disseminator of public opinion–related
information, but also as a public opinion manipulator who could generate
positive publicity and public approval of the president. By relying on personal contacts in Congress to assess public opinion on President Hoover's
behalf, MacLafferty essentially defined public opinion for Hoover as the con-
fluence of congressional opinion and public approval. Members of Congress
served as barometers of public opinion by relaying to the president, via
MacLafferty, that audience participation and media publicity were sparse.
Rather than accepting that wooing members of Congress was an integral
function of the presidency, Hoover rejected the notion that currying congressional favor was viable, stating that Republican members of Congress were
disloyal to him and hastened his political and policy agendas.[21] Hoover had
no good reason to trust their version of what constituted public opinion and
every reason to distrust the congressmen. As the economy sputtered, some
congressmen blamed Hoover. The 1930 midterm elections showed tepid support for Hoover, as the Democrats gained fifty-three seats in the House, and
eight seats in the Senate. Congressmen thought Hoover was tone deaf on the
economy; Hoover thought they were self-interested political renegades.

Hoover systematically attempted to gauge public opinion. He did so secretly, indicating that public opinion data were a valuable commodity not to
be shared with others. Finally, he attempted to identify citizens' attitudes by
disengaging himself from Congress. The Hoover presidency began a trend –
circumventing Congress in order to measure public opinion directly.

FDR

Hoover's grasp to locate public opinion, borne out of a nearly impossible working relationship with Congress, was followed by the presidency
of Franklin Delano Roosevelt. The FDR administration's strong interest in
public opinion research can be attributed partly to FDR's interest in reor-
ganizing the executive branch so it could measure public opinion without

had been poorly received. For example, Joslin claims that Hoover said after his failure to
win reelection in 1932 that, "Perhaps my tactics have been wrong. Now what I have tried
to do has been to save the people. They don't know what they have missed. They are not
appreciative. What I should have done was to have waited until they were half drowned and
waded in and tried to save them. They would have known what it was all about." HCHA,
Joslin Diary, January 9,1933, Box 10.
[21] HCHA, MacLafferty Diary, November 16, 1932; also see ibid., December 13, 1932.

Congress' knowledge.[22] FDR did not hide his desire to reorganize the executive branch, as evidenced by his explicitly expressed endorsement of the 1936 Brownlow Report. As such, FDR's administration marked the commencement of an unprecedented growth of the executive branch and the beginning of a personalized presidency. Richard Neustadt describes the Roosevelt White House as especially personalized to meet FDR's needs, encouraging competition among his advisers, and in the process, providing Roosevelt with multiple avenues for accessing information.[23] But the rise of the administrative presidency during the Roosevelt administration is more complex than a rise in the number of presidential staffers, for the advent of the modern social survey precipitated a new function of the executive branch, namely the gauging of public opinion without the consent of Congress, parties, and the media.[24]

FDR's dealings with Congress were repeatedly tense, even allowing for the inherent conflict set up by constitutional differentiation between the executive and legislative branches. In large part, the tension arose because FDR occasionally tried to defy, subvert, and sabotage Congress, best demonstrated by his court-packing plan and attempt to purge Congress of anti–New Deal Democrats. These maneuvers exacerbated frictional relations between Congress and the administration, and were reflected by changes in the composition of Congress. In 1936, Democrats held 333 House seats. But the 76th Congress resulted in a Republican gain of eighty seats, and in 1942 the GOP gained an additional forty-seven seats. In the Senate, Roosevelt's Democrats also took a drubbing, as the Republicans gained twenty-one seats from 1938 to 1942.[25] FDR could not depend on congressional allies to assess public opinion, in part because his party was losing control of Congress – the institution traditionally purported to speak for the public at large. Additionally, as Republicans defeated Democrats, employing Congress as a conduit between the executive branch and the public was a recipe for failure. For a president seeking increased autonomy from Congress, trusting congressional Democrats to give him a sense of public opinion was political suicide. Some of those Democrats regretted seeing their colleagues lose. The purge was an unmitigated failure and arguably reinforced FDR's sense that Congress should not be trusted – to gauge public opinion, or to do anything other than pass the president's policies.

[22] See Leila A. Sussman, "FDR and the White House Mail," for a detailed analysis of the FDR administration's reading of White House mail.

[23] Richard E. Neustadt, "Approaches to Staffing the Presidency," *American Political Science Review* 54 (1963): 855–864.

[24] For more on the rise of the administrative presidency during the FDR presidency, see Milkis, *The President and the Parties*; Euchner, "Public Support and Opinion"; and Wayne, *The Legislative Presidency*.

[25] Harold W. Stanley and Richard G. Niemi, *Vital Statistics on American Politics, Third Edition*. Washington, DC: CQ Press, 1992, pp. 122–125.

With the coming of World War II, a strong executive branch was vitally important to Roosevelt, and as war became imminent, FDR turned to opinion polls to assess public backing for the war. The eventual need to galvanize the country for a war effort had become apparent. For FDR, remaining beholden to Congress was no longer a viable option. He needed to defeat the spreading isolationist sentiment and polls provided a means to ascertain views for or against the war. In the spring of 1940 adviser Anna Rosenberg began showing FDR Gallup poll data provided by Hadley Cantril, director of the Office of Public Opinion Research at Princeton University.[26] FDR and his advisers were particularly interested in poll results showing trends of opinion about American assistance to Britain and on American intervention in the war.[27] While FDR's idea for lend-lease seemed to come out of nowhere and was even called a "flash of almost clairvoyant knowledge and understanding" by Labor Secretary Frances Perkins, inside information supplied by Cantril on the public's view toward aid to Britain had been available to the president for months.[28] The results showed a growing receptivity toward lending war materials to the British. On March 7, 1941, four days before lend-lease was signed into law, Cantril directly contacted FDR with the following proposal:

Mrs. [Anna] Rosenberg thought you might like to have on hand some of the findings of my public opinion research... I shall be delighted to keep this information up to date for you if you will tell Mrs. Rosenberg to whom I should send new material. I shall be glad to make the facilities available to you at any time. We can get confidential information on questions you suggest, follow up any hunch you may care to see tested regarding the determinants of opinion, and provide you with the answers to any questions ever asked by the Gallup or Fortune polls... The Gallup poll particularly has accumulated a vast amount of information that has never been published... Although my general aim is the academic search for truth, I am at present more interested in using the facilities to see that we may continue to search for truth in the next few decades.[29]

FDR temporarily arrogated Congress' power to measure public opinion, discovering that his views about military intervention matched public sentiment. Congress, ensconced in its traditional representative role, was left with nothing to disavow, especially as public opinion frequently approved of FDR's policies.

[26] Cantril describes his relationship with FDR's advisers in some detail in Hadley Cantril, *The Human Dimension: Experiences in Policy Research*. New Brunswick, NJ: Rutgers University Press, 1967. Also see Doris Kearns Goodwin, *No Ordinary Time: Franklin and Eleanor Roosevelt: The Home Front in World War II*. New York: Simon and Schuster, 1994, for further analysis of the Lend-Lease program.

[27] See Cantril, *The Human Dimension*, 35–36, and Betty Houchin Winfield, *FDR and the News Media*. New York: Columbia University Press, 1994, p. 219.

[28] Goodwin, *No Ordinary Time*, p. 193.

[29] Franklin Delano Roosevelt Library [FDRL] 1941, Gallup Polls, Box 857.

Although most of the surveys were written either by Cantril or Gallup, Cantril's March 7, 1941 letter opened the door for White House advisers to help write poll questions. A one sentence note from Assistant Solicitor General Oscar Cox to Economic Assistant to the White House Isador Lubin, dated May 3, 1943, read, "Here is a copy of the pamphlet on public relations to the National Resources Planning Board proposals, as well as to some of the questions that I got Cantril to ask." Another letter from Cox to Jerome Bruner of the Office of Public Opinion Research listed revisions to three questions.[30]

By 1942, poll data were disseminated by Cantril and his partner Gerard Lambert to White House advisers at Lambert's house in Washington, D.C., where they "deliberately made a point of being seen as little as possible in Government offices or agencies in order to minimize curiosity and preserve the informality of our relationships."[31] Cantril's successful attempts to be discrete in discussing these matters were further documented in a memorandum from Cantril to Samuel Rosenman, the president's aide and frequent speech-writer, in which Cantril wrote, "No doubt you have told Mrs. Roosevelt that because of the confidential nature of our work we are anxious to soft-pedal the fact that we have our own privately financed polling mechanism and that we never want this fact published."[32]

Whereas Lawrence Jacobs and Robert Shapiro's work reveals how the Nixon administration sought secrecy of poll data to manipulate and distort public opinion, Cantril's polls helped FDR and his advisers manipulate public opinion only in a narrow sense.[33] Polls did not change public opinion, but rather polls educated the Roosevelt administration as to where public opinion was located, thereby enabling them to market policies to specific constituencies. The privacy of the polls further substantiates the desire not to share information with Congress. Cantril noted that the polls' secrecy was to "guide the President and other civilian war leaders in bracing people for the long, hard road ahead and for occasional setbacks."[34] No doubt, some of those setbacks concerned the receptivity of the American public to engage in military action in Europe. Cantril polled, for example, about how the bombing of Rome might affect U.S. Catholics' morale and support for the war, and whether or not the United States should create refugee camps for persons persecuted by the Nazis.[35] Because the administration wanted to

---

[30] FDRL 1943, Cox Papers, Box 100.

[31] Cantril, *The Human Dimension*, pp. 39–40.

[32] FDRL 1943, Rosenman Files.

[33] Lawrence R. Jacobs and Robert Y. Shapiro, "Presidential Manipulation of Polls and Public Opinion: The Nixon Administration and the Pollsters," *Political Science Quarterly* 110 (1995–1996) [http://epn.org/psnixo.html], and "The Rise of Presidential Polling: The Nixon White House in Historical Perspective."

[34] Cantril, *The Human Dimension*, p. 52.

[35] Ibid., 53–54. The refugee camp poll question is a fascinating one, and reads as follows: "It has been proposed that our government offer now temporary protection and refuge to those

Presidents Herbert Hoover and Franklin Delano Roosevelt (Courtesy of the FDR Library)

know how the public would react to policies not yet codified into law, and because they were aware of accusations of being beholden to public opinion, it was all the more important not to look like a machinating ruler eagerly seeking and assuaging public opinion.[36] Criticisms of Roosevelt would only have been amplified if Cantril's polls and meetings were discovered by members of Congress. The polls were secret – establishing presidential autonomy as they informed the administration of public opinion.

In a semiautobiographical work, *The Human Dimension,* Cantril provides numerous examples of when the administration paid attention to his data. For example, Cantril writes, "A few days after turning in the [farming] report to Judge Rosenman, Lambert and I got letters from the President

people in Europe who have been persecuted by the Nazis but have escaped, and are now homeless, and could save themselves by coming here. The plan proposes that these people would be kept in special camps in this country for the duration of the war. They would not be allowed to have jobs outside the camps. When the war is over, they would all be returned to their native lands. Would you approve or disapprove of this plan?" FDRL 1944, Rosenman Files, Poll Report from Cantril, April 14, 1944.

[36] See, for example, Robert Dallek, *Franklin D. Roosevelt and American Foreign Policy, 1932–1945.* New York: Oxford University Press, 1979, p. 336.

commending the report as both surprising and informative."[37] Some poll reports were read directly by FDR. When asked on August 9, 1940 if he would like to see Princeton Public Opinion Poll reports "from time to time," FDR responded affirmatively.[38] Roosevelt acknowledged receipt of polls in an October 28, 1943 letter to Lambert, in which he stated that "the report [was] most interesting and instructive and I am sure that it will be very useful."[39] Ten months later, on August 24, 1944, Roosevelt, through his private secretary Grace Tully, commended Cantril for sending him poll reports, "as they keep him [FDR] in touch with what people are thinking."[40] Cantril's polls gave Roosevelt more than a snapshot of the public mood; they increased the autonomy of the presidency by assuming within the executive branch a traditional function of Congress, that of assessing public opinion. Roosevelt's successor, however, would show far less interest in utilizing this resource.

TRUMAN

President Truman disdained polls, claiming that he "never paid any attention to the polls myself because in my judgment they did not represent a true cross section of American opinion." He continued with a statement that echoed President Hoover's distinction between opinion and facts. "I did not believe that the major components of our society, such as agriculture, management, and labor, were adequately sampled. I also know that the polls did not represent facts but mere speculation, and I have always placed my faith in the known facts ... A man who is influenced by the polls or is afraid to make decisions which may make him unpopular is not a man to represent the welfare of the country."[41] Truman's pejorative comments about polls, in his memoirs and public papers, alluded to the *Literary Digest* debacle:

[W]hen those people vote, they are going to throw the Galluping polls right in the ashcan – you watch 'em. There are going to be more red-faced pollsters on November the 3rd than there were in 1936, when the Literary Digest said that Roosevelt shouldn't be elected.[42]

Polls were not Truman's friend, but neither was Congress. Although Truman served as a senator and retained friendships with some of his former

[37] Cantril, *Human Dimension*, p. 71. Also see pp. 55–74.
[38] FDRL 1940, Gallup Polls, Box 857.
[39] FDRL 1943, PPF, Box 5470.
[40] Ibid.
[41] Harry S. Truman, *Memoirs by Harry S. Truman, Volume Two: Years of Trial and Hope.* New York: Macmillan, 1956, pp. 177, 196.
[42] Harry S. Truman, *Public Papers of the Presidents of the United States.* Washington, DC: General Services Administration, 1956, p. 920.

colleagues, he had great difficulty maneuvering bills through the legislative branch.[43] Alonzo Hamby describes Truman as being "acutely aware of the seething resentment that he and many of his colleagues had felt at being pushed around by a strong president. Overconfident in his ability to deal with leading members of Congress on a personal basis, he believed that conciliation and quiet negotiations might yield more results than demands."[44]

Truman struck a conciliatory note in his 1947 State of the Union address, but Republicans and the administration failed to find a way to cooperate. Truman fought with the Republican 80th Congress over numerous bills, perhaps most notably the Taft-Hartley Labor Bill in 1947. During his presidential tenure, 180 bills were vetoed by Truman and twelve of them, Taft-Hartley included, were overridden by Congress. The vetoes and overrides reflected the near contempt Congress had for Truman. The President's calling of a special congressional session in 1948 only intensified the animosity between the two branches; Republican Senator Charles Brooks of Illinois said about the special session: "[N]ever in the history of American politics has a Chief Executive stooped so low."[45] Truman's calls for civil rights legislation alienated his fellow Democrats and farming policies seemed to rile members from both parties. Ironically, an exception to these continual disagreements was the establishment of a Commission on the Organization of the Executive Branch (headed by former President Herbert Hoover). Truman remains an anomaly, as his frictions with Congress did not precipitate a desire by him or his aides to conduct private polls.

EISENHOWER

President Eisenhower forged excellent relations with Republican Congressman Charles Halleck, who was House Majority Leader when Eisenhower took office in 1953 and became Minority Leader in 1955 when the Democrats gained control of both the House and the Senate. Still, Eisenhower's relations with other Republicans were strained. While Eisenhower historians Robert Branyan and Lawrence Larsen have categorized the president's relations

---

[43] For excellent analyses of Truman's relations with Congress and its members, see David McCullough, *Truman.* New York: Simon and Schuster, 1992; Alonzo L. Hamby, *Man of the People: A Life of Harry S. Truman.* New York: Oxford University Press, 1995; Alonzo L. Hamby, *Beyond the New Deal: Harry S. Truman and American Liberalism.* New York: Columbia University Press, 1973; Roy Jenkins, *Truman.* New York: Harper & Row, 1986; and Donald R. McCoy, *The Presidency of Harry S. Truman.* Lawrence: University Press of Kansas, 1984. Privately, Truman expressed views about individual members of Congress that were sometimes tart if not profane. See Hamby, *Man of the People,* p. 469.

[44] Hamby, *Man of the People,* p. 363, citing Francis H. Heller, ed., *The Truman White House: The Administration of the Presidency, 1945–1953.* Lawrence: Regents Press of Kansas, 1980, pp. 227–230.

[45] Cited in Jenkins, *Truman,* p. 131.

with Congress as "generally good," they also note that on many occasions, the president's sanguine personal relations with members of Congress did not translate into harmony between the two branches of government. For example, Ohio Senator John Bricker and his proposal for a constitutional amendment limiting presidential authority frustrated Eisenhower. Wisconsin Senator Joseph McCarthy's hunt for Communists was also a burden to the president, who wrote in his diary that "nothing will be so effective in combating his particular kind of troublemaking as to ignore him."[46] Former Speaker of the House Joseph Martin from Massachusetts questioned Eisenhower's low tariff policies and Senators Homer Capehart and William Jenner of Indiana, William Langer of North Dakota, and McCarthy of Wisconsin frequently feuded with the president on legislative matters. Former Majority Leader William Knowland of California, while retaining a personal friendship with the president, "consistently quarreled with any programs that seemed tolerant of communist nations."[47]

A poll conducted in 1953 by Alfred Politz Research, Inc. demonstrates how Eisenhower staffers secretly and independently polled about foreign policy matters. An abridged list of the Politz poll questions includes the following questions:

- Would you be in favor of driving the Communists out of all Korea if it meant ... (by sex, age, and education)
  a. A complete draft of military manpower in this country?
  b. The government taking complete control of prices, wages, and production in this country?
  c. Other countries withdrawing their soldiers from Korea leaving the United States to fight alone?
  d. Great increases in the number of killed and wounded American soldiers?
  e. A full-scale war with Communist China on China mainland?
- Would you still be in favor of the United States increasing its help to fight Communists in French Indo-China if it meant ... (by sex and education)
  a. A complete draft of military manpower?
  b. The United States would become involved in a full-scale war with Communist China?

[46] See Dwight David Eisenhower Diary, April 1, 1953, cited in Craig Allen, *Eisenhower and the Mass Media: Peace, Prosperity and Prime-Time TV*. Chapel Hill: University of North Carolina Press, 1993, p. 19, fn. 27.
[47] See Robert L. Branyan and Lawrence H. Larsen, *The Eisenhower Administration 1953–1961: A Documentary History*. New York: Random House, 1971. The quotation cited is from Branyan and Larsen, p. 429. Also see Harry Z. Scheele, "Executive-Legislative Relations: Eisenhower and Halleck." In *Reexamining the Eisenhower Presidency*, edited by Shirley Anne Warshaw. Westport, CT: Greenwood Press, 1993, 133–152.

   c. American soldiers fighting in Indo-China?
   d. The United States supplying most of the men and money?
   e. The United States helping without United Nations' cooperation?
   f. Reducing U.S. strength in Europe?
   g. The United States backing French-colonial policy?
   h. Less defense of the United States against air attack?
- There has been some talk lately of a conference among the governments of the United States, Soviet Russia, England, and France with the idea of trying to bring about more peaceful relations among these countries. Do you think it would be a good idea for this country to work actively toward such a conference or not? (by age, sex, economic status, and education)
- How do you feel about the United States helping to fight the Communists in Indo-China, if the Communists seem to be going to invade the whole country? Are you in favor of the United States helping or not? (by sex, age, economic status, and education)[48]

The Politz poll questions appear to have been designed to assess both the degree and intensity to which Americans favored military involvement in Indo-China. There were no memoranda accompanying the poll and it is unclear who read the poll or what impact if any it had on Eisenhower's foreign policies. Given the poll's questions and its classified status, it looks as if the poll were intended to assess public opinion – secretly and independently of Congress and the media – about military intervention in southeast Asia.

Additionally, the Eisenhower administration's State Department confidentially commissioned polls, perhaps without even the president's knowledge. For thirteen years (beginning in the Truman administration in 1944), the State Department hired the National Opinion Research Center (NORC) to conduct polls. Prior to this, Hadley Cantril had conducted surveys for the State Department in 1943. The NORC contract was confidentially funded from a discretionary fund marked for "Emergencies in the Diplomatic and Consular Service."[49] The State Department contract explicitly stated that "No Member of or Delegate of Congress or Resident Commissioner, shall be admitted to any share or part of this contract, or to any benefit that may arise therefrom." When members of Congress learned of the executive branch's attempts to gauge public opinion in a February 8, 1957 *Washington Star* article, they saw executive branch polling as a usurpation of their powers. The House Government Operations Committee held hearings about the

---

[48] Dwight David Eisenhower Library [DDEL], Alfred Politz Research, Inc., n.d., Box 105. A memo not attached to this poll notes that the Politz poll was conducted sometime before August 18, 1953. DDEL, DDE Confidential, "State, Department of (through Sept. 1953) (11)," Box 67.
[49] Converse, *History of Survey Research in the United States*, p. 322.

State Department polls, and some members accused the executive branch of intentionally concealing its public opinion polling operations. The House Government Operations Subcommittee on International Operations initiated an investigation, revealing that the State Department secretly had been commissioning polls and that they did not consider Congress' interpretation of public opinion to constitute genuine public opinion.[50] Discussions among H. Schuler Foster, chief of the State Department's Division of Public Studies, Congressman Victor Knox (R-VA), and Congressman Glenard Lipscomb (R-CA) revealed the State Department's keen interest in seeking autonomy from Congress.

KNOX: [T]he Secretary [of State] is limited by making use of the agency of Government to which public opinion is intended to be formally expressed, namely, the Congress.

FOSTER: But, Mr. Knox, the primary purpose of Congress, of course, as you and I realize, is to enact laws, and not to convey from week to week, and day to day, the opinions of the American people on all the topics, foreign and domestic.

KNOX: Well, now, Mr. Foster, you are aware of the fact that the Secretary of State often appears before committees of Congress and testifies, which from the questions that are propounded to the Secretary and his answers to them, certainly gives him some indication as to what public opinion is, as far as Congress is concerned, does it not?

FOSTER: Yes. I would think it would be more accurate, Mr. Knox, to call that congressional opinion, or perhaps, committee opinion.

KNOX: Are you inclined to believe that the Members of Congress are not representing the people who elected them to Congress in the manner which was in their best judgment, and in conformity with the opinion of the people who elected them?

FOSTER: I, of course, did not say that, Mr. Knox, but you know many Members of Congress seem to find it helpful themselves to conduct polls, in order to improve their understanding of the thinking of their constituents on these questions.

KNOX: If that is true, and I think it is true, it certainly should reflect in their statements to the Department or other agencies of the Government, should it not?

FOSTER: I think it does. We ourselves, make a careful study of all those that are listed in the *Congressional Record*.

---

[50] State Department Hearings, 85th Congress, H1612-1, June 21–July 11, 1957, p. 208.

KNOX: Well, Congress is not enough. You feel you should go beyond that. You don't think the opinion of Congress represents the American people.

FOSTER: I would not think, Mr. Knox, that would be the most reliable place in which to get information on what all of the people across the country are thinking about all of the various topics of foreign affairs concerning which the State Department needs to know; what they are thinking.[51]

. . . .

LIPSCOMB: Can you tell us why the arrangement was made to pay for these polls out of the Emergencies in the diplomatic and consular services funds?

FOSTER: It was because, as I was just trying to explain to Mr. [Henry] Reuss [D-WI], it was desired to keep the existence of the operation from the knowledge of other governments.

LIPSCOMB: Were there any other reasons; to keep the knowledge of its existence from Congress, for instance?

FOSTER: I have no idea of that.[52]

It is clear that distrust abounded between the legislative and executive branches as it related to measuring public opinion. According to Lipscomb, the executive branch was usurping a function of Congress, and doing so without Congress' knowledge. Foster replied by saying that the polls were secretly conducted because it would have been embarrassing if our allies learned that Americans did not think of them favorably. Lipscomb found this response unsatisfactory, arguing instead this was simply an excuse for hiding polls from Congress.

Knox and Lipscomb argued that the legislative branch, not the executive branch, was the proper institutional gauge of public opinion. On the other hand, Foster thought it was inaccurate to equate a member of Congress' interpretation of public opinion with actual public sentiment. One can only speculate if their objections to the State Department's polling were motivated by Republican Party infighting, as their objections to the State Department polls concerned whether or not Congress' role as assessor of public opinion was being usurped by an executive branch headed by Republicans. No doubt, certain members of Congress were especially critical of the State Department, especially those who thought of State Department employees as careerist bureaucrats who were losing the Cold War. Still, the hearings were chaired by a Democrat, not a Republican, and the arguments made against the State Department polling were not rooted in partisan rhetoric, but rather in differences over the proper functions of the legislative and executive branches.

[51] Ibid., 206–207.
[52] Ibid., 216.

The final congressional committee report rebuked the State Department for the illegal use of appropriated funds and their evasive testimony before its subcommittee.

It should be noted that throughout Eisenhower's tenure as president, senior administration officials (including Chief of Staff Sherman Adams, Press Secretary James Hagerty, and aides C.D. Jackson and Bryce Harlow) received public opinion–related data from a variety of sources, including members of Congress.[53] But the dearth of questionnaires sent by members of Congress during Eisenhower's eight-year tenure as president (sixteen surveys sent by thirteen Congressmen) further substantiates that presidents did not actively seek assessments of public opinion from Congress and that only a few members of the legislative branch considered it their duty to inform the White House of their appraisals of constituents' opinions.[54]

The tide had turned toward a radical expansion of presidential polling. For the last time, the presidents' advisers received and interpreted these polls under the duress of congressional dissent. As presidential polling became more commonplace (and institutionalized), members of Congress eventually envisioned the functions of the presidency to include monitoring local and national sentiment on a whole host of issues. As will be shown in Chapter 4, this trend of directly measuring public opinion via private polls endured in subsequent presidential administrations.

[53] See DDEL, "Polls," Files 156-B, Boxes 1218, 1219.
[54] The brief, standard format of the thank-you notes written by Adams and Hagerty to the senders of the polls suggests that the unsolicited poll data were not carefully read. Congressmen sending their surveys were Henderson (OH), Ostertag (NY), Hosmer (CA), Quigley (Democrat – PA) (2 surveys), Corbett (PA) (3 surveys), Gwinn (NY), McGregor, (OH), Martin (IA) (2 surveys), Bass (NH), Latham (NY), Scrivner (KS), Keating (NY), and Wilson (CA).

4

Dodging the Hill

Presidential Polling in the Post-Eisenhower Years

> The obvious weakness of government by opinion is the difficulty in ascertaining it.[1]

This chapter delineates how Presidents Kennedy through Nixon's strained relations with Congress help explain their desire to poll autonomously and privately. One development that emerged during the Kennedy presidency was the rise of the pollster (in this case, Lou Harris) as a key adviser. LBJ's presidency continued this trend; Oliver Quayle, who once worked for Harris, conducted polls for the Johnson administration. Johnson frequently sought to assess citizens' views by conducting and interpreting local polls as national snapshots of the public's mood. President Nixon recognized more than his predecessors how polls could be used to advance his agenda. He appointed his chief of staff, H.R. Haldeman, to be the primary point man for measuring public opinion. Haldeman's power as it related to gauging public opinion was unparalleled; he streamlined presidential polling operations in irreversible ways. In each of these presidencies, one recurring theme emerges – presidents opted to use private polls with great frequency and did so largely without congressional interference.

JFK

As John F. Kennedy won the White House in 1960, twenty Democratic members of Congress lost their seats. Press Secretary Pierre Salinger described executive-legislative relations during the Kennedy years as "virulent."[2] One reason may be because some of Kennedy's advisers thought that "bringing pressure on Capitol Hill by appealing 'over the heads' of Congress to the

---

[1] Bryce, *American Commonwealth*, p. 315.
[2] Pierre Salinger, *With Kennedy*. New York: Doubleday, 1966, p. 337.

people" would work.[3] Kennedy adviser Ted Sorensen concurred, writing that the president thought mobilizing public opinion to be a high priority.[4] Kennedy's advisers spoke repeatedly of developing a systematic strategy for going public, but they also knew that such appeals could backfire. If the president's image and persona could aid them in advancing their policy agenda, it could also damage them if members of Congress remained firmly opposed to the president's policies.

As Lawrence Jacobs notes in his book *The Health of Nations*, the administration tried to marshal public support for the president's health care proposal with a series of thirty rallies in May 1962.[5] The going public strategy failed, further weakening already tenuous ties with Congress. Republicans, angered at JFK's victory over Vice President Nixon, thought Kennedy to be antibusiness. Senator Bricker of Ohio, for example, bemoaned President Kennedy's denouncing of steel companies for raising prices as a "display of dictatorial power."[6] But the biggest obstacle facing the administration was that many serving in Congress were Southern and did not share the president's political style or agenda. Arthur Schlesinger writes of Kennedy's strained relations with the southern congressional contingent:

There were too many new ideas, coming too fast, couched in too cool and analytical a tone and implying too critical a view of American society. Instead of being reassured, many Congressmen felt threatened. And the President himself, despite those fourteen years in Congress, had always been something of an alien on the Hill ... A country Congressman from Tennessee told David Brinkley in 1962, 'All that Mozart string music and ballet dancing down there and all that fox hunting and London clothes. He's too elegant for me. I can't talk to him.'[7]

By all accounts, White House congressional liaison Lawrence O'Brien served admirably, but he did not remove the obstacles (institutional and personal) that generated tensions between the two branches. According to Kennedy biographer Richard Reeves, some of the fault in Kennedy's legislative strategy could be attributed to the president's personal style; "There was only so much time," Reeves writes, "he was willing to spend with, or even think about, his old colleagues."[8]

Relations worsened between the administration and Capitol Hill Democrats when seventeen Senate Democrats decided that Vice President Johnson

[3] Arthur M. Schlesinger, Jr., *A Thousand Days: John F. Kennedy in the White House*. Boston: Houghton Mifflin, 1965, p. 724.
[4] Theodore C. Sorensen, *Kennedy*. New York: Harper & Row, 1965.
[5] Lawrence R. Jacobs, *The Health of Nations: Public Opinion and the Making of American and British Health Policy*. Ithaca, NY: Cornell University Press, 1993, esp. pp. 140–148.
[6] Schlesinger, *A Thousand Days*, p. 639.
[7] Ibid., 710.
[8] Richard Reeves, *President Kennedy: Profile of Power*. New York: Simon and Schuster, 1993, p. 431.

Senator Hubert H. Humphrey and President John Kennedy, 9/17/63 (Courtesy of the JFK Library)

should not lead the Senate Democratic caucus because they thought it was an intrusion by the executive branch.[9] In November 1962, the Republicans won four new House seats, further weakening the administration's ability to pass legislation. When James MacGregor Burns proposed to the American Political Science Association a presidential commission investigating executive-legislative relations, President Kennedy dismissed the idea as unnecessary; Congress, he thought, needed to reform itself.[10] When asked if his legislative programs were receiving "the proper degree of support from the Democratic majorities in the House and Senate," Kennedy bluntly replied in the negative, and suggested that his legislative agenda would succeed only if more Democrats were elected.[11] Congress passed some legislation the president wanted (for example, tariff bill, an increase in the minimum wage, the Peace Corps), but other bills, such as getting medical care under social security, or the president's education bill, either were defeated on the floor, or died in committee, never making it to the full House or Senate for a vote.[12]

---

[9] Schlesinger, *A Thousand Days*, p. 706.

[10] Ibid., 712.

[11] Reeves, *President Kennedy*, p. 325, citing *Public Papers of the Presidents: John F. Kennedy, 1961–1963*, 3 vols. Washington, DC: Government Printing Office, 1962–1964, [June 27, 1962].

[12] See Hugh Sidey, *John F. Kennedy, President*. New York: Atheneum, 1964.

In short, President Kennedy's exchanges with Congress did not generate a desire for the president to rely on Congress as the vehicle to gauge public opinion for the administration. Instead, Kennedy relied on Lou Harris, who polled extensively during Kennedy's presidential campaign. Much of Harris' polling stemmed from a desire to seek autonomy from the Democratic Party and the media, and will therefore be discussed in greater length in Chapters 5 and 6. Nonetheless, there is some evidence that some of Harris' polls were designed to complement congressional appraisals of public opinion, if not bypass them altogether. A January 1962 poll of West Virginians included a variety of questions about potential policy initiatives – the traditional domain of Congress – such as whether citizens favored or opposed serving liquor by the drink. Only in the last two pages of the poll report were there analyses of presidential performance.[13] Two other Harris polls also revealed a concern for ascertaining public opinion on various policies before Congress. A January 1963 Harris poll, entitled "Polls – 1963 Wheat Referendum," spanned 116 pages. The cover page states that it was prepared for the Farmer's Grain Terminal Association (GTA), but the prose intimates that it was written for members of the administration to read, as exemplified by a sentence in the second to last page of the report:

What we are suggesting is that it would be a vast mistake for GTA or the Farmers Union or the Department or the Secretary or the President to engage in a mass media campaign to get out the vote or to urge a 'yes' vote.[14]

Similarly, Harris Poll "Polls – Political Climate in the State of Florida, December 1961" included various questions about Governor Farris Bryant, Senator George Smathers and Cuba. Specifically, Harris asked Floridians if they favored U.S. troops invading Cuba, whether trade with Cuba should be cut off or continued, and how receptive they were to Cuban refugees. These examples show that the Kennedy administration sought a means of gauging public opinion without congressional interference. In order to provide the Kennedy administration with this type of poll-related information, Harris "piggy-backed" poll questions about domestic and foreign policies onto surveys designed for other clients. The administration willingly and secretly received these reports, enabling them to procure information about policies without engaging Congress in discussing those policies.

Another important development is Harris' direct contact with the president. In an October 4, 1962 memorandum, for example, Harris' prose is written for and to the president, not his advisers.

It is my belief that you are more in control of this election then ever before . . . By their recklessness in Cuba, they have cast doubt on our position in Berlin. You can then

[13] John F. Kennedy Library [JFKL], "Harris Poll #1101," 'Polls – First and Fourth C.D.'s in West Virginia, January, 1962,' President's Office Files [POF], Box 104.
[14] JFKL, "Polls – 1963 Wheat Referendum, January 1963," 115, POF, Box 105.

state that if it came to it, we will stand by the freedom of West Berlin, even if we have to do it alone … You can then conclude that you had hoped these honest differences over health care or no health care … would be the subject of honest debate.[15]

Similarly, in a December 12, 1962 memo, Harris recommended to "commit your administration to a three point reduction in the corporate tax over a five year period (from 52 to 49 percent)."[16] By using phrases like "you can then conclude" and "your administration," Harris wrote his poll reports specifically for Kennedy. The personal relationship between pollster and president had been established.

The Kennedy administration also received polls from Joseph Napolitan. Like Harris' polls, Napolitan's surveys often included questions about policies pending before Congress. In one poll, Napolitan asked a general question, "What do you think of the Peace Corps, Medicare, the Crisis in Cuba?" revealing that Napolitan also used the private polls to locate public opinion in policy domains.[17] Napolitan's polls were piggy-back polls initially designed for gubernatorial, senatorial, and congressional candidates. When asked about how the White House received his polls, Napolitan stated that he sent polls to the White House without being asked. "When Kennedy and Johnson were president, it was my policy to send copies of my polls to the White House – with the candidate's permission, of course."[18]

Napolitan believed polls were of paramount importance to President Kennedy and other politicians:

It is true that presidents (and other officeholders as well) depend more on polls now than they did 30 years ago, but one reason for this is that polling has become much more sophisticated, and it is possible now to conduct a national poll overnight, which was unheard of in the Kennedy-Johnson years. But presidents utilize many sources of information. Polls may be the most important (and probably the most reliable), but I don't know of any president who has relied on polls for his information to the exclusion of the other sources.[19]

[15] JFKL, "Polls – General," Harris to the President, October 4, 1962, POF, Box 105.
[16] JFKL, "Polls – General," Harris to the President, December 12, 1962, POF, Box 105. Additional references to President Kennedy as "you" can be found in this document.
[17] JFKL, "Polls – Political Attitudes, Pennsylvania, April 1963," Joseph Napolitan Associates, Survey No. PA -163S, POF 105.
[18] Letter from Joe Napolitan to this author, February 27, 1995. When asked if he recalled directly ever talking to President Kennedy about polls, Napolitan answered: "In the United States, the only time I recall discussing my polls directly with the president occurred the night before the election in Massachusetts in 1962, Ted Kennedy's first campaign for the senate. I was asked to wait, alone, in a room at the Statler Hotel in Boston. Eventually President Kennedy strode into the room and said, 'Hi Joe. What do the polls show?' I told him Ted would win easily and Endicott Peabody, the Democratic candidate for governor, whose campaign I was managing, would squeak by. That's exactly what happened. Kennedy's questions that night were concerned almost exclusively with demographic and geographic findings around the state." Ibid.
[19] See Napolitan correspondence.

To Napolitan, presidents lent more credence to polls because of their su-
perior reliability. President Kennedy's increased reliance on Harris' public
opinion research shows that polls had emerged as a key instrument to gauge
public opinion. Furthermore, Napolitan's sending his polls voluntarily to
the Kennedy administration served an important function in the evolution
of presidential polling. While they were not explicitly designed to assist
President Kennedy to employ a going public strategy, they did enable him not
to rely on Congress as the primary conduit between the presidency and the
citizenry. Assessing public opinion no longer required listening or catering to
Congress, but rather required that a presidential administration hire private
pollsters whose confidential data for other candidates could be disseminated
to senior White House advisers. Hired pollsters, not Congress, ensured the
confidential collecting and administering of public opinion information and
began to replace members of Congress as discussion partners concerning
policy initiatives and public sentiment.[20]

LBJ

Lyndon Johnson noted in his autobiography, *The Vantage Point*, that in
October of 1963, just before President Kennedy was assassinated, a newspaper column noted that "Congress is beginning to look like a sit-down
strike."[21] Johnson's personal relationships with various senators, most notably Republican Everett Dirksen of Illinois and Democrat Richard Russell
of Georgia, were immeasurably valuable in getting some of the New Frontier
and Great Society legislation out of committee for full votes on the floor.[22]
Johnson's understanding of Congress and his appreciation for how members
of Congress perceived the presidency aided him in trying to reduce conflict
between the two branches. Johnson frequently briefed members of Congress
in advance of his policy announcements and provided them with perks, such
as invitations to the White House, all in order to foster amicable relations,
and optimally, fidelity toward the administration. According to Johnson biographer Doris Kearns, "the scope and intensity of [his] participation in the
legislative process were unprecedented."[23]

Johnson's personal interaction with legislators did not preclude him from
measuring public opinion independently of them. To the contrary, his desire

[20] Most of the poll reports from Harris and Napolitan were marked "CONFIDENTIAL."
[21] Lyndon Baines Johnson, *The Vantage Point: Perspectives of the Presidency 1963–1969*. New
York: Holt, Rinehart and Winston, 1971, p. 34.
[22] For various interpretations of Johnson's dealings with Congress, see Irving Bernstein, *Guns
or Butter: The Presidency of Lyndon Johnson*. New York: Oxford University Press, 1996;
Robert Dallek, *Flawed Giant: Lyndon Johnson and His Times 1961–1973*. New York:
Oxford University Press, 1998; Doris Kearns, *Lyndon Johnson and the American Dream*.
New York: Harper & Row, 1976, p. 225; and Taylor Branch, *Pillar of Fire: America in the
King Years 1963–65*. New York: Simon and Schuster, 1998, pp. 523, 563, 583–584, 594.
[23] Kearns, *Lyndon Johnson and the American Dream*, p. 225.

to push for his policy agenda demanded that he not rely on Congress to ascertain the voice of the people, in part because he knew that some of his former Senate colleagues (Dirksen and Russell, among others) opposed the policies he was promoting. In the words of Johnson biographer Robert Dallek, unpredictability was a political weapon to be used by Congress, especially as Johnson continued to embrace civil rights against the wishes of his Southern colleagues, and as his administration slowly escalated the war in Vietnam, against the wishes of congressional liberals.[24] Hostility toward civil rights and trouble in Vietnam devastated the administration in 1966 when Republicans gained forty-seven seats in the House, three in the Senate, and eight governorships. When Johnson tried to push for a tax increase in 1967, liberals balked, hoping to force the administration to temper if not abandon the war effort. Johnson's unpopular policies, combined with losses of congressional allies, necessitated independence in gauging of public opinion; his private polls served as the instrument of separation from Congress in the sense that the Johnson administration could locate, and if need be, seek to manipulate public opinion, without congressional interference or obstructions.

Lou Harris' former vice president, Oliver Quayle, privately polled for President Johnson. While in office, the Johnson administration downplayed the extent to which polls were internally analyzed, but memoranda show that Johnson's advisers avidly perused poll data, especially as it related to Vietnam. Questions about Vietnam saturated Quayle's polls during 1965 and 1966. Quayle asked a variety of specific questions about Vietnam in these polls and his comments indicate that a primary purpose of these polls was not so much to manipulate public opinion as it was to identify the electorate's positions about the war. A sampling of Quayle's frequently asked poll questions apropos Vietnam is listed below:

- Which statement do you most agree with?
  We should go all out (short of using nuclear weapons) and either win or force negotiations.
  We should do as we are: Keep on fighting a limited war, but increase military operations as necessary while seeking negotiations.
  We should stay in Viet Nam, but reduce military operations.
  We should get out of Viet Nam now.
  Not sure.[25]
- Which statement do you most agree with?
  "Pure Hawk" I disagree with our present policy; we are not going far enough. We should go further, such as carrying the war more into North Viet Nam.

---

[24] Dallek, *Flawed Giant*, p. ix. Also see Johnson, *The Vantage Point*, pp. 322–329, 440–444, for Johnson's review of presidential-congressional relations.

[25] Lyndon Baines Johnson Library [LBJL], 1965 Quayle polls, Fred Panzer Files, Boxes 171–175. (Note: This question is asked as early as June 1965.)

"LBJ Hawk" I agree with what we are doing, but we should increase our military effort to win a clear military victory.

"LBJ Dove" I agree with what we are doing, but we should do more to bring about negotiations, such as a cease-fire request.

"Pure Dove" I disagree with present policy. We shouldn't be there. We shouldn't be bombing North Viet Nam and should pull our troops out now.

Not sure.[26]

- What is your attitude toward:
  A temporary pause in Viet Nam.
  A temporary cease fire in Viet Nam.
  All out bombing if pause and cease fire fail.
  Increasing troops, with higher levels of loss of life but shortened war.
  Use of napalm.
  Not to use atomic weapons.
  Allowing Viet Cong represented in Government of South Viet Nam as a means to end war.
  A neutralist government in South Viet Nam as a means to end war.[27]
- Do you favor increasing taxes to help pay for war, or decreasing domestic programs?[28]

Johnson sought to assess public opinion about Vietnam much like FDR examined citizens' views about particulars of World War II. Quayle sought to determine the policy positions of the respondents, their overall familiarity with the current events surrounding the issue and their willingness to alter their positions (for example, favoring a tax increase, endorsing a different military strategy given certain circumstances).

In LBJ's case, however, Quayle's Vietnam questions sometimes sought to locate public opinion by providing answers that were described as "LBJ Hawk" and "LBJ Dove" respectively. The president's stated positions, therefore, serve as axes from which the president's pollster then determined how responsive the public was toward the administration's Vietnam policies. It is also worth noting that these questions differed by region. Although it is possible that White House advisers specifically and secretly directed Quayle to ask specific questions of certain constituencies, especially considering the emphasis placed on state-by-state analyses of public opinion by the presidential electoral system, the absence of archival data indicate that this is highly implausible. While there is one memorandum showing that White House aides once tinkered with Quayle's poll wording, there is only one such memorandum, suggesting that Johnson's advisers were

---

[26] LBJL, Quayle Poll 333, Bayonne, New Jersey, Fred Panzer Files.
[27] LBJL, Quayle Poll 326, 22nd C.D. California, March 1966, Fred Panzer Files.
[28] LBJL, Quayle Poll 332, New Hampshire, June 1966, Fred Panzer Files.

not carefully crafting specific Vietnam-related questions.[29] A more likely scenario is that the polls were not being used to distinguish Michigan voters from California voters, but rather were used as snapshots of public opinion at a certain time. Rather, Quayle used these local polls as vehicles to assess public opinion.[30]

Quayle's original poll reports were filtered to Johnson in a two-to-five page summarized form.[31] In 1965 through mid-1967, for example, Albert H. Cantril summarized or analyzed polls in various memoranda, which he sent to Hayes Redmon. Redmon frequently forwarded this information to Press Secretary Bill Moyers, who would usually send a memo to President Johnson with "President's Night Reading" written on or clipped to the top. Albert Cantril notes that a majority of his memos used national polls conducted by parties other than Quayle to gauge public opinion on current issues, and on issues likely to be discussed in forthcoming months.[32]

Quayle also conducted a poll in Vietnam, obtaining methodological assistance by academics Paul Lazarsfeld and Warren Miller.[33] In his report, Quayle noted that the purpose of this poll was to

provide the government of the Republic of South Viet Nam and the government of the United States of America with information which will add to the total knowledge about the struggle in this nation. Specifically, this new knowledge will assist the United

[29] It is possible that White House question-wording initiatives were not done in writing, and that the absence of archival data merely signifies the astute political instincts of Johnson's advisers who successfully crafted questions without leaving a paper trail. But the dearth of data showing White House involvement in question wording suggests that Quayle, not the administration, determined what to ask.

[30] Perhaps Quayle was testing which question wording would result in the most favorable response for Johnson, but again, the absence of archival data fail to substantiate this claim, as there are no indications that Johnson used the regional data to go public or to encourage Quayle to utilize one question and ignore another. The going public strategy may have been implemented without a paper trail, but a random survey of Johnson's phone logs and travel schedule indicates that the president neither immediately contacted members of Congress nor visited regions from which he just received piggy-back polls. To confirm that these polls were not instruments for going public, I analyzed logs and schedules for ten dates between 1966 and 1967. First I ascertained when a particular poll report would have been received by the Johnson White House by estimating the received date from the date provided by Quayle. I then attempted to find a personal contact from Johnson to a member of Congress or senator from that state, or in the case of a personal visit, to the region itself, beginning with the date, subtracting seven days (in case I estimated incorrectly) and adding twenty-one days (providing the president with ample time to contact the member of Congress). I abandoned this effort after ten attempts found no personal contacts with the president following his receiving poll data.

[31] In 1964, Douglass Cater and Horace Busby analyzed polls. In 1967, after the departure of Redmon and his supervisor, Press Secretary Bill Moyers, Marvin Watson, and later Fred Panzer were assigned to analyze the private polls.

[32] LBJL, Albert H. Cantril CHRON FILE.

[33] Miller eventually abandoned his connection to this poll after expressing concerns about its methodology. Personal conversation with Warren Miller, December 1994.

States in gauging its total role in South Viet Nam, militarily, economic, and, above all, political. It will also assist the GVN in its own efforts to develop and execute policies which will better serve its people and, ultimately, provide the nation with stable and efficient government. Finally, at long last, the people of this war torn land have had a chance to make their own voices and opinions heard and considered.[34]

Here again, there are no archival data showing that the president informed Congress of this poll before it was conducted, substantiating the argument that presidential polls served as instruments of separation from Congress, not as tools to be shared with Congress. If LBJ's private polls served to replace Congress, then the Nixon White House catapulted presidential polling to even greater heights.

NIXON

After defeating Vice President Hubert Humphrey, Richard Nixon created the Lindsay Task Force on Organization of the Executive Branch. Later, in April 1969, he appointed Roy L. Ash, founder and chief executive officer of Litton Industries, to head the President's Advisory Council on Executive Organization (PACEO), which was designed largely to implement the recommendations of the Lindsay Task Force. According to Nixon adviser Leonard Garment, President Nixon believed that "in order to reduce *federal* power, it was first necessary to increase *presidential* power."[35] What emerged was a new federalism that sought to circumvent the Washington bureaucracy and an executive branch in which decision making was highly centralized among White House advisers.[36]

President Nixon not only adopted a prevailing mind set that presupposed an activist presidency, he wholeheartedly endorsed it. Stanley Kutler quotes Nixon as saying, "I thought it was absurd for members of Congress to complain that the executive branch had stolen power from them. Modern presidents had merely stepped into the vacuum created when Congress failed to discipline itself sufficiently to play a strong policy-making role."[37] Governmental power, he later said, was so disconnected that it resembled "fragmented fiefdoms" that had a "hobbling effect" on efficiency.[38]

Not since Zachary Taylor had a first-term president won the White House without having party control in at least one branch of Congress. Democrats were already hostile toward Nixon and his attacks on the status quo were

[34] LBJL, Quayle Poll 245, January 1966, Fred Panzer Files, Box 177.
[35] Hoff, *Nixon Reconsidered*, p. 67. Italics in original.
[36] Ibid.
[37] Stanley I. Kutler, *The Wars of Watergate: The Last Crisis of Richard Nixon*. New York: Knopf, 1990, p. 127, citing Richard M. Nixon, *RN: The Memoirs of Richard Nixon, Vol. I*. New York: Warner Books, 1979, p. 512. [Note: The quotation cited by Kutler could not be located on the corresponding page of Nixon's memoirs.]
[38] Richard M. Nixon, cited in Kutler, *The Wars of Watergate*, p. 139.

perceived as attempts to aggrandize power. Unlike his predecessor, conciliation with Congress was not President Nixon's forte. In his memoirs, he writes how he was determined to "knock heads together in order to get things done" in Congress, and how he recognized early in his presidency that resistance from Congress would be the norm, rather than the exception.[39] In 1969, he unsuccessfully appointed to the Supreme Court Clement F. Haynesworth and G. Harrold Carswell, signaling both dissension from Congress and the administration's unwillingness to navigate appointments through the Democratically controlled Congress. After the Democrats gained nine House seats and eleven governorships (while losing two Senate seats) in 1970, President Nixon once again deployed an offensive strategy against Congress. When the Senate repealed the Gulf of Tonkin Resolution, Nixon's advisers and surrogates insinuated that Congress was abetting the enemy.[40]

What emerged was a presidency in which information was sought to increase presidential power and autonomy, so much so that Thomas W. Benham, vice president of ORC, the polling firm commissioned by the Nixon White House, once referred to "the voracious White House appetite for information."[41] Recognizing that monitoring public opinion was vital to his success, President Nixon appointed his chief of staff, H.R. Haldeman, to be the primary point man for measuring and interpreting public opinion. Haldeman was a former advertising executive whose familiarity with surveys stemmed from his experience in marketing. According to his diaries, Haldeman was told by Nixon that the White House was an isolation tank that required his staff to "get in touch" with the average American.[42] Haldeman controlled who received White House polls and he severely limited their visibility to others. When Charles Colson asked to see an April 1971 poll about veterans, Haldeman denied the request, stating that "the President has ordered that no one is to see it."[43] Murray Chotiner, President Nixon's political counselor, asked to receive "the results of any polls that are taken," but was told by Haldeman that he would receive "all pertinent polling information" and that he was welcome to offer his thoughts to Nixon aide Jeb

[39] Nixon, *RN*, p. 414.

[40] Kutler, *The Wars of Watergate*, p. 157.

[41] Richard Milhous Nixon Project at the National Archives [RMNP@NA], "Polls Chron July–August 1971," Note from Benham to Strachan, July 9, 1971, H.R. Haldeman [HRH] Files, Box 335. This point is also addressed in Jacobs and Shapiro, "Presidential Manipulation of Polls and Public Opinion."

[42] Haldeman, *Haldeman Diaries*, January 29, 1969. Also see Jacobs and Shapiro, "The Rise of Presidential Polling," p. 165.

[43] RMNP@NA, "ORC 4-28-30/71 Veterans Survey," Memorandum from Larry Higby to H.R. Haldeman (about Colson's request), May 4, 1971, Haldeman Files, Box 349. In addition to checking off that Colson could not see the poll, Haldeman also wrote the following cryptic message: "And we can pay for it – the front man was in case we released it."

Magruder about what polling items have been asked and what should be included in future polls.[44] By July 1971, Haldeman streamlined the gathering of polls in the White House. He asked his assistant, Larry Higby, to make sure that all polls were included in the poll books, replete with a cover sheet, title, the date, survey answers, and complete questionnaire. While Harry O'Neill, ORC's pollster, noted that several members of the White House staff worked with him in developing questions and press releases, Haldeman was in charge; he decided what should be seen, who should see it, and when.[45]

Haldeman conceptualized poll data as corresponding to "principal news events and principal Presidential activities."[46] Presidential popularity ratings were tracked and tabulated, and sometimes the president's approval rating was linearly documented with specific events (for example, Vietnam speech, Cambodia) identified in the chart's peaks and valleys.[47] Events inevitably shaped opinions, particularly opinions about the president, and as such, opinions helped determine which events to highlight or downplay in the media, and therefore opinions had to be monitored.

Haldeman also believed that poll data could be used as a means to advance the administration's legislative agenda. "The President was concerned as a result of the meeting with the Senators yesterday afternoon that we hadn't gotten the favorable poll data to them," Haldeman wrote. "And that they weren't aware of the ORC poll released last weekend, showing a shift in approval of the President's handling of the Vietnam War."[48] Two days later, Larry Higby wrote Haldeman with a "standard operating procedure for distribution of any future polls to the Hill."[49] Higby said that the problem with poll distribution arose in part because Nixon "mentioned some figures that we had not been instructed to distribute. (These are the figures that you gave [Republican National Committee] Chairman Dole.)"[50]

To Nixon, poll data were a valuable commodity, so much so that if ORC poll data were being sent to Republican members of Congress, they in return should send their polls to the administration. A July 29, 1969 memorandum

44 RMNP@NA, "1970 Polls IIB," Memorandum from Chotiner to Haldeman, January 21, 1970, and memorandum from Haldeman to Chotiner, January 23, 1970, Harry Dent Files, Box 10.
45 Telephone interview with Harry O'Neill, June 7, 1996.
46 RMNP@NA, Memorandum from Stephen Bull via Dwight L. Chapin to H.R. Haldeman, April 9, 1970, Stephen Bull Files, Box 5.
47 These poll sheets contained the approval, disapproval, and no opinion percentages, and the poll's release date. See RMNP@NA, "Polls," Memorandum and attachment from Gordon Strachan to Charles Colson, Gordon Strachan Files, Box 10.
48 RMNP@NA, "Polls Chron March–April 1971 [I of II]," Memorandum from Haldeman to Clark Mac Gregor, April 21, 1971, Haldeman Files, Box 334.
49 Ibid., Memorandum from Larry Higby to H.R. Haldeman, April 23, 1971, Box 334.
50 Ibid.

from Assistant to the President Bryce Harlow to Harry Dent reveals a plan to collect congressional surveys:

I want to report that Lyn Nofziger is working on ways to make effective use of Congressional and other polls. He is also studying ways to make them available for the President's perusal. We expect to have a breakdown shortly of polls taken to data this year by Republican Congressmen. Additionally, Lyn plans to determine whether individual members will be willing to ask their constituents their opinion on a few specific issues, using their newsletters as vehicles. At this time it does not appear that any of the members are planning full-fledged polls. Finally, Lyn is working with the National Committee to see if it can be a collection point for polls taken in states and districts around the country. He will keep me informed of his progress.[51]

President Nixon envisioned Republican congressional polls as instruments to advance his policies. Paradoxically, Haldeman's yearning to read and use congressional poll data was countered by his lack of a planned, going public strategy. In a note to Magruder, Haldeman argued that local polls showing high presidential approval would help deter candidates from running against the President.

From time to time as people are in here for appointments, and this especially applies to Congressmen and candidates, they indicate polls from their states show a very high approval rating for the President. These polls from the states should be collected and Magruder should set up a plan for feeding them out gradually – not all at once – to keep up the point of the President's standing in the states and to show the desire of the people throughout the country for the President's support in the election ... This will help to build the idea that running against the President is dangerous. This should be done for the national effect, not for the local effect. A very high standing in a particular state can have a national effect, especially as it is repeated.[52]

Showing members of Congress Nixon's strength in polls (as measured by his popularity and the approval of his agenda) yielded political dividends. Local polls showing support for President Nixon were to be disseminated to enhance the president's popularity in order to ward off presidential challengers. While there is no evidence that this plan to amass GOP polls came to fruition, both Harlow and Haldeman's suggestions underscore how President Nixon and his advisers studied polls and attempted to exploit them for their electoral and legislative purposes.

Haldeman and Nixon understood that poll data affected legislators' decisions. Referring to a point made by the president, Haldeman wrote, "[P]olls directly affect our ability to govern, because of their influence on Congressmen, foreign leaders, etc...."[53] Additionally, according to

---

[51] RMNP@NA, "1970 Polls IIB," Memorandum for the Staff Secretary, July 29, 1969, Harry Dent Files, Box 10.
[52] RMNP@NA, "1970 Poll(s) Other 2 of 2," Confidential Memorandum for Mr. Magruder, September 26, 1970, Harry Dent Files, Box 10.
[53] Haldeman, *Haldeman Diaries*, January 19, 1971.

Rowland Evans and Robert Novak, authors of *Nixon in the White House* and journalists who covered the Nixon administration, Haldeman thought of Congress as "an awkward and obnoxious obstacle, a hostile foreign power." They continued:

Haldeman, in particular, favored a take-it-or-leave-it, the-hell-with-them attitude in dealing with Congress. The other extreme was the conviction, later dimmed by events, that the way to get Congress to do the President's bidding was precisely the same as the way to get gullible housewives to buy soap – in other words, by using every public-relations and ad-man technique, to go out and sell ... they continued to think [this would work], long after [Bryce] Harlow, with the wisdom and experience, had tried to disabuse them of this idea.[54]

White House officials tried to intimidate or woo members of Congress – specifically Democratic senators. White House staffer William E. Timmons asked Harry Dent for inclusion of a poll question that he explicitly stated would be used for persuading senators to vote for a certain bill.

If you are planning any professional polls for candidates or the White House, could you arrange to ask a question on the SAFEGUARD PHASE II system? This information would be most helpful in squeezing certain Democrat Senators on this year's ABM [Anti-ballistic missile] vote ... Please let me know if there's a possibility for a piggy-back question.[55]

Dent responded to Timmons by saying that this request had been passed on to "our professional pollster."[56] No question in the 1970 poll archives could be found explicitly asking about Safeguard Phase II, and as such, the request should not be interpreted as a critical event. Still, the purpose of the request, regardless of its implementation, indicated that a Nixon adviser envisioned polls to be used to convince members of Congress that certain policies were popular with the electorate and therefore worthy of particular votes.[57] Additionally, Timmons' request shows how politicized the Nixon polling operation was: Poll questions could be added to a questionnaire if they could be politically justified. Poll answers were not just about seeking public attitudes, but about seeking political power.

Although Nixon's advisers initially wanted to obtain polls from Republican members of Congress, they also did not want Congress to question how they were paying for polls. The issue of federal funding for polls arose as early

---

54 Rowland Evans, Jr., and Robert D. Novak, *Nixon in the White House: The Frustration of Power.* New York: Random House, 1971, p. 109.
55 RMNP@NA, "1970 Polls IIA," Memorandum from William E. Timmons to Harry Dent, February 25, 1970, Harry S. Dent Files, Box 10.
56 Ibid., Note from Dent to Timmons, February 26, 1970.
57 A list of polls filed in the Trude Brown Safe indicated that the White House received some state and congressional polls. See RMNP@NA, "Polls Chron March–April 1971 [I of II]," Haldeman [HRH] Files, Box 334.

as 1970, when Larry Higby contacted Alexander Haig of the National Security Council [NSC] about the NSC's "doing their own polling with Federal funds."[58] Haig thought such an idea was unwise because it "would be impossible to do and still maintain the degree of security required with regard to the information received."[59] Similarly, a June 30, 1971 memorandum from Jon Huntsman to H.R. Haldeman discussed ways to finance polls conducted by the Opinion Research Corporation (ORC):

It was determined that no other agencies or councils can proceed with these expenditures legally or contractually. [The executive branch's] Domestic Council cannot do this because they are already overextended in this area for FY '71 and they are also concerned about congressional relations should they be audited.[60]

One week later, staff secretary to the president, John Campbell, wrote a memorandum to John Ehrlichman about funding of polls conducted for the Domestic [Policy] Council. Campbell reiterated Huntsman's concerns that members of Congress may object to the White House's funding of polls and specifically the use of the president's de facto polling firm, ORC, as the winner of a future Domestic Council poll contract.

The cons with using Domestic Council funds are:
1. Basically . . . a disclosure of this contract during the political season of 1972 might be embarrassing to the President.
2. Although the chances are slim, the possibility does exist that Ken [Cole?] would be asked during budget testimony next year on the Council's FY '73 budget about the contracts the Council has had and the firms we used.
3. Of interest is the fact that the White House, although it has had funds available in the past, its books are never audited by GAO and it is never probed by Congressional committees, had felt it *too risky* to do any polling with White House funds and always used outside funds.[61]

Nixon's advisers feared receiving negative attention if Congress learned about the White House's extensive use of polls. Although they never mentioned the congressional hearings during the Eisenhower years, Nixon's advisers realized that congressional audits showing private polling by the Nixon White House would be politically devastating. It was too risky for the executive branch to pay for polls for two reasons. First, the polls were private; they were not for congressional perusal. Second, they had political overtones, and as a result, could not be paid for with governmental funds. So the White House resorted to outside funding, namely, the RNC, and private

[58] RMNP@NA, "Memorandum for HRH from GS," Memorandum from Higby to Haldeman, December 9, 1970, HRH Files, Box 342.
[59] Ibid.
[60] RMNP@NA, "[CF] PR 15 Public Opinion Polls [1971–74] [1 of 2]," Memorandum from Huntsman to Haldeman, June 30, 1971, Box 53.
[61] RMNP@NA, "[CF] Public Opinion Polls [1971–74] [1 of 2]," Memorandum from Campbell to Ehrlichman, July 7, 1971, Box 53.

persons. Colson was the contact of one source for poll payments. When asked at one point if he could raise money to pay for some polls, Colson responded in the negative, saying, "I would rather not because it is a drain from a more important use later and is a little bit dangerous."[62] In another instance, Haldeman informed Colson that he could not see a poll, adding that the payment for polls was aided by a secret source which Nixon officials disguised by falsely attributing funding to a "front man." "And we can pay for it," reads a handwritten note by Haldeman, ". . . the front man was in case we released it."[63]

Many of the ORC polls began with two of the three following questions:[64]

1. How do you rate the job President Nixon and his administration have done so far – excellent, good, only fair, or poor? 2. Since Richard Nixon has become President, has your opinion of him become more favorable or less favorable than it was before? 3. Do you approve or disapprove of the way Richard Nixon is handling his job as President?

In addition to these questions, it is hard to imagine a topic about which ORC did not poll. O'Neill noted that Haldeman and his staff "really knew what they were doing when it came to polls. They asked questions before and after certain issues and actions made news."[65] Polls in the Nixon Archives confirm O'Neill's point. Below is a sample of Nixon's private poll questions:[66]

- This week the Lyndon B. Johnson Library will be opened in Texas. Do you think this library is a good idea or not?
- President Nixon participated in a televised interview last week with the commentators of the three networks. Did you see that television program?
- Have you heard, seen, or read about President Nixon's decision to send a rescue mission to Son Tay, North Vietnam to free American POWs?
- Do you approve or disapprove of President Nixon's decision to send a rescue mission to Son Tay, North Vietnam to free American POWs?
- Would you approve of further attempts to rescue American prisoners of war including another rescue mission?

[62] Charles Colson, in Lawrence R. Jacobs and Robert Y. Shapiro, "The Rise of Presidential Polling: The Nixon White House in Historical Perspective," pp. 171–172, citing RMNP@NA, Memorandum from Colson to Jack Gleason, April 18, 1970, Charles Colson Files, Box 100.
[63] RMNP@NA, "ORC 4-28-30/71 Veterans Survey," Memorandum from Larry Higby to H.R. Haldeman (about Colson's request), May 4, 1971, Haldeman Files, Box 349.
[64] See RMNP@NA, ORC polls in HRH Files, Boxes 130–420.
[65] Conversation with Harry O'Neill, May 19, 1995.
[66] These poll questions can be found in HRH Files, Boxes 334, 340, 408–410. Note: This is a sampling of questions; it is not a comprehensive list, nor does it indicate how often these questions were asked.

- In 1972 there will be another presidential election. Suppose this election were being held today and the candidates were Richard Nixon and Edmund Muskie, [sic] which one would you vote for?[67]
- Plans have been announced for a series of demonstrations in the next few weeks to protest the war in Vietnam. Do you favor or oppose these demonstrations?
- The United States is on the verge of a nervous breakdown (strongly agree, somewhat agree, somewhat disagree, strongly disagree, no opinion).
- A proposal has been made in Congress to require the U.S. government to bring home all U.S. troops before the end of this year. Would you like to have your congressman vote for or against this proposal?
- Do you approve of the way the Washington police handled the [antiwar] demonstrators?
- Do you feel that in his attacks on American industry, consumer advocate Ralph Nader has done more good than harm, or more harm than good?
- Is this the way you would have probably voted before President Nixon's trip to China, or has his trip caused you to change your mind?
- Have you seen, read, or heard about the so-called "Watergate" incident last June, when five men were arrested while trying to break in and bug the Democratic National Committee headquarters at the Watergate Hotel?
- Who do you think put these men up to the break-in and bugging attempt at the Democratic National Committee headquarters – President Nixon, President Nixon's campaign committee, the Republican Party, or Cuban exiles?
- Do you think President Nixon was responsible for the break-in and bugging attempt at the Democratic National Committee headquarters, or not?
- Do you believe this whole break-in and bugging attempt at the Democratic National Committee headquarters is just more politics, or is it something serious?[68]

The ORC polls captured the pulse of current events. O'Neill commented about how certain questions were asked on some surveys and not others:

We wanted to ask the approval question. That was a stand-by. Others – it depended on what was going on. The nice thing about asking a question more than once is that you don't necessarily have to ask it every two weeks to see a trend. You can put one

---

[67] December 1–3, 1970, ORC Poll. Note that questions 7 through 10 of the same poll replace Muskie with Senators Edward Kennedy, Hubert Humphrey, George McGovern, and Mayor John Lindsay respectively. Moreover, the "who would you vote for" question is repeatedly asked by ORC throughout 1972. See RMNP@NA, HRH Files, Boxes 408–410.

[68] This Watergate-related question was found in the January 12–14, 1973 poll. RMNP@NA, "Spending Poll," HRH Files, Box 170. This poll report suggests that Watergate-related questions appear to have been asked first in an August 29–31, 1972 poll.

in, take it out, and put it back later. Generally, current events determined the poll's contents. They wanted to see what people thought about what was going on.[69]

In this regard, the ORC polls functioned as if they were media polls, asking about day-to-day activities that showed what Americans favored, opposed, enjoyed, or disdained. As Haldeman connected poll data to events, ORC asked about these events, and reams of internal memoranda noted changes in these poll data over time.

David R. Derge, president of Behavioral Research Associates in Bloomington, Indiana, provided analyses of ORC polls from 1969 through part of 1971. Analyses were about five pages long and contained advice on how better to market the administration's policies. Derge's advice paralleled that of Cantril, Harris, and Quayle, as he frequently suggested ways to increase publicity and expand coverage for the president. But Derge served another function; he was a Ph.D. and polling specialist at Southern Illinois and later at the University of Indiana and his academic credentials added legitimacy to Nixon's polling operation. Derge helped design questions as well as interpret the answers, and once "met with Nixon and Kissinger to hammer out ... the wording of a question in the Oval Office."[70] O'Neill elaborated on Derge's role, describing him as a professional, competent interpreter of polls.

You have to remember that this is before the pollster is part of the in-group – the inner circle. [Patrick] Caddell changes that, when he becomes Carter's strategist, guru, and pollster. But these are the days when the administration is developing their use of polls, without having the pollster as the insider. Derge acts as a go-between for the White House and ORC. We [ORC] had a good relationship with him. Lovely guy, and smart ... I can't recall any conflicts between Derge and us. We got along.[71]

Although there is some evidence that Haldeman grew impatient with Derge's summaries ("what we need is analysis, not highlights"), Derge provided advice on how to conduct the surveys and how to interpret them.[72] The Nixon White House advisers enjoyed the fruits of several experts' labor, and in so doing, gained further appreciation for their private polling operation.

President Nixon read some of these polls and their accompanying analyses. In a lengthy memorandum dated July 9, 1971 from Assistant Director of the Domestic Policy Council John C. Whitaker to John D. Ehrlichman, Whitaker responded to President Nixon's criticism of a May 1971 ORC poll about the environment. Nixon claimed that the poll suffered from not asking respondents their views about the environment in the context of personal

[69] Conversation with Harry O'Neill, May 19, 1995.
[70] Derge, interview with Jacobs, May 17, 1993, in Jacobs and Shapiro, "The Rise of Presidential Polling," p. 173.
[71] O'Neill interview.
[72] RMNP@NA, "Memorandum from Derge to Haldeman," Handwritten note by Haldeman to Higby on March 25, 1971, HRH Files, Box 334.

Harry O'Neill (Courtesy of Harry O'Neill)

tradeoffs, specifically job or income loss. Whitaker noted that the next set of polls tried to relate the environment to the voter personally in key states:

For Texas   Do you think it would or would not be worth it to close down plants and create some unemployment in order to clean up the Houston Ship Channel? *For California*   Do you think it would or would not be worth it to ration the use of automobiles and use of electricity in order to clean up San Francisco Bay? *For Illinois*   Do you think it would or would not be worth it to close down plants and create some unemployment in order to clean up the Chicago River and the shores of Lake Michigan? Do you think it would or would not be worth it to close down plants and create some unemployment in order to clean up the Ohio River? *For New Jersey*   Do you think it would or would not be worth it to close down plants and create some unemployment in order to clean up the Raritan Bay? I really want to see how strong the issue is in terms of tradeoff, but knowing [sic] full well almost the entire public doesn't see it as a tradeoff question."[73]

The multitude of ORC questions, the frequency with which they polled, the speed with which they interpreted their polls, the tracking of the answers

---

[73] RMNP@NA, Whitaker to Ehrlichman, 9 July 1971, Response to Log P-1775, "Polls [From CFOA 762][2 of 4]," Whitaker Files, Box 92.

by the White House, President Nixon's perusal of poll data, and the evidence that national questions were tailored to individual states all indicate that ORC and the Nixon White House escalated presidential polling to an unprecedented level. Presidential surveys were now commonly employed instruments to see what the public knew about current events and how President Nixon could advance his agenda based on that knowledge. Polls were used with great frequency – almost biweekly at times – to monitor day-to-day current events. Haldeman's experience with surveys from his work in advertising resulted in an ability to organize and administer a polling operation that sought to obtain and manipulate poll data from a variety of sources.

Haldeman did not plan on using polls to go public as Kernell describes the going public strategy. Rather, Haldeman's version of going public was generic and national, as compared to specific and statewide. He did not use tailor-made polls to persuade individual members of Congress to support the president, but he repeatedly desired to circulate polls that showed a popular president in the hopes that they cumulatively and nationally would reinforce the president's political strength.

The tight reigns over access to poll data by Haldeman, the secrecy underlying the polls, breadth of the ORC polls, and multiple use of Derge and O'Neill in creating and interpreting polls are proof that Nixon's polling operation surpassed his predecessors. President Nixon had helped institutionalize presidential polling, and in doing so, had obviated Congress' function of interpreting public opinion.

CONCLUSION

Several common themes can be identified in the trajectory of how presidential polling became institutionalized. First, the presidential polling apparatus with respect to Congress became ever more active with each successive administration. President Hoover intentionally avoided meeting directly with members of Congress, opting instead to locate public opinion in part by having a former member of Congress serve to measure public opinion for him. Hoover also adopted other measures of public opinion, which will be addressed in subsequent chapters. Hoover's presidency is particularly prescient because of the privacy attached to public opinion data, the nexus between public opinion and presidential public relations, and the administration's attempt to replace Congress as the institutional conduit between the president and the people.

FDR expanded the role of presidential public opinion research beyond monitoring congressional opinions. Instead, he used private polls as a direct conduit to the masses, trying to figure out how to market his ideas and wartime strategies. In many ways, the onset of the war made this use of polling possible, for an understanding of domestic public opinion could be used to improve the ability of the executive branch to implement military actions, especially those that were potentially unpopular. Here again, Cantril's polling for the Roosevelt administration was done without congressional interference. Furthermore, Cantril's academic credentials, his working relationship with Gallup, and his analyses impressed the president, who personally read the poll data for information about what Americans were thinking about his policies.

In the late 1940s and early 1950s, the State Department secretly began to use polls and intentionally hid their polling contract from Congress. Congressional hearings about these polls reveal how reluctant the executive branch was to rely on the legislative branch for assessments of the citizenry. Rather, the executive branch sought unfiltered, secret gauges of public sentiment, and private polls offered them the means to obviate Congress.

Louis Harris began to personalize presidential polling by fostering frequent contacts with President Kennedy. Harris' polling for Kennedy retained the secrecy of his predecessor Hadley Cantril. Harris' polls served as vehicles to measure public opinion without congressional interference. The Johnson administration sometimes used Oliver Quayle's state and congressional polls to measure public opinion.[74] Quayle's multiple Vietnam-related poll questions, for example, signify an eagerness to identify what the public was thinking and a desire to market the administration's policies to the public.

Finally, President Nixon's private polling operation signifies yet another turning point in the evolution of presidential polling. Collectively, the secrecy and frequency of the polls (they were kept in a safe and conducted fortnightly), the strict limitations as to who had access to presidential poll data, the suggestions that polls could be used to intimidate members of Congress, and the breadth and depth of the ORC poll questions resulted in a transformation of the presidency. Because of the activism sought by Nixon and implemented by Haldeman, the Nixon administration revolutionized how polls were to be used by future chief executives. Public opinion was now a precious commodity that could be located privately, extensively, and without Congress.

The anomaly among these presidents is Harry Truman, whose spurning of polls preceded the pundits and pollsters' erroneous prediction that New York State Governor Thomas E. Dewey would defeat Truman in the 1948 presidential election. Truman's distrust of polls was exacerbated by his 1948 victory, but the flawed polls of 1948 were not the cause of his disdain for polling.[75] William Doyle, in his book about White House tapes, notes that

---

[74] Fewer than a quarter of Albert Cantril's memos concerned Quayle's polls of states and congressional districts. See fn. 32.

[75] Benedict K. Zobrist, Director of the Harry S. Truman Library, noted that "the White House files for the Truman administration failed to indicate that President Truman or his staff ever made use of public opinion polls as an administrative tool. While there is some evidence in

Truman rebuffed using the tapes available to chief executives, much like he disregarded private polls as vehicles to measure public sentiment.[76] One can only speculate as to why Truman avoided private polling. Perhaps it was his skepticism in modern social scientific techniques, his reluctance to replace what he thought was commonsense with technology, or his political upbringing that inculcated him with an appreciation of political parties as being the proper organization for locating public opinion. No doubt the Pendergast machine measured public opinion in traditional ways – through the media and by talking with constituents. That method proved successful for Truman throughout his political life; perhaps he saw no reason to change a system that was working.

As will be shown in Chapter 5, the relationship between the presidency and the political parties also played a significant role in the evolution of presidential polling. As presidents and presidential candidates employed public opinion polls with increasing frequency, political parties covered the costs associated with private polling, often without seeing the results. From Hoover, a Republican Party black sheep who assessed straw poll results to chart his popularity, to Nixon, whose zeal for secrecy led him to withhold valuable poll data from the RNC, the national political parties witnessed their traditional function of assessing public opinion rapidly shift to the presidency.

the files that copies of the Gallup and other polls were occasionally referred to Truman for his information, we could find nothing to indicate that he made use of such information in making decisions" Letter from Zobrist to this author, November 7, 1991.

[76] William Doyle, *Inside the Oval Office: White House Tapes from FDR to Clinton*. New York: Kodansha International, 1999.

5

Take the Money and Poll

Parties and the Public Opinion Presidency

Throughout the twentieth century, congressional and party leadership have frequently overlapped. Presidents do not trust these leaders to provide independent gauges of public opinion. This chapter begins by analyzing how President Hoover did not rely on the Republican Party to measure public opinion for him. The chapter continues chronologically through the Nixon administration, documenting how strained relations between presidents and their parties generate a need by the executive branch to gauge public opinion autonomously. Over time, presidential polls become more accepted as a political tool. For Kennedy, television, not political parties, was the best conduit for increasing voter turnout, improving Kennedy's image, and assuaging citizens' fears about his religion. In the case of the Nixon White House, the GOP received sanitized polling data after Nixon's advisers culled the survey responses. Parties' financial coffers sometimes subsidize presidents' polls even though presidents don't trust their parties to serve as the institutional conduit between themselves and the American people.

Presidents often have been dependent on parties for obtaining poll data, in ways that deserve further explication. During election time, some presidential candidates established links between themselves and a key party leader (for example, the National Committee Chair). This personal connection serves as a conduit of poll-related information. As president, this relationship changes; the personal connection with the party operative frequently endures, but over time, the presidency has sought to distance the national party committee from being a recipient of private poll data. What has resulted is a process where parties now pay for presidents' private polls, even as the parties do not have access to the polls for which they have paid.

HOOVER

Before he became president, Hoover was not popular with the GOP party elite, in part because they questioned Hoover's party loyalty. While Hoover

74

was a registered Republican, he worked in the Wilson Administration as the director of the Food Administration, during which he wrote that "We must have united support for the President" and attended Democratic Party luncheons during the war. Such moves outraged the RNC, which interpreted Hoover as endorsing Democrats, and specifically a Democratic Congress.[1] In fact, on January 2, 1920, Franklin Roosevelt wrote to Hugh Gibson, the American minister in Poland, saying that Hoover "is certainly a wonder, and I wish that we could make him President of the United States. There could not be a better one."[2]

Additionally, Republican operatives saw Hoover as a self-advertising foreign policy interventionist who rose to popularity without progressing through the party ranks. Hoover's trajectory to the presidency included several unsuccessful attempts by his opponents to block his candidacy at the GOP convention in Kansas City. They felt that Hoover was not one of them – he did not emerge through the traditional Republican Party organization, he did not participate in the writing of the 1928 Republican platform, and he did not enjoy or employ partisan politics.[3] His money, organization, and image, and not his party connections, enabled him to capture the Republican presidential nomination in 1928.[4]

A comment at the annual Gridiron Dinner in 1932 captures Hoover's distaste for traditional partisan politics. Hoover lashed out against partisanship in times of crisis, exclaiming that political parties have "a positive responsibility to leadership and to patriotic action which overrides partisanship."[5] Given his views of partisanship as unnecessarily confrontational, one would have expected Hoover and his advisers to gauge public opinion in a matter that was consistent with Hoover's nonpartisan proclivities. Recognizing that support from party loyalists was likely to be tepid, Hoover's 1928 campaign actively solicited support from outside the traditional party operatives and loyalists. Hoover and his allies forged a strategy that circumvented the Republican Party organization by creating their own campaign, independent of the traditional vote-getting mechanisms employed by political parties of the era. Because Hoover had cultivated his image as a presidential contender

[1] David Burner, *Herbert Hoover: A Public Life*. New York: Knopf, 1979, p. 150.
[2] Franklin Roosevelt, in *Herbert Hoover and Franklin D. Roosevelt: A Documentary History*, edited by Timothy Walsh and Dwight M. Miller. Westport, CT: Greenwood Press, 1998, p. 6.
[3] Hoover's aide James MacLafferty shared the sentiment that Hoover "became President against the wishes of the leaders of the Republican party and they have never truly liked him. Many of them secretly worked against him or were cool in what they did for him," HCHA, MacLafferty Diary, November 16, 1932. Also see Martin L. Fausold, *The Presidency of Herbert C. Hoover*. Lawrence: University of Kansas Press, 1985, pp. 23–24; and Wilfred E. Binkley, *American Political Parties: Their Natural History*.
[4] Fausold, *The Presidency of Herbert C. Hoover*, p. 22.
[5] Hoover 1934, II, p. 160.

as the secretary of commerce, most notably by chairing the Mississippi Flood Committee, many citizens knew of Hoover before his candidacy because they had read headlines about him or had seen movies produced by the Commerce Department that showed Hoover doing relief work. His pervasive presence in the news provided Secretary Hoover with a powerful instrument for a presidential contender – name recognition.[6]

Continuing the campaign outside of traditional party operatives, Hoover's advisers tracked the straw polls, then considered to be the most reliable and valid measure of public opinion data as it related to elections.[7] States were listed alphabetically and then tabulated with the weekly percentage straw poll vote for both Hoover (noted with a capital H) and his Democratic presidential opponent Al Smith (noted with a capital S).[8] Additional straw poll data include a September 1928 survey commissioned by the *National Republic* that asked "newspaper editors and other subscribers" a series of questions such as, "What issue or issues seem to be uppermost in the minds of the voters of your locality," "Judging from the present outlook, how do you think your state will go, and by how much? If you have made no further inquiry beyond your own locality, we suggest that you base this guess on the drift in your own neighborhood," and "Do you expect a light or a heavy vote?"[9]

Other data suggest that locating public opinion was a highly politicized enterprise. Edward Anthony, the New York State Director of Publicity for the Republican National Committee, compiled a poll of persons recognized in *Who's Who* for the Hoover campaign. An accompanying memorandum reveals how measuring public opinion and partisanship were intertwined.

The results were Hoover 8,762 and Smith 1,270. This was quite a straw in the wind thing at the time, but it not only gave us a story that was carried by AP, UP, Universal, and INS, but it gave us the names of prominent people whom we could suggest as chairmen of committees. It was a gold mine – these 8,700 names. We got many of them to work hard for the Chief's election.[10]

Public opinion had a political undertone, especially as the straw poll was sent to Hoover's advisers by a Republican Party chair and because the opinions directly concerned citizens' views for Hoover's reelection.

Such straw poll data were routinely sent to Hoover's advisers, most all of it showing Hoover defeating his Democratic opponent Al Smith. When

---

[6] See Joan Hoff Wilson, *Herbert Hoover: Forgotten Progressive*. Boston: Little Brown, 1975; Burner, *Herbert Hoover*, p. 198; Fausold, *The Presidency of Herbert C. Hoover*.

[7] Jay M. Shafritz, *HarperCollins Dictionary of American Government and Politics*. New York: Harper Perennial, 1992, p. 446.

[8] HCHA, "Polls-Surveys," Campaigns and Transitions, Box 161.

[9] HCHA, Campaigns and Transitions, Box 161.

[10] Ibid., and HCHA, Oral History Interview with Edward Anthony, July 12, 1970.

the straw polls showed Hoover trailing, one adviser claimed the polls were flawed. Ernest Walker Sawyer, a Republican loyalist and friend of both Hoover and Secretary of Interior Ray Wilbur, periodically provided summaries of Hearst and *Literary Digest* straw polls. Sawyer once commented that the Hearst polls were possibly tainted with an anti-Hoover bias. Although an October Hearst straw poll showed no new trends in eight states, Sawyer wrote that "these are states which we expect Hoover to be gaining." He questioned the methodology of the *Digest* poll, asking Wilbur why the *Digest* poll had counted over two million voters when twenty million had not yet been counted. "There must be something wrong with the counting to get jammed up like that. Perhaps they are holding back the votes?"[11]

The 1932 Hoover-Curtis campaign also tracked the *Literary Digest* straw polls, comparing their 1924 and 1928 results, and describing them as an accurate barometer of the forthcoming election because of the polls' scientific quality. When data showed that the GOP ticket was leading the Democrats, Hoover-Curtis campaign chairman William H. Hill issued a press statement for "immediate release" saying that although actual election returns "will show some deviations from these scientific statistics . . . the result of this study points so overwhelmingly to the popular leaning to Hoover everywhere, that I believe it clinches any doubt that may have been felt as to the certainty of a Hoover victory at the polls."[12]

While some of the data purported to be scientific, some of the polls were simply whatever Hoover's advisers could obtain. Straw polls conducted by college students, for example, were received and read by Secretary of the Interior Ray Wilbur.[13] Other poll-related data for the Hoover campaign were sent by RNC operatives. Lewis Strauss, the vice treasurer of the Republican National Committee, for example, was a major distributor and recipient of straw poll data. On October 21, 1932, Strauss received a poll from J. David Houser, president of The Houser Associates, in which approximately five thousand personal, face-to-face interviews were made in fourteen areas centered around large cities. According to the seventeen-page poll report, interviewers "worked out from these cities as centers, and interviewed both the rural and urban dwellers . . . A careful attempt was made to get a sampling

[11] HCHA, "Political – 1932," Ernest Walker Sawyer, Ray Wilbur Papers, October 19, 1932.
[12] HCHA, "Polls," Presidential Papers – Press Relations, Box 1203.
[13] Archives contained election-related information about students from Harvard, Massachusetts Institute of Technology, Columbia University, the University of Washington, the University of Minnesota, Cornell, the University of California, Whittier, Park College, Presbyterian Theological Seminary, Sarah Lawrence, Washington State University, Colgate, University of Southern California, Lawrence, Ohio State, University of Detroit, Amherst, Haverford, Oberlin, Antioch, Buffalo Teachers College, and Hamilton. See HCHA, Wilbur Papers, "Political – 1932," Wilbur Papers, Box 97.

among each economic class group."[14] Respondents were divided into five
categories – loyal Republicans, Hoover supporters who voted for Smith in
1928, loyal Democrats, Roosevelt supporters who voted for Hoover in 1928,
and Norman Thomas supporters. Questions about prohibition, the depression, the tariff, relations with Europe, and "significant beliefs" were asked,
and computations were made to show the differences between the Hoover
and Roosevelt supporters.

Strauss became a personal conduit between the Hoover presidency and
the GOP in the 1932 campaign. In addition to collecting the Houser poll,
Strauss amassed and interpreted many straw polls, including those published
in Hearst newspapers. His data were divided into three columns – states
solidly for Hoover, states lately showing a plurality of Hoover votes which
formerly had reported a Franklin Roosevelt majority, and other states where
Roosevelt's lead was precipitating. Each state's electoral votes were also
noted. The Hoover campaign concentrated in assessing public opinion only
in states where Hoover was leading or gaining popularity, as the report
explicitly read "States definitely [for] Roosevelt not included." Their analysis was flawed, showing Hoover defeating FDR with 272 electoral votes,
with another 76 electoral votes for Hoover in states where FDR's lead was
supposedly weakening.[15]

The RNC repeatedly released straw poll data, all of it showing Hoover
leading Roosevelt. One RNC press release concerned Mr. Lloyd A. Pfeiffer,
a traveling salesman whose trip to nine states indicated that "the business
men are buying goods, only and if, President Hoover is reelected."[16] An
October 25, 1932 press release declared Hoover would defeat Roosevelt with
an electoral college vote of 369 to 70, based on a poll taken at a Chicago Ford
assembly plant. "Combining these figures," the release continued, "with
the results of four polls announced... from Parks College, Parkville, Mo.,
Presbyterian Theological Seminary and Ryan Car Works, Chicago, and the
directors of the Audit Bureau of Circulation give Hoover slightly more than
71% of the total vote; Roosevelt slightly more than 19% and Thomas just
under 10%."[17]

Hoover did not rely on parties to measure public opinion for him. As will
be shown in Chapter 6, clerks in the Hoover White House rigorously tabulated newspaper editorials, documenting both the positions taken by editors,
and the circulations of the newspapers. To some extent, these tabulations

[14] The cities mentioned are New York, Boston, Pittsburgh, Cleveland, Chicago, Denver, Tulsa,
New Orleans, Los Angeles, Kansas City, Atlanta, San Francisco, Seattle, and Oklahoma City.
[15] HCHA, "Campaign of 1932 – Polls," Lewis L. Strauss Papers, Box 16. Hearst endorsed
John Garner for President in January 1932; there is no mention of Hearst's anti-Hoover
sentiments in these reports.
[16] Ibid.
[17] HCHA, Presidential Papers – Press Relations, "Polls," Box 1203.

were an independent means by which Hoover's advisers sought autonomous gauges of public opinion. Hoover's successor, Franklin Roosevelt, vigorously solicited measures of the public mood independent of the Democratic Party. In this regard, the Hoover presidency serves as an important transition between the semidependence on parties and outright autonomy from them.

FDR

FDR's complex relationship with the Democratic Party promulgated his desire to gain autonomy from it. Charles LaCerra, author of *Franklin Delano Roosevelt and Tammany Hall of New York*, contends that FDR and the New York State Democratic Party had an ongoing love-hate partnership.[18] FDR began his political career as an antimachine reformer, campaigning against the political bosses and forming counterorganizations designed to tame political patronage. Slowly, he abandoned his antipathy for the New York City party bosses, growing to appreciate their organizational skills and ability to connect with the common citizen. When running for the United States Senate in 1914, FDR's friend Louis Howe advised FDR not to speak ill of Tammany, lest they mobilize around a friendlier primary opponent. However FDR retained his anti-Tammany edge and the bosses found a primary challenger in Ambassador to Germany James W. Gerard, who defeated FDR in New York state's first senatorial primary.

Having learned that alienating the city bosses was tantamount to political suicide, FDR chose a more amicable strategy, at least temporarily. As assistant secretary to the Navy, FDR asked Woodrow Wilson about getting involved in local New York politics. "My judgment is that it would be best if members of the administration should use as much influence as possible," suggested Wilson, "but say as little as possible."[19] Roosevelt eventually campaigned for Tammany-backed gubernatorial candidate Alfred E. Smith, but the Tammany forces still disdained FDR. In 1920, they advanced his name as a vice-presidential candidate, largely because they sensed a Republican victory and thought that by showcasing FDR as a national loser they could permanently eradicate his political ambitions. "We've got to get rid of him once and for all," DNC Committeeman and Tammany man Norman Mack said. "I tell you. He's a troublemaker."[20]

---

[18] Excellent (and sometimes contradictory) analyses of FDR's interaction with the Democratic Party can be found in James MacGregor Burns, *Roosevelt: The Lion and the Fox*. New York: Harvest, 1956; Lyle W. Dorsett, *FDR and the City Bosses*. Port Washington, NY: Kennikat Press, 1977; Milkis, *The President and the Parties*; Sean J. Savage, *Roosevelt: The Party Leader 1932–1945*. Lexington: University Press of Kentucky, 1991; and Arthur M. Schlesinger, *The Age of Roosevelt, The Crisis of the Old Order, 1919–1933*. Boston: Houghton Mifflin, 1957.

[19] Burns, *Roosevelt: The Lion and the Fox*, p. 56.

[20] Walter Myers, "FDR vs. The Democratic Party," *Esquire* 59 (March 1959), 115.

The Democrats lost in 1920, but FDR's tenure as a private citizen was short lived as he sought to develop the national Democratic Party and his stature in it. In 1921, he suggested to the DNC that they hold periodic conferences and establish permanent office headquarters in Washington, D.C. By 1925, *The New York Times* reported Tammany leader George Olvany, Brooklyn party boss John H. McCooey, and New York City Mayor Jimmy Walker meeting at Roosevelt's home. In 1928, Roosevelt won the governorship of New York previously occupied by Al Smith, who unsuccessfully sought the presidency. By this time, FDR had learned the valuable lessons of compromise provided to him by Wilson, Howe, and adviser Sam Rosenman. Roosevelt retained political appointments originally made by Smith, regularly met with Democratic Party bosses during his tenure as governor and periodically sought advice from Tammany bosses. But FDR also occasionally attempted to curb Tammany's power. This ambiguous, vacillating relationship did not win him friends in the press, his most notable critic being the editorialist Walter Lippmann, who described FDR as weak, evasive, and indecisive.[21]

Having won the presidency handily in 1936, FDR faced a party dilemma in the United States Senate. Majority Leader Joe Robinson had suddenly died; New Deal stalwart Alben Barkley from Kentucky and the more conservative Pat Harrison from Mississippi both wanted the job. Roosevelt fought for Barkley, who won, but the victory was pyrrhic, as the narrow margin of 38–37 revealed that Roosevelt had burned political capital he would need in the future. Nonetheless, with the counsel of Tommy Corcoran and Harold Ickes, FDR sought in 1938 to purge the Democratic Party of anti–New Dealers, much like Woodrow Wilson's misfired attempt in 1918 to cleanse Congress of contrary Democratic Senator Vardaman (Mississippi) and Representatives Slayden (Texas) and Huddleston (Alabama). FDR personally campaigned against Democratic Senators Millard Tydings (Maryland) and Walter George (Georgia) and indirectly against others, including Democratic incumbent Governor Charles H. Martin (Oregon). All except Martin won handily in their respective primaries and general elections; the Oregon

---

[21] Walter Lippmann, in *Interpretations, 1931–1932*, edited by Allan Nevins. New York: Macmillan, 1932, pp. 250–251. During his first presidential term, FDR involved himself in local New York Democratic Party matters. By intentionally endorsing Joseph V. McKee in the New York City mayoral race to split the Democratic vote, FDR sought a political fight with Tammany bosses. With national Democrats Roosevelt angered House Speaker William B. Bankhead and Majority Leader Sam Rayburn by not consulting with them over congressional appointees, as well as Pittsburgh, Pennsylvania party boss David Lawrence and three Democratic members of Congress by hastily postponing a White House meeting with them. See Savage, *Roosevelt: The Party Leader*, p. 32, Burns, *Roosevelt: The Lion and the Fox*, p. 349. According to Savage and Dorsett, FDR periodically met with party bosses throughout his third and fourth terms and the bosses grew fond of his New Deal policies, in part because they aided urban voters who lived where party machines were strong. See Dorsett, *FDR and the City Bosses*.

gubernatorial race was ultimately won by a Republican. Roosevelt's war on party rebels not only failed miserably, it backfired. Republicans gained eighty House seats and eight Senate seats.

Sean Savage argues that the purge of 1938 aided Democratic Party liberalism "by dramatically publicizing the ideological-policy differences and conflicts between the liberal and conservative elements of the Party."[22] In *The President and the Parties*, Sidney Milkis contends that Roosevelt's unsuccessful purge weakened the party in organizational manpower as it simultaneously strengthened the power of the executive branch to pursue FDR's own agenda.[23] Long-term benefits of defining the Democratic Party aside, the purge generated enduring tensions between the executive branch and party leaders.

Before the attempted purge, FDR and the national Democratic Party had tried to use polls as a means to develop their party organization. In 1928, a man by the name of Emil Hurja offered to work for John J. Raskob, who was then chairman of the DNC.

You do the same test to public opinion that you do to ore. In mining you take several samples from the face of the ore, pulverize them, and find out what the average pay per ton will be. In politics, you take sections of voters, check new trends against past performances, establish the percentage of shift among different voting strata, supplement this information with reports from competent observers in the field, and you can accurately predict an election result.[24]

Raskob declined Hurja's offer, but his replacement James Farley did not. Farley found Hurja's maps and statistical analyses invaluable political instruments. Farley's early allegiance to FDR stemmed from when Farley chaired the New York State Democratic Party, and to both Farley and the president, polls and politics were inextricably connected. They were to be used as instruments for both gauging public opinion and devices to exert political power. In the mid-1930s, as chairman of the Democratic National Committee, Farley frequently commissioned polls under the guidance of Hurja. Hurja introduced himself to Frank C. Walker, one of Roosevelt's financial supporters,

---

[22] Savage, *Roosevelt: The Party Leader 1932–1945*, p. 157.

[23] See Milkis, *The President and the Parties*, and Burns, *Roosevelt: The Lion and the Fox*, pp. 346–347. Farley warned FDR not to pursue the attempted purge and the dismal failure of the Democrats in 1938 hindered Farley's presidential ambitions. Farley and FDR ultimately became political adversaries after Roosevelt sought a third term. Farley quit as DNC Chairman and was replaced by Bronx Democratic Party boss Edward J. Flynn, who worked to restore party cohesion before eventually being nominated as Ambassador to Australia in 1942. Flynn was replaced by former DNC treasurer Frank Walker, who simultaneously served as Postmaster General. About a year later, St. Louis Democrat activist Bob Hennegan replaced Walker, seeking to "resolve intra-party conflicts and assure Roosevelt's renomination." See Savage, *Roosevelt: The Party Leader 1932–1945*, p. 102.

[24] Thomas Sugrue, "Farley's Guess Man," *American Magazine* (May 1936): 87.

as a "good Democrat" who would employ his knowledge of statistics for no remuneration.[25] Farley helped Hurja get a job as an administrative assistant in the Department of the Interior. He stayed there until Interior Secretary Harold L. Ickes objected and was then moved to DNC headquarters.

Emil Hurja on the cover of *Time* magazine, 3/2/36 (Courtesy of Timepix)

FDR appointed Farley postmaster general, and Farley became a de facto "patronage czar" in the Roosevelt administration as he retained his role as DNC chair.[26] To Farley, loyal career appointees made good workers, and therefore good public policy. Patronage appointees would "work for a higher thing than mere self; they want to have the party and the principles it stands for to succeed."[27]

With the assistance of Hurja, Farley established a rigorous system of rewarding Democratic supporters with federal jobs. Hurja amassed a plethora of public opinion data including straw votes at county fairs and

[25] Ibid.

[26] Savage, *Roosevelt: The Party Leader 1932–1945*, p. 83.

[27] Henry F. Pringle, "Who's on the Payroll," *American Magazine* 117 (November 1933): 19. Not all appointees were Democrats. In 1934, national Democratic Party leaders investigated the number of Republican patronage appointees as it demanded more Democratic distribution of jobs. A proposal to cease patronage, suggested by Senator George Norris (R-NE), died, in part because no one took seriously his disdain for political appointments based solely on merit. For a detailed analysis of FDR's patronage policies, see Paul P. Van Riper, *History of the United States Civil Service*. New York: Row, Peters, 1958.

newspaper editorial opinions.[28] For Hurja, it was perfectly appropriate for the Democratic Party to be the organization for "handling," "collecting," "tabulating," and "charting ... newspaper polls, radio polls, straw ballots, etc. in whatever districts they are conducted, computing the results in percentages, so that a current estimate is always available of sentiment."[29]

Hurja personally linked poll data to the national Democratic Party and the Roosevelt administration. The Democratic Party used Hurja's analyses for Roosevelt's presidential campaign, and afterward, Hurja was hired to employ his statistical skills to help decide who would receive patronage jobs, undermining the old-fashioned party patronage system. Hurja's survey research would locate regions replete with FDR loyalists and would reward them by recommending a patronage contract or job. Other times, a politically vulnerable district that needed a boost from the administration would receive one, also in the form of patronage jobs. The local Democratic party recommended loyalists for patronage jobs, but now the executive branch, via Hurja's polling, decided who received which jobs and where. That Hurja's polling and patronage distribution initially were conducted under the auspices of the Democratic Party organization does not signify a departure from FDR's desire to shift control from the party to the White House. Hurja's calculations to determine the recipients of political jobs significantly altered the make-up of government employment rosters. Whereas patronage jobs were once decided locally, the new system guaranteed loyalty to FDR through the executive branch:

Traditionally these jobs had been given out wholesale on a hit-or-miss basis for Congressmen to distribute to their friends and party workers. Hurja dramatically changed that and revolutionized the system for the New Deal ... If the Congressman had voted against the President, his friends were not likely to get jobs.[30]

FDR was aware of Hurja's work and directed him to pursue his polling endeavors.

Pursuant to your expressed desire on my visit to Hyde Park, I arranged for a postcard poll of the cities embraced in your Western tour, the ballots to hit two days after your visit. The result surpassed my expectations. I had not supposed that a visit would bring such material improvement in the voting expectations of the cities visited. We had polled the identical cities in October, so we had the best type of comparable figures ... While it is probably not good practice to apply the city increases shown to the entire state, yet the improvement applied to the state adjusted *Literary Digest* percentages works these transformations ...[31]

[28] See Melvin G. Holli, "Emil E. Hurja: Michigan's Presidential Pollster," *Michigan Historical Review* 21 (1995): 125–138, and Ray Tucker, "Chart and Graph Man," *Collier's* 95 (1935): 28–29.

[29] FDRL 1936, Hurja Papers, Box 70.

[30] Holli, "Emil E. Hurja: Michigan's Presidential Pollster," pp. 133–134.

[31] FDRL 1936, Hurja Papers, Memorandum from Hurja to FDR, October 24, 1936, Box 70.

When Hurja's methods proved accurate in 1936, his reputation as a political soothsayer was established. Hurja's face reached the cover of *Time* with the heading, "Democracy's Emil's Hurja: He counts his elections before they are hatched."[32] A *Collier's* article described Hurja as the "prophet extraordinary of the Democratic party," who "with questionnaires and frequent samplings of public opinion . . . checks up reaction to administration policies, to presidential speeches and conferences, to the attitude of congressional blocs on both sides of the aisle, to Republican lines of attack."[33]

In addition to perusing Gallup polls, Hurja catalogued letters received by the DNC, and even studied "house-to-house polls privately taken by bookmakers who place election bets."[34] The *Time* article described how "Hurja's value to the Party consisted chiefly in keeping well out of the spotlight" and how he "went to Washington to apply modern business methods to political patronage."[35] Regardless of the biases inherent in Hurja's analyses, his polling for the DNC changed how public opinion was measured for politicians. Whereas the *Literary Digest* relied on the size of the sample to ascertain validity, Hurja appears to have sought geographic and economic diversity in his polls.

Hurja's analyses were an integral part of FDR's attempt to strengthen the executive branch by making it less dependent on Democratic Party bosses. While Hurja's analyses were not tantamount to the surveys that Hadley Cantril would later conduct for FDR, they served as an important precursor to Cantril's questionnaires and to the institutionalization of presidential polling via the party. Hurja, via Chairman Farley, originally introduced Roosevelt to using primitive polls as political weapons. Ultimately, when modern polls with more sophisticated sampling techniques were developed, FDR used Cantril's private polls to gain autonomy (and with it, political power) by measuring public opinion without his party's consent or input. Presidential polls and politics had become inextricably intertwined, even as modern surveys were being developed.

EISENHOWER

The Eisenhower campaigns and administration routinely used public polls as a means to gauge public opinion. The primary source of the poll data was the then president of the advertising firm Young and Rubicam, Sigurd "Sig" Larmon. Larmon, a mentor of George Gallup and a friend of both Eisenhower and his Chief of Staff Sherman Adams, supplied the Eisenhower White House advisers with public opinion information and public relations

---

[32] "Democracy's Emil Hurja," *Time* 27 (March 2, 1936): 16–18.
[33] Tucker, "Chart and Graph Man."
[34] "Democracy's Emil Hurja," p. 18.
[35] Ibid.

advice throughout the 1952 campaign and during Eisenhower's tenure as president.[36]

Larmon's advice apropos public opinion was frequently delivered in the form of recommendations for party leaders. In an undated memorandum entitled "Suggestions for the Republican National Committee," Larmon stated that polls were a necessary tool for winning the presidency.

The first and most important step in preparing for 1952 is to find out exactly what the public does think about political issues and parties, and probe as accurately as possible into the reasons why these attitudes prevail – and how they might have changed. For example, what does the public think about:

- The Republican Party? Why?
- Republican leaders such as Taft, Dewey, Stassen, etc. Why?
- Eisenhower and MacArthur. Why?
- The Democratic Party and its leaders. Why?
- What do they want our domestic policies to accomplish?
- What do they want our foreign policy to be?

...With such facts and attitudes available for analysis and study, then Republican leaders are in a position to critically examine and re-evaluate every plank in the platform – every important statement made or proposed by Republican leaders...[37]

According to Larmon, polls helped party leaders assess citizens' views of candidates, political parties, and policies. Larmon also noted that campaigns required constant reevaluation and that polls helped advisers implement changes ("execute corrective action") in campaign strategies. For Larmon, polls aided presidents in working with party leaders. Party leaders, however, were not the conduits of public opinion – polls were. Rather, the goal was to aid elected officials and party officials to stay "on message" – a message that was articulated by President Eisenhower with the use of his private polls.

The Eisenhower presidential campaigns accepted occasional polls provided to them by the RNC, but Eisenhower's personal relationship with Larmon provided the president with direct access to Gallup's polls. Only when Richard Nixon took office in 1969 were all institutions, other than the presidency, considered suspiciously limiting to the autonomy of the chief executive.

---

[36] See DDEL, "Opinion Poll 1952 Presidential Race," Staff Files: Committee for Eisenhower, Young and Rubicam 1952–61, Box 3; "Correspondence of Sig Larmon," Young and Rubicam Files, 1952, Box 1; "Young and Rubicam," Young and Rubicam Files, Box 5; "Political Notebook 1952," Box 5; and DDE Central General File 156-B, "Public Opinion Polls '52–'53 (Surveys) (2)," Box 1218; "Polls" "1954 (1)," "1955 (1)," "1954 (2)," "1955 (3)," Box 1219.

[37] DDEL, "Correspondence of S. Larmon," Young and Rubicam File, Box 5.

KENNEDY

The first sign of Louis Harris' polling for the Kennedy campaign appeared in an October 1957 Harris poll, entitled "An Analysis of a Trial Pairing of Vice President Richard M. Nixon vs. Senator John F. Kennedy For the Presidency of the United States, Conducted for [New Haven, Connecticut] Mayor Richard C. Lee, October 1957." The eleven-page poll report included cross tabulations of how New Havenites would vote in a race between Nixon and Kennedy and breakdowns of this information by "key groups" (Irish, Italians, Jews, White Protestants, and Blacks). In a series of open-ended questions, respondents were asked to decipher what voters thought of the two candidates. Their answers documented eight major and four minor aspects of Kennedy's appeal. A brief examination of Kennedy's negative characteristics was included, as was an even briefer description of Nixon's positive and negative characteristics.

Harris' campaign polling covered twenty-seven states over the course of nineteen months. Two issues – television and religion – permeated the Harris campaign poll reports. Repeatedly during the campaign, Harris suggested that Kennedy increase his television exposure. To Harris, Kennedy's appearances on television enabled voters to see that Kennedy was intelligent and good-looking. Television, not political parties, was the best conduit for increasing voter turnout, improving Kennedy's image, and assuaging citizens' fears about his religion. Below is a sampling of Harris' recommendations as they related to Kennedy and television:

The reason for the heavy reliance on TV spots by the Senator is that he cannot rely on the local candidates to do much to help him on Election Day.[38]

It [Ohio] must be given a top priority with heavy TV spots, especially on the bread and butter issues.[39]

If the Senator's schedule does not permit his stumping the state again the Houston ministers meeting should be used repeatedly on Tennessee TV. (Even if he can get back to the state TV repeats of the meeting should be used to reinforce his stand.)[40]

Certainly both the party and citizens' organizations should be appraised of the Philadelphia situation. Clearly, one way to improve it is a successful registration drive there and perhaps a greater amount of local television, radio, and media advertising than is now allocated.[41]

Basically there is nothing about the Kennedy image in Ohio that cannot be helped substantially by personal campaigning and far more exposure on television than has been the case up to now.[42]

[38] JFKL, Washington Poll #858, RFK Pre-Administration Political Files, Box 44.
[39] JFKL, Ohio Poll #808, RFK Pre-Administration, Political Files, Box 45.
[40] JFKL, Tennessee Poll #853, RFK Pre-Administration, Political Files, Box 45.
[41] JFKL, Pennsylvania Poll #802, RFK Pre-Administration, Political Files, Box 45.
[42] JFKL, Ohio Poll, September 6, 1960, RFK Pre-Administration, Political Files, Box 45.

Convinced that television cameras exposed Kennedy as witty, candid, and smart, Harris advised Kennedy to abandon the party in favor of pursuing a campaign strategy that emphasized his strengths. To Harris, the poll data all pointed to the same conclusion – relying on the traditional strategies of the Democratic Party was futile – Senator Kennedy needed to establish autonomy from his party by being on television; if he did otherwise, he would not win the presidency.

The other major theme that transcended the campaign poll reports was Harris' analysis of religious attitudes. In addition to frequently breaking down voter preferences by religion (usually "Protestant" and "Catholic"), Harris also undertook an extensive inquiry about religious and political attitudes. Questions asking if respondents were concerned about Kennedy's religious affiliation were cited in at least thirty-seven of the sixty-nine campaign poll reports.

When respondents expressed concern over Kennedy's Catholicism, Harris cooly described them as bigoted, simultaneously seeking to woo them to the Kennedy camp, or to get them to stay home. "It is immediately apparent that the vast bulk of the bigoted Nixon vote here has gone decisively over to Vice President Nixon," Harris wrote on one occasion. "It is also heartening to see that by a solid 2-to-1 margin the undecided vote is not bigoted."[43]

Harris envisioned Kennedy's Catholicism to transcend party identification as a predominant issue in determining how citizens would vote. "Degrees of bigotry" (a term used by Harris) were measured on a state-to-state basis. The following examples of Harris' analyses reveal his concern about religion as an important issue to be addressed in various states.

The degree of religious bigotry in Minnesota remains constant but is still high. With this high prejudice against a Catholic there is reason to be concerned that this can hurt even more in the last week of the campaign. This is among the highest states for religious bigotry we have found outside the southern bible belt. It will be important here for the Senator to hit the religious issue on television because if he can turn it for the state, 11 electoral votes might in the end hinge on it.[44]

The third over-all issue which must be hit by the Senator during his final tour is religious bias. Prejudice has not increased – fortunately – but it is still the major block to the Senator's victory in Maine. He has reached his maximum potential among the Catholic voters – and must depend upon increased support from the Protestant voters if he is to win ... In Maine, the Senator must bluntly and directly once again state his unequivocal belief in the complete separation of Church and State.[45]

Today, only the Republican and Independent Catholics intend to cross over into the Democratic primary. This is the way it must be kept until primary day. For the only conceivable trigger that could bring them into that contest is if they suddenly felt that

43 Ibid.
44 JFKL, Minnesota Poll #844, RFK Pre-Administration, Political Files, Box 44.
45 JFKL, Maine Poll #913, RFK Pre-Administration, Political Files, Box 44.

the Catholics were supposedly pulling off a coup to elect Senator Kennedy . . . Given this potential powder keg, it is undoubtedly the better part of wisdom for Senator Kennedy not only to avoid all appearances before Catholic groups, but also to shun any major pronouncements on the religious issue here in Wisconsin. Certainly at this time a final church and state speech would be wholly out of order.[46]

According to Harris, Kennedy was to tailor his rhetoric and campaign strategy based on the religious or prejudicial tenor of the state in which he was campaigning. In Minnesota, Harris recommended that Kennedy attack the religious issue on television. In Maine, Harris argued that in order to gain Protestant votes, Kennedy was to articulate his belief in the separation of church and state, ostensibly to assuage the fears of Protestants. Finally in Wisconsin, Harris indicated that religion was helping Kennedy in bringing Catholic Republicans and Independents to "cross over" and vote in the Democratic primary, but that overexposure of support among Catholics may backfire. In each of these recommendations, media exposure replaced the party as the means to achieve Kennedy's electoral ends.

Evidence that Harris poll data were excluded from the DNC's perusal can be found in a memorandum sent by George Belknap of the DNC to Robert Kennedy, asking permission to read sections of Harris' polls:

I realize that the Harris reports can't be circulated. However, there are sections of the reports which don't pose any security problems and which could be of considerable use in the DNC . . . Would it be possible for me to have access to reproduction of the issue sections of the Harris studies?[47]

While it is unclear whether Kennedy allowed the DNC to receive Harris' polls, the autonomy of presidential polling had been established. Releasing private polls to the party leaders was considered a possible security risk. Moreover, the president's advisers, not his party, were to receive the unfiltered poll data. Harris sent his poll data to Robert Kennedy; the party would receive poll information only if Kennedy wanted the data distributed beyond his purview.

Computer simulations were also used by the Democratic Party to predict changes in public opinion over the course of the Kennedy campaign and to test the validity of Harris' strategies about religion. Created by Ithiel de Sola Pool, a Massachusetts Institute of Technology political scientist, and Yale University psychologist Robert Abelson, the Simulmatics Corporation used poll data from a variety of sources to simulate and predict the 1960 election based on changes in voting behavior by certain demographic groups.

---

[46] JFKL, Wisconsin Democratic Primary of 3rd, 7th, and 9th Congressional Districts, 12, 7 March 1960, RFK Pre-Administration, Political Files, Box 45.

[47] JFKL, "Poll: George Belknap 6/20/60–8/20/60 & undated," Memorandum from Dr. George Belknap to Robert Kennedy, September 25, 1960, RFK Papers, Pre-Administration, Political Files, Box 45.

Simulmatics assembled and collated public opinion poll results from the previous decade to create computerized profiles of 480 different types of Americans.[48] Pool, Abelson, and Popkin employed computer simulations to test "what effect the increased emphasis on the Catholic issue has."[49] Following Paul Lazarsfeld and his colleagues at Columbia University, Pool argued that social factors determined how citizens will vote:

> Issues are not the most important factor in a campaign. Lazarsfeld and others have shown that social milieu and party are much more important than issues in determining a voter's decision. The candidate's image and personality may also be more important in determining the election outcome. But these are things about which the candidate can do little. He controls the issues he talks about. He has much less control of who he is and who the voters are.[50]

The simulations did not play a prominent role in the Kennedy campaign, in part because of resistance by the DNC that the Simulmatics data was of dubious value.[51] The Simulmatics project served as a historical precursor to same-day, telephone tracking polls. The party's computer simulations meant that one could measure public opinion of a specific demographic group repeatedly over time (for example, a married, male farmer living in the West) as they simultaneously attempted to measure the marginal differences in public opinion when a candidate adjusted his campaign rhetoric or issue positions.

In ways similar to the Eisenhower era, the Democratic Party and the Kennedy presidency engaged in a cordial, shallow relationship concerning measuring public opinion. The DNC was out of the loop receiving Harris' polls, but they did receive copies of polls sent by other pollsters.

JOHNSON

President Johnson's complicated relationship with the Democratic National Committee reveals itself in the way his administration worked with the DNC to create a private polling operation. Johnson inherited a national party operation that was largely comprised of Kennedy supporters. DNC Chairman

---

[48] Stephen Mills, *The New Machine Men: Polls and Persuasion in Australian Politics.* Ringwood, VIC, Australia: Penguin Books, 1986, pp. 204–205. For a more detailed discussion about the 1960 election computer simulations, see Ithiel de Sola Pool and Robert P. Abelson, "The Simulmatics Project," *Public Opinion Quarterly* 25 (1961): 167–183; Ithiel de Sola Pool, Robert P. Abelson, and Samuel L. Popkin, *Candidates, Issues, and Strategies: A Computer Simulation of the 1960 Presidential Election.* Cambridge, MA: MIT Press, 1964. Simulmatics also became the focus of a best-selling novel, Eugene Burdick's, *The 480.* New York: Dell, 1964.

[49] JFKL, "Poll: George Belknap 6/20/60–8/20/60 & undated," Memorandum from Dr. George Belknap to Robert Kennedy and Steve Smith, August 29, 1960, RFK Papers, Pre-Administration, Political Files, Box 45.

[50] See Pool, et al., *Candidates, Issues, and Strategies,* pp. 8–9.

[51] See Belknap memo, fn. 52.

John Bailey, for example, was a Connecticut party boss, and many of his deputies were loyal Northern liberals. Predictably, Johnson had mixed views about this inheritance. To him, excessive partisanship frequently hindered good government and inhibited presidential power. After his landslide victory over Barry Goldwater in 1964, Johnson thought that the DNC was doing more harm than good. In his book *The Party's Over*, David Broder noted that Johnson significantly slashed the DNC's budget after winning the 1964 election, reducing their staff and having their long-distance telephone lines removed.[52] On the other hand, several members of the Johnson administration forged personal ties with DNC Finance Chairman Arthur Krim, who ultimately served as a conduit between the White House and Democratic pollsters. Krim fostered Johnson's private polling operation by distancing the Johnson White House from the DNC bureaucracy and streamlining polling with Krim's office at the helm, simultaneously establishing the DNC as the payer of presidential polls.

Johnson apparently had an affinity for reading polls. Although Eric Goldman asserts that the prepresidential Lyndon Johnson disdained public opinion polls, Robert Caro provides a different point of view, arguing that Johnson employed them throughout his career.

No politician in Texas had ever used polls as Johnson wanted to use them ... Johnson wanted polling done not monthly but weekly, and each week he wanted nearly identical polls done not by one firm but by two or three. 'He wanted to be able to compare them on every point,' Ed Clark recalls ... as Johnson explained to his adviser what type of polls he wanted, the perceptive of them realized that their Chief was talking about something new to politics; he wanted polls that revealed not only voter preferences but the depth of those preferences, how the preferences were changing – and how they might be changed ...[53]

When Johnson assumed the presidency, neither the DNC nor the White House had systematically coordinated a way to gather presidential-related poll data. The early Johnson White House advisers documented poll data as they received them, with little concern about the ideological or methodological biases that might have infused the data. One pollster, John Kraft, suggested that the DNC "attempt some sort of coordination" in collecting poll data.[54] An October 3, 1964 document entitled "34 States Have Replied," sent from presidential confidante Clifton Carter to the president, reveals the

---

[52] David S. Broder, *The Party's Over: The Failure of Politics in America*. New York: Harper & Row, 1971, p. 62. Also see Kearns, *Lyndon Johnson and the American Dream*, pp. 244–245.

[53] Eric F. Goldman, *The Tragedy of Lyndon Johnson*. New York: Knopf, 1969, p. 169; Robert A. Caro, "Annals of Politics: The Johnson Years: The Old and the New," *New Yorker*, January 22, 1990, p. 58.

[54] Lyndon Baines Johnson Library [LBJL], "PR16 "1-22-64–2-10-64," Letter from John Kraft to Earle Clements, White House [WH] Central File PR16.

dearth of poll-related information sent to the president.[55] The memorandum listed twenty-four states, the date of the last poll taken in that state, the source of the poll, the region in which the poll was taken, and state poll results pitting President Johnson against Republican presidential opponent Barry Goldwater. Some polls were given by friends of the White House (for example, organized labor); others had no known source. Next to four of these states listed were asterisks noting that the results were "Not thought accurately to represent voter sentiment," and five of the states had question marks in the column marked "Source of poll."[56] One of the thirty-four states had the AFL-CIO listed as a poll source, and three of the states had Democratic Party organizations listed as a poll source.[57]

LBJ was rumored to have been enamored with polling after reading Oliver Quayle's poll analyses during the 1960 presidential campaign. "That boy seems to know what he's doin'," Johnson apparently said about Quayle.[58]

President Lyndon B. Johnson and Oliver Quayle in the Oval Office (Courtesy of the LBJ Library)

The first effort to institutionalize the Johnson-Quayle polling operation was made by United Artists Chairman Arthur Krim, who also served as the DNC's finance chair. Krim forged personal ties between Quayle and

[55] LBJL, "34 STATES HAVE REPLIED," "10/1/64–10/28/64," October 3, 1964, Summary – Noon, Saturday, October 3 – RE POLLS, White House Central File PR 16, Box 345. Also see Horace Busby Files, Box 34.
[56] Ibid.
[57] Ibid.
[58] William H. Honan, "Johnson May Not Have Poll Fever, But He Has a 'Good Case of the Poll Sniffles,'" *The New York Times Magazine*, August 21, 1966, pp. 34–69.

Johnson's key advisers and found financial backing for the president's polling operations. Communications among Quayle, Krim, and the White House aides were direct and comprehensive, as evidenced by the following memorandum from Johnson adviser W. Marvin Watson to the president:

Krim has also contacted Mr. Quayle. Quayle is not set up for personal interviews, however he can: a.) Make 200 telephone samplings tomorrow on reaction to the speech. This could not be released. b.) By Friday night, make a sampling of 500 individuals (by telephone) in 20 metropolitan markets. This may be used for publicity and would show reaction to the State of the Union Message. c.) Make a national telephone survey covering: 1.) reaction to the speech, and 2.) pairing the five possible Republican candidates against Wallace and the President. If authorized to begin in the morning (Thursday, January 18) Quayle could have the results by Monday night, January 22. Cost would be $9,500. [Note: Next to Section c is a handwritten note that reads 1-18-67 ASKED A.K. TO GO AHEAD.][59]

Watson's comment that the poll "could be used for publicity" reveals how Johnson's advisers thought of polls as instruments for manipulating public opinion. In response to one poll analysis in 1964, Johnson advised his speech-writers to incorporate it by accordingly emphasizing and deemphasizing certain issues of importance to voters.[60] By sending word that he wanted speech writers to take note of Quayle's polls, the president acknowledged that the polls had multiple functions in his overall role as president and presidential candidate. Private polls identified public opinion, and helped shape it.

Further evidence of Krim's intermediary role can be found in additional memoranda sent among White House advisers:

Mr. Krim called and said that Oliver Quayle had told him of a telephone survey that he had made in North Carolina on February 1, 2, and 3 for Terry Sanford. Some 200 persons who have voted in Democratic Primaries were interviewed by phone with the following results.[61]

The Johnson White House did not coordinate polls for itself, but rather relied on Quayle and Krim. Krim and Quayle's roles as polling gatekeepers limited the autonomy of the Johnson White House in accumulating and interpreting poll data. In fact, Quayle's independence from the White House and his loyalty to the Democratic Party resulted in his hiding questions from the White House. In a 1968 letter, Quayle instructed Krim not to show the White House specific poll questions.

Here is the sample depth questionnaire you asked for using New York as a typical state. I do repeat my request that it be for the limited eyes discussed, that no copies

---

[59] LBJL, "Arthur Krim," Letter from Watson to the President, January 17, 1968, Marvin Watson Files, Box 26.
[60] LBJL, Note from Douglas Cater to Horace Busby, October 12, 1964, Busby Files, Box 41.
[61] LBJL, "North Carolina," Letter from Watson to President, February 6, 1968, Marvin Watson Files, Box 13 (1373B).

be made, and that when you are finished it be returned to me. The reason for this is that we normally do *not* submit questionnaires. Neither Walter Jenkins nor Bill Moyers saw questionnaires in 1964, even on our first survey.[62]

Quayle controlled what poll data would be sent to the White House and what data would remain in his purview. The president's pollster determined what information would be interpreted by White House advisers.

Two memoranda show that Johnson's adviser Fred Panzer sought to revise poll questions, particularly about Vietnam. In a June 28, 1967 note from Panzer to White House Chief of Staff Jim Jones, Panzer noted "a few points for Mr. Krim's guidance," and then proceeded to include suggestions about question wording, ordering, and responses.[63] In another memorandum written about six months later, Panzer wrote, "the words in the third bracket sound very technical but they would only confuse people. Perhaps Quayle can simplify. If not, they could be omitted."[64] Panzer's note to Jones intimated that Jones would forward recommendations to Krim, raising questions about why revisions were not directly sent to Quayle, who appeared to author the questions, but instead were filtered through a party operative. The first case reveals Krim's role as a power broker between Quayle and the administration. By suggesting that he amend poll questions, or at minimum, forward amendments to Quayle, Panzer indicates how his role was one of suggesting revisions of polls, not mandating them. The second memo suggests that Quayle was contacted directly about poll revisions, indicating that Quayle, although having some power in limiting what poll questions the administration's advisers might have seen, was asked by Panzer to change or omit what were considered to be confusing questions. The presidential branch was in the business of creating and revising polls. Panzer, Krim, and Quayle's roles grew simultaneously, and in the process, they functioned to institutionalize private polls as desirable and valuable.

With regard to requesting specific survey items, Fred Panzer once wrote Watson about Under Secretary of State Nicholas deB. Katzenbach's request for old and new poll data on Vietnam:

However, Mr. Katzenbach also mentions several questions that he would like asked. So far as I know, none of these have been asked so a new poll would have to be undertaken. Mr. Katzenbach mentions Lloyd Free as the man who could do some independent analyses for State. I agree that Free is a highly competent and responsible public opinion researcher. But he is also Nelson Rockefeller's pollster. My own feeling

---

[62] LBJL, "Arthur Krim," Letter from Quayle to Krim, January 31, 1968, Marvin Watson Files, Box 26.

[63] LBJL, Memorandum from Panzer to Jones, June 28, 1967, WH Central File, Box 348.

[64] LBJL, "11-22-67–12-27-67," Memorandum from Panzer to Watson, November 30, 1967, WH Central Files, PR 16, Box 350.

is that State contract with IDA or Rand or some other think tank to have this work done...[65]

Katzenbach's request for Vietnam-related poll data was hampered by presidential politics, as Lloyd Free's relationship with Republican presidential candidate Nelson Rockefeller precluded his firm from conducting the poll. Katzenbach's note signifies that Johnson's cabinet secretary asked the White House advisers' permission to poll instead of commissioning a survey on his own. Katzenbach did not have autonomy over how his office used polls. Rather, he recognized that Johnson's key advisers were the people to whom he had to appeal his request for a poll. Johnson's advisers had created a systematic means of collecting, creating, and distributing private polls.

Civil rights and race repeatedly emerged as important themes in Quayle's 1964 polls. Quayle argued that some white voters' willingness to vote for a Democrat was hindered by their prejudice toward black citizens. "Backlash," according to Quayle, signified the number of Democrats who would vote Republican. "Frontlash" signified the number of Republicans who would vote Democratic. Quayle created a "presidential backlash index," designed to measure how many Democratic voters would abandon the Johnson-Humphrey ticket for the Goldwater-Miller ticket. According to Quayle, "backlash" by white voters against Johnson-Humphrey stemmed from anti–civil rights attitudes, even though no question was asked if the propensity to vote Republican (or disaffection with the Democratic ticket) emanated from racial attitudes. Similarly, there was no evidence that the "frontlash" stemmed from the racial attitudes of Republicans. Moreover, there was no attempt to see if these racial attitudes affected the local (that is, nonpresidential) races for which Quayle was also polling. Rather, after establishing that some Democrats had anti–civil rights attitudes, Quayle then measured the intensity of these views, and concluded that Democrats with high levels of prejudice were more likely to vote for the Goldwater-Miller ticket, inferring that this intense prejudice among some voters was a critical factor in winning over swing voters.

The backlash index was repeatedly cited in Quayle's 1964 polls, as Quayle considered it to be vitally important. The index showed that Quayle, like Harris, employed a reelection strategy based on poll data. Just as Harris argued that religion and television were important variables in Kennedy's victory over Nixon, Quayle concluded that racial attitudes were a critical factor in the 1964 election. Quayle's backlash index ostensibly identified which states' voters would vote Republican because of their racial attitudes, when in actuality it merely identified voters who disagreed with the Democrats' pro–civil rights platform. Given the intensity of their antipathy toward civil

[65] LBJL, "Public Opinion Polls (1967)," Memorandum from Panzer to Watson, November 2, 1967, WH CF PR16, Box 82.

rights, Quayle concluded that these voters would not vote for the Democratic presidential ticket. Quayle's 1964 piggy-back polls, not party bosses, were employed to substantiate a theory to be used in the reelection of the president.

Tensions between Quayle and the Johnson White House flared in October 1966, when a *New York Times* reporter, William Honan, wrote a *New York Times Magazine* article implying that President Johnson suffered from "poll fever."[66] In the article, Quayle boasted to Honan how he served as the president's pollster and how the White House avidly combed his poll data. Admitting to being the president's pollster was considered a betrayal of the president's trust, as these polls were administered confidentially. Furthermore, by revealing that the president privately polled, Quayle had undermined the president's autonomy as he simultaneously tarnished Johnson as being beholden to the whims of the public. Shortly after the article's publication, W. Marvin Watson attempted to dispel the perception that Johnson was addicted to polls by telling Honan that Quayle was not the president's pollster and that polls were merely one of several instruments by which the president measured public opinion. Quayle was reprimanded by Watson, as evidenced by a memo from Watson to President Johnson:

> Ollie Quayle came by today and assured me that this meeting, and any meeting in the White House, and his job, if any, with the White House, will always remain off the record and confidential. He said he only wants to help the president ... Quayle says he has enough business for himself. He believes the President is going to win in 1968. He looks forward to working with us if we so decide.[67]

While no one stated that the Honan article led to Quayle's departure, Quayle's publicity bothered the White House and despite his professed loyalty to the president, the Johnson White House virtually ceased to receive Quayle's poll reports soon after the *Times* article was published. In 1967, there were three Quayle poll reports in the Johnson archives compared with twenty-seven polls from other Democratic Party–affiliated pollsters, most notably Joseph Napolitan, a Democratic pollster from Springfield, Massachusetts.[68] Like Quayle, Napolitan used congressional polls as vehicles

---

[66] Honan, "Johnson May Not Have Poll Fever."

[67] LBJL, Letter from Watson to the President, December 5, 1967, Tuesday, 7:30 p.m., "Arthur Krim," Marvin Watson Files, Box 26.

[68] The first part of this argument, namely that the Johnson White House discontinued receiving Quayle's polls because of Quayle's publicizing Johnson's affinity for polls, is found in Jacobs and Shapiro, in which the authors write that "Johnson suspended his links to Quayle because the pollster had become too visible." See Lawrence R. Jacobs and Robert Y. Shapiro, "Disorganized Democracy: The Institutionalization of Polling and Public Opinion Analysis During the Kennedy, Johnson, and Nixon Presidencies," paper prepared for presentation at the annual meeting of the American Political Science Association, September 1–4, 1994, New York, NY, p. 22, fn. 74. The footnote cites a variety of memos, including a memo from Moyers to Jacobsen, March 28, 1967 (LBJL, forwarded to LBJ from Watson on March 30, 1967, Marvin Watson Files, Box 27), but does not cite a particular sentence or paragraph

to piggy-back questions that were of interest to the Johnson administration. Napolitan downplayed his role as a presidential pollster:

When Kennedy and Johnson were president, it was my policy to send copies of my polls to the White House – with the candidate's permission, of course. In those days the White House did not do much independent polling, certainly nothing of the magnitude used by recent presidents, and the staff was happy to receive copies of current state and congressional district surveys.[69]

Both Quayle and Napolitan's local polls were used as if they were national snapshots of public opinion. Despite the administration's reaction to Quayle's comments in the *Times* article, Oliver Quayle reemerged as a pollster for the Democrats, sending at least nine poll reports to Johnson's key advisers devoted to the president's reelection efforts. Quayle's December poll of 247 New Hampshire Democratic primary voters is of particular interest, as it indicates how his questions were used to discredit Johnson's potential primary opponent, Eugene McCarthy. The poll included the following questions:

• Reaction to the following statements:
  "I think less of Eugene McCarthy because he opposed JFK in 1960 and backed Adlai Stevenson."
  "I tend to think less of Eugene McCarthy because he wants us to knuckle under to the communists."
• Attitude toward a policy leader who had said,
  "He's not Catholic enough, Irish enough, and not liberal enough to be president."[70]

This poll, paid for by the DNC, obviated party bosses as determinants of planning a campaign strategy. Quayle's poll data were designed to assess the ideological, political, and policy views of New Hampshire's Democratic voters in order to implement specific campaign strategies for the New Hampshire primary. Quayle underscored his role as a campaign strategist in his poll summary:

He [Senator McIntyre] will aid this effort and his name should be featured prominently . . . Our recommendation about making abundant use of McIntyre is even stronger with Mr. [Governor] King . . . We think those running the campaign

---

from these memos. The relationship between the president's pollster and the ostensibly negative publicity he receives in the media is a recurring theme in many of the works by Jacobs and Shapiro. See Bibliography.

[69] Correspondence from Joseph Napolitan to this author, March 1995. Also see LBJL, Survey of Political Attitudes, Massachusetts, August 1964, "Politics 2 of 2," Moyers Files, Box 40, and Survey of Political Climate in Wisconsin, March 1968, p. 1, "Texas-Wyoming," Fred Panzer Files, Box 223.

[70] LBJL, New Hampshire Study # 1072, Panzer Files, Box 174.

for a Johnson write-in should consider a flyer and/or television and radio spots that show (or tell of) the President together with General Westmoreland . . . identification with the General is a distinct plus.[71]

Advancing the president's campaign bid was not limited to determining which persons and issues should be highlighted or downplayed. Quayle's New Hampshire poll recommended ways to discredit Senator Eugene McCarthy, whom Quayle envisioned as the most dangerous threat to Johnson's reelection bid:

If McCarthy goes, a major effort must be made to have him come through as 'the extreme candidate,' 'the appeasement candidate,' or 'the surrender candidate.' And if the preceding phrases seem a little extreme themselves, then we suggest consideration of such alternatives as 'the knuckle under candidate,' or 'the back down candidate' . . . McCarthy has always been more interested in dissension than anything else, and here he is at it again. It would make a good TV spot . . . This is more evidence that McCarthy can be hurt if the issue becomes give in versus stand firm on Viet Nam.[72]

In what appears to be an early use of polls to see how to attack a political opponent, Quayle's DNC-funded New Hampshire poll suggested that Johnson's campaign employ certain advertising strategies based on responses to poll questions concerning citizens' impressions of McCarthy. The use of private polls to discredit McCarthy is particularly significant because it reveals how Johnson's fight for reelection entailed using ammunition – polls – garnered from outside the traditional party apparatus. Not only had the president's private pollster replaced party operatives as a key strategist, but by using his polling instrument to attack a fellow Democrat, Quayle (and in the process, Johnson's campaign) had promulgated independence away from parties by presidential candidates.

More evidence that Quayle's later polls were designed specifically for the president's reelection campaign can be found in questions that asked which words and phrases best described McCarthy and Johnson and then sorting the words into positive and negative categories.[73] Quayle was looking for phrases ("word profiles") that could later be used in television commercials or campaign speeches. Another poll given to New Yorkers in February of 1968 confirms this point. Respondents were asked to surmise what television shows Nixon, Johnson, Romney, and Wallace would watch if they were in their living rooms.[74] The television show question may have been asked to determine what times to buy television advertisements, or it may have been asked to see how citizens perceive candidates (for example, as funny or

[71] Ibid., 8, 9, 32.
[72] Ibid., 11, 51.
[73] Ibid., 53, 61.
[74] LBJL, Study 968, New York, February 1968, Panzer Files.

serious). By 1968, presidential polls were no longer objective instruments to measure public opinion; they had become politicized instruments that also measured public opinion.

With the exception of one citation, I could find no evidence to show that President Johnson used his polls to advance a going public strategy.[75] Rather, the president's private polling operation served to manipulate or monitor public opinion. By personally relying on Krim for polling funding, Johnson's advisers further distanced themselves from the national, state, and local party apparatuses that could have served as institutions for measuring the public's mood. State party leaders and other DNC operatives played little role in amassing or interpreting presidential poll data.[76] Rather, Johnson's advisers valued Krim's limited, personal ties to them. Krim helped finance Johnson's polls, as he kept them private and devoid of attention from other party leaders and the press.

NIXON

For President Nixon, poll data assumed an immeasurable value. Accordingly, his administration was reluctant to share its polls with others, even those who aided his reelection efforts. Specifically, he wanted some questions to be seen by "his eyes only," and not shown to the Republican National Committee – even though it was paying for the polls and had been accustomed to receiving presentations at its meetings. Sometimes, two survey

---

[75] Bruce Altschuler, *LBJ and the Polls*. Gainesville: University of Florida Press, 1990, p. 54. Senator Pell is ostensibly shown a Quayle poll of Rhode Islanders showing support for Johnson's Viet Nam policies. I investigated whether or not Johnson visited or spoke with members of Congress within a two-week period after receiving a poll report from the region of the elected official. For example, if a New York poll report was received "for the president's night reading" on the 1st of the month, I then looked at the White House diary logs to see if New York state elected officials met with Johnson, or if Johnson visited New York, from the 2nd through the 15th of the month. This investigation was aborted after multiple failed attempts to link the president's receiving of the polls with any possible meetings or visits by Johnson. The White House logs, however, are limited to meetings and telephone calls with the President, not his advisers. Still, this attempt to link the President's poll data with visits from specific politicians suggests that Johnson used poll data as a representative snapshot of opinions, rather than as a vehicle to advance a detailed or prearranged going public strategy.

[76] A review of the White House Diary Logs indicates that Johnson's meetings with Democratic Party state chairs were usually brief ceremonial functions confined to large groups. From 1964 through 1968, only five state party chairs telephoned the president or personally met with him in the Oval Office, at his ranch in Texas, or on Air Force One. Only ten of them met or telephoned him more than three times within a year, and these meetings were usually for fewer than fifteen minutes. LBJL, White House Diary Logs 1964–1968. The diary log data show one state party chair voluntarily sending DNC poll results to the White House. See LBJL, "Public Opinion Polls (1966) 3 of 5," Letter from Nancy Ferguson Bush to Marvin Watson, October 10, 1966, Confidential Files PR16, Box 81.

questionnaires were prepared, one for the RNC's perusal, and another for the White House.

> [RNC Chairman Rogers] Morton understands that the President wants some questions and answers for 'his eyes only.' Thus, whatever questions the President wants to ask should be given to Dirge [sic] and Dirge should prepare a separate questionnaire for Morton to see, prior to going into the field. This would be a sanitized version. Then, when Dirge gets the results, he should have one set of results for the President and a sanitized version for Morton. This way, I don't think we will have any problem at all with Morton and the National Committee.[77]

Morton understood and expected that the president's poll data would differ from the poll data he received. Morton's tacit approval of receiving a sanitized poll report made clear the relationship between the White House and the RNC. The White House determined the ground rules under which the GOP operated. In short, the GOP paid for the White House's polls, but the White House decided what should be asked in private polls and who should see the answers.[78]

To some degree, the Republican Party infrastructure embraced this subservient role assigned to it by Nixon. State party chairs provided some Nixon aides with poll data, enabling the Nixon White House to collect public opinion polls from local party operatives. On January 19, 1970, Thomas Reed, a member of the California Executive Committee of the RNC, informed Harry Dent that the California GOP was planning a statewide poll in February. "I assume you would like to know how the President's popularity stands compared to earlier polls and that you would like an open ended question regarding the most important problem facing the United States. I am already planning to include those."[79] A handwritten note confirms that state party chairs donated poll data to Dent.[80] Reed, who knew Dent, volunteered to include specific poll questions in the California survey. Not surprisingly, Dent accepted the offer to include a poll question on behalf of the administration. Nixon's aides valued poll data and gladly received them from party operatives.

President Nixon enjoyed politics and his polls helped him market his past and future policy agendas:

> I think that a poll re: Derge, but not one where we go for 3,000 or 4,000 personal interviews, but one where you ask the right questions and do it on a basis of 800–900

---

[77] RMNP@NA, Memorandum from Haldeman to Harry S. Dent, August 19, 1969, HRH Files, Box 134.

[78] Also see August 19 and 26, 1969 Memoranda, Haldeman Files, Box 134. Jacobs and Shapiro argue that the RNC objected to the arrangement whereby they paid for polls they did not see. See Jacobs and Shapiro, "The Rise of Presidential Polling," p. 185, fn. 90.

[79] RMNP@NA, "1970 Polls IIB," Letter from Reed to Dent, January 19, 1970, Harry Dent Files, Box 10.

[80] RMNP@NA, "1970 Poll(s) Other 2 of 2," Unauthorized handwritten note to Harry Dent, Harry Dent Files, Box 10.

interviews, would be useful on the major issues. For example, what is the opinion of those polled on whether the Administration takes a hard enough line on crime, dope, etc. In other words, the same in-depth questions that Derge asked in his May or June poll – I can't recall when it was asked, but the last one he took in depth. Let's get answers to those questions as we go into the last two years to see what we have to do.[81]

Polls were so valuable that they were not to be shared. Haldeman and Nixon limited access so strictly that polls were kept in a safe.[82] Within the White House, access to poll data required permission by Haldeman. By limiting access of private poll data, Haldeman ensured that poll data would only be seen by key Nixon advisers, and in the process, provided increased autonomy for Nixon from the RNC and Congress.

Derge's role as polling adviser parallels that of Cantril, Harris, and Quayle. For Derge, polls were vehicles to advance marketing and expand coverage for the president. By recommending heavier publicity for certain issues, Derge advocated that the president's private polls should be used both to locate public opinion and to steer it. This point is exemplified by his comments linking beliefs about U.S. military superiority over the Soviet Union to U.S. military prestige "in the publicity programs." Derge was a key adviser for Nixon's staff, secretly making recommendations about future polls and doing so with great latitude and autonomy.[83]

More than a year before the 1972 elections, Nixon's pollsters began planning how to use public opinion–related data to aid them in their reelection efforts. Thomas Benham, vice president of ORC, suggested in May 1971 that the Nixon reelection campaign conduct focus groups to test a "suitable slogan or theme," and that a "four-wave program of large-scale interviews in key battleground states" be employed to identify citizens' views on key issues. Benham recommended using a three-wave panel, a poll specifically designed to assess President Nixon's image, and a special survey of young voters. Benham also noted that the campaign could take advantage of ORC's General Public Caravan – "an omnibus research vehicle on which individual questions can be placed without the necessity to finance a separate research study each time." Benham explicitly discouraged the Nixon campaign from using computer simulation techniques used by Ithiel de Sola Pool and his colleagues in the 1960s:

An effort was made [to do simulations] during the Kennedy campaign of 1960, but as we understand it, the politicians who made the decisions did not take it too seriously, although the authors claim that their techniques successfully pointed to

[81] RMNP@NA, Memorandum from The President to H.R. Haldeman, November 30 , 1970, "Derge and Benham Memos 1 of 3," Haldeman Files, Box 340.
[82] RMNP@NA, Note from Gordon Strachan to LP [?], July 2, 1971, "HRH Derge Polls, Late '70 – Early '71," Haldeman Files, Box 340.
[83] See Jacobs and Shapiro, "Presidential Manipulation of Polls and Public Opinion."

useful campaign tactics... At this time, however, we do not feel we can endorse or reject simulation as a tool for developing campaign strategy during 1972.[84]

Private polls were also used to test the effectiveness of campaign propaganda films. One memo from an unsigned author, written on noncampaign stationary, indicates that two documentaries about Nixon were shown to two audiences. Both audiences viewed the documentaries and then were asked a series of questions about the president. The author concluded that one of the films, *The Nixon Years*, was the more "effective of the two films, [and] should receive predominant use during the re-election campaign communicating to voters."[85]

Soon after the Nixon image study commenced, Jeb Magruder and Higby wrote Haldeman and Attorney General Mitchell with a plan for how best to use polling during the 1972 reelection:

In the battleground states, we will be particularly interested in identifying and communicating with the ambivalent votes... A highly targeted polling program would then be used to identify the issues and attitudes that will most strongly determine these votes. Those findings would be the basis for individual contacts through mail, telephone or personal visits by local campaign workers. Variations on this technique have been used effectively in several state elections. Notably Reagan in 1970 in San Francisco County, with DMI [Decision Making Information, Inc.] as the vendor.[86]

By and large, Benham's advice was taken, but ORC was not the sole benefactor in serving the Nixon campaign. Robert Teeter, director of Market Opinion Research (MOR), became the polling director for President Nixon's reelection effort and MOR commissioned many of the president's campaign's polls. In a letter to Attorney General (and Campaign Manager) John Mitchell, Teeter suggested that the Committee for the Re-Election of the President (CREEP) hire several firms to poll for the president and the GOP. Teeter noted that four polling firms had sent proposals to the reelection committee, including ORC, MOR, DMI, and Cambridge Opinion Studies of New York (also known as Cambridge).

Using more than one vendor has several advantages. It gives the President's campaign access to large amounts of trend data, experience, and expertise these firms have built up in certain states. It gives us access to more of the advanced thinking and new techniques that have been developed within the party during the past few years.

Teeter proposed hiring the first three of the four firms cited above, including his own. Each firm did not necessarily know that the other was

84 RMNP@NA, "Polling Memoranda," Benham to Haldeman, May 5, 1971, HRH Files, Box 263.
85 RMNP@NA, "[CF] Public Opinion Polls [2 of 2]," Unauthorized memorandum filed 9/7/1972, Box 53.
86 RMNP@NA, "Polling Memoranda," Higby/Magruder to Haldeman/Attorney General, Undated Draft, HRH Files, Box 263.

polling for Nixon.[87] Polls in "target states" and "important primary states" were launched in November 1971 and concluded just before the November 1972 election. The MOR polls differed from the ORC polls in two significant ways. First, unlike the ORC poll summaries that were a few pages, the MOR poll reports were frequently over 150 pages. While ORC's analysis succinctly stated the highlights of the poll, MOR analyses sometimes included all poll results. Second, most of these polls were conducted statewide and included several questions for state and local candidates. The surveys also contained several questions about the presidential race, asking about national and international issues (taxes, crime, Vietnam, the economy) and respondents' approval and disapproval of Nixon, Vice President Agnew, and George McGovern. Teeter also suggested that CREEP coordinate their polling activities with state parties.

> Obviously, the potential problem would be in the handling of the data . . . Data security can be adequately assured in several ways, and the problem will be dealt with on a case-by-case basis . . . In addition to target states, there will be opportunities for participation in statewide polls being done by Republican vendors in places where we are not doing our own polls.[88]

To a great extent, Teeter's proposal was implemented. In a January 3, 1972 memorandum from Teeter to Haldeman, Teeter noted that nineteen state polls had already been or were about to be going in the field.[89] Here again, it is apparent that Nixon's advisers collected polls from party operatives without having to reciprocate by delivering sensitive poll data. To the contrary, both the Nixon reelection campaign and the White House received poll data from a variety of sources, limiting access of these polls to everyone except Haldeman and some of his subordinates.

Harry O'Neill of ORC had little contact with Teeter during Nixon's tenure, but did not suspect that Teeter's polls were conducted as an institutional check on his own ORC polls.

> Perhaps their polling with Teeter was possible evidence of the White House's paranoia over information, but never did I ever hear from anyone in the Nixon White House, 'Hey, how come you got X for an answer? Teeter got Y.'[90]

Similarly, Teeter was aware of the extent to which ORC had been conducting private polls for the Nixon administration.

[87] RMNP@NA, "Polls 11–12/1971," Memorandum from Robert M. Teeter to the Attorney General, November 17, 1971, Box 335.

[88] Ibid.

[89] RMNP@NA, "Jan–Feb 1972, Memorandum from Teeter to Haldeman," January 3, 1972, Haldeman Files, Box 335.

[90] O'Neill interview, June 7, 1996.

Yes, I was aware the Administration was receiving polls from ORC during 1972. ORC had been polling directly for the White House during the first Nixon Administration and continued to do so during 1972. I was using them to do some polling for the campaign and they were also commissioned to do additional polling for the White House by Bob Haldeman's staff during the same period. While I was aware this was occurring I did not know the extent of it until well after the '72 election.[91]

The genius of President Nixon's polling operation lay in the ability to amass and interpret polls from a variety of allies, all of whose loyalty to the president overrode their allegiance to the GOP. By hiring ORC primarily for internal White House polls and MOR for campaign polls, the Nixon White House was able to obtain a plethora of insights and data they sought, without depending on any one source of information. By working with ORC and MOR, and by letting each organization know that they were both working for the president, Nixon's advisers did not worry about jealousy or hostility among their pollsters. To the contrary – the pollsters respected one another. Their loyalty to the president grew as they identified key groups and issues to be used for campaign and policy propaganda.

Some of Nixon's poll questions suggest that the intersection of administrating and campaigning ultimately worked to Nixon's detriment. One question, for example, read, "Should the government give financial aid to parochial schools so their students won't be dumped into the public school system?" By designing a question likely to evoke a particular answer, the Nixon administration used polls to produce propaganda allegedly to advance a policy agenda.[92] But to state that this question, or others like it, shows how the Nixon presidency transformed White House polling into a political operation is to ignore the evolution of presidential polling. Polls had already become political instruments. Parties were being replaced by in-house polls. Haldeman's experience with surveys from his work in advertising resulted in an ability to organize and administer a complex polling operation that sought to obtain and manipulate poll data from a variety of sources. Doing so demanded clear and proper channels for accessing poll data and presumed a belief that the presidency was the legitimate institution for measuring public opinion.

The breadth of the ORC and MOR polls, the staffers' diligence in getting advances of poll data, the tight reins over access to poll data by Haldeman, the secrecy underlying the internal polls, the tacit acceptance by the RNC to accept a subservient role, the use of polls to alter schedules and produce propaganda, and the constant drumbeat of publicity that surrounded poll data were proof that Nixon's polling operation surpassed all other presidents

[91] Letter from Robert M. Teeter, June 20, 1996.
[92] Gerald R. Ford Library [GRFL], ORC Poll, Jan. 3–20, 1972, Question 22-14, Teeter Files.

and that his polling served in part to replace the power of his own party.[93] Presidential polls were no longer piggy-backed surveys that included information that was of peripheral interest to the president. They were now fortnightly instruments designed to see what the public knew about current events and to shape public opinion, both about the president's image and policies.

Chapter 6 will reveal that the evolution of presidential polling is also shaped by the fractious relationship between the presidency and the media. As presidents sought to exploit the media for their own advantage, they soon learned that their private polls could circumvent the media, much like they did in obviating Congress. Whereas Presidents Hoover through Eisenhower used the media as a means to measure public opinion, future presidents used their private polls to develop a presidential image, thereby attempting to manipulate public opinion in the media.

---

[93] Memoranda among White House staffers indicated that President Nixon's speechwriters occasionally obtained some poll reports. Jeb Magruder contacted White House speech writer Pat Buchanan to "make effective use" of a poll that the White House received before it was released by the Republican National Committee. See RMNP@NA, "1970 Polls IIB," Jeb Magruder to Pat Buchanan, Lyn Nofziger, and Harry Dent, November 25, 1969, Harry Dent Files, Box 10.

6

The Media Are Not the Messengers

> There is a pronounced need for a complete overhauling of our Government 'sales department,' both domestic and foreign. This country as the father of advertising and public relations has done a bad job in selling itself, its history, its aims-hopes-dreams to the 'man on the street' of the countries into which it has poured billions, and of our own country.[1]

> The president's most persistent problem in staying in touch with reality lies in his staff.[2]

The media must report the facts, and in doing so, they perform the vital role of informing the citizenry. Facts are presented to them by political actors, including presidents, who seek to manipulate events in order to pursue a desired outcome. Somewhere in between the educative function of the media, and the desires by presidents to show themselves in the best possible light, lies the role of private public opinion polls. The conflicting nature of the two institutions underscores why a president doesn't want to depend on the media as the means by which citizens' views are assessed. This is not to say that members of the media intentionally distort public opinion data, but rather that their function as a potential investigator of the presidency necessitates that a president not think of the media as an ally on which to rely. This chapter reveals that, prior to the advent of polls, President Hoover compiled statistical evaluations of newspaper editorials as a means to gauge public opinion. Once modern polls were created, however, FDR abandoned newspapers as a scientific gauge of public opinion and began to use private polls. Throughout the 1940s, 1950s, 1960s, and 1970s, presidents read newspapers and monitored media survey data. However the autonomy

---

[1] Dwight Eisenhower, DDEL, "DDE Diary – November 1953 (1)," Ann Whitman File, October 1953, A75-22, Box 3.
[2] George E. Reedy, *The Twilight of the Presidency*. New York: New American Library/World Publishing, 1970, p. 85.

presidents gained by using private polls mitigated the value and potency of the media as a primary gauge of the public mood.[3]

THE PRE-FDR ERA

Jean Converse astutely notes that as long as there have been elections, citizens have tried to predict them. Tom Smith has written about what he has labeled proto-straw polls of 1824, "the first contested election to be decided largely by popular vote."[4] Smith documents how newspaper editors acted as political soothsayers and how "poll books" were sometimes left out at public places such as taverns for people to write in their political preferences. According to Smith, while these straw polls were not sponsored or conducted by newspapers, "acceptance of the value of these straw polls rested heavily on the partisan leanings of the editors."[5] Similarly, Richard Jensen's analysis of the elections of 1898 also indicates that "generally the Republican [newspaper] owners released only glad tidings" of secret polls conducted by partisan groups.[6]

Hoover's presidency recognized the partisan nature of the media and his presidential tenure paralleled the blossoming of the public relations industry. Edward Bernays, arguably the founder of public relations, advanced the belief that politicians should promote themselves by employing propagandistic techniques.[7] For Bernays, manipulating public opinion was an important function of successful political leaders. "Fortunately," Bernays wrote in his book *Propaganda*, "the sincere and gifted politician is able, by the instrument of propaganda, to mold and form the will of the people."[8] Bernays' theories were hailed as "science" in the *American Mercury* and in *The New York Times* as having "overwhelming national importance."[9] As stated in

---

[3] The term "media poll" used in this chapter refers to public opinion data that have been gathered by private polling companies such as Gallup and Harris, or polls conducted by news services for public consumption.

[4] Tom W. Smith, "The First Straw?: A Study of the Origins of Election Polls," *Public Opinion Quarterly* 54 (1990): 31.

[5] Ibid., 26, 29–30.

[6] Richard Jensen, *The Winning of the Midwest: Social and Political Conflict, 1888–1896.* Chicago: University of Chicago Press, 1971, p. 56. Also see Jensen, "Democracy by the Numbers," *Public Opinion* (Spring 1980): 53–59; "American Election Analysis: A Case History of Methodological Innovation and Diffusion." In *Politics and the Social Sciences*, edited by Seymour Martin Lipset. New York: Oxford University Press, 1969, pp. 226–243; and "History and the Political Scientist." In Ibid., 1–28.

[7] For more on Bernays, see Bernays, *Propaganda*; William Leach, *Land of Desire: Merchants, Power, and the Rise of a New American Culture.* New York: Pantheon, 1993; and Larry Tye, *The Father of Spin: Edward L. Bernays and the Birth of Public Relations.* New York: Crown, 1998.

[8] Bernays, *Propaganda*, p. 92.

[9] Henry F. Pringle, "The Mass Psychologist," *American Mercury* 19 (1930): 155; Herman J. Mankiewicz, "The Virtuous Press Agent," *The New York Times*, April 6, 1924, Sec. 3, 2.

Chapter 2, President Hoover found Bernays' work valuable and invited him to the White House one month before the 1932 election to discuss a last-minute plan for winning reelection.[10]

President Hoover knew from his days as secretary of commerce that good press relations were essential for advancing one's political agenda. He adopted several institutional events, such as the press conference, intended to promote closer ties between the press and the presidency, but Hoover never embraced the folksy nature of his predecessor Calvin Coolidge. By taking reporters on vacation with him and by using the radio to communicate directly to the people, Coolidge enjoyed generally positive press coverage, promulgating the view that presidents should appeal to the masses by having unfiltered relations with the press.[11]

Once elected as president, Hoover sought to develop a "more intimate relationship with the press" by deciding to meet with White House reporters directly and regularly.[12] Accordingly, reporters and editorialists initially welcomed the Hoover presidency, but tensions with the media quickly ensued, in part because Hoover and his press secretary, George Akerson, began to censor questions from the media.[13] By insisting that reporters direct their questions to him by first submitting them to Akerson, Hoover antagonized the press as he was seeking to woo them.

Hoover's reluctance to trust the media as an unbiased conduit of public opinion and mass communication was due in part to the Democrats' hiring of Charles Michelson as their publicity director. Michelson, a former Washington bureau chief of the *New York World*, discredited Hoover as he simultaneously extolled Democratic party ideas. Hoover resented Michelson's attacks, and grew to distrust the media, dismissing rare accolades from them. On June 23, 1931, Press Secretary Ted Joslin showed Hoover newspaper editorials praising his fiscal prudence. Hoover responded, "Everything is pleasing now, but there may well be a groundswell against my proposal. Don't you forget this for a minute."[14] President Hoover thought of the media as unreliable and untrustworthy organs of public opinion. As a result, his relations

---

[10] Tye, *The Father of Spin*, p. 79. Tye cites an undated memo found in the Bernays Papers located in the Library of Congress.

[11] Elmer E. Cornwell, Jr., "Coolidge and Presidential Leadership," *Public Opinion Quarterly* 21 (1957): 265–278; James E. Pollard, *The Presidents and the Press*. New York: Macmillan, 1947, pp. 697–736.

[12] HCHA, Presidential Papers – Press Relations #2, Herbert C. Hoover, March 7, 1929, Box 1180.

[13] HCHA, MacLafferty Diary, December 13, 1930; Pollard, *The Presidents and the Press*, p. 739; Fausold, *The Presidency of Herbert C. Hoover*, p. 47; Donald R. McCoy, "To the White House: Herbert Hoover August 1927–March 1929." In *The Hoover Presidency: A Reappraisal*, edited by Martin L. Fausold. Albany, NY: SUNY Press, 1974, p. 45; Wilson, *Herbert Hoover: Forgotten Progressive*, pp. 81, 123; Burner, *Herbert Hoover: A Public Life*.

[14] HCHA, Joslin Diary, June 23, 1931, Box 10.

with the media were antagonistically symbiotic; they were biased, but, absent viable alternatives, he read their reports for their assessments of public sentiment.

Hoover was not the first president to use media reports to measure public opinion. President Lincoln gauged public opinion by communicating privately with military and personal correspondents, reading newspaper articles given to him by his private secretaries, reviewing communications among elected officials, and by receiving delegations of interested groups of citizens.[15] Robert Hilderbrand has written about how Presidents McKinley, [Theodore] Roosevelt, and Wilson all used the press to gauge public opinion.[16] Massachusetts Governor Calvin Coolidge visited the editorial rooms to "paw over the Massachusetts newspapers, talk with the editorial writers, [and] read the Associated Press dispatches as they were coming in," and as president, he read national newspapers for about an hour on a daily basis.[17]

Hoover, however, was the first president to gauge public opinion systematically by creating a confidential quantifiable measurement of newspaper content. Hoover had his executive clerks, Rudolph Forster and M.C. Latta, confidentially read and analyze newspaper editorials. Six linear feet of these editorial analyses from 1929 to 1932 are boxed in the Hoover Presidential Library. These reports listed which newspapers favored or opposed particular political and policy issues. When editorials and issues provided more nuanced interpretations beyond pro-con/favor-against responses, the reports divided issues into categories, totaling the number of editorials that took a respective position. A letter code key describing each newspaper usually was attached to this document (for example, Q = qualified approval or disapproval; Z = syndicated or chain paper editorial; R = Republican paper; H = Hearst paper; 1 = criticism well founded but Congress won't heed it).[18]

For example, the newspaper editorials that followed the November 1930 midterm elections were divided into eleven categories – "See Result as Rebuke to President," "Outcome is Rebuke to Administration," "See Voters Rebuking G.O.P. Leadership (Nat'l/and/or State)," "Result is a Rebuke to Congress," "Chief Factor Believed to Be Depression," "Wet-Dry Issue Most Important Factor," "Vote Shows Repudiation of 'Straddlers,'" "Forecast Chaos in Congress," "Expresses Increasing Independence of Voters," "See Results as Repudiation of 'Reaction and Privilege,'" and "See Tariff as Factor in Results." For each category, the names of newspapers whose editorials

[15] Hans L. Trefousse, *Lincoln's Decision for Emancipation*. Philadelphia: J.B. Lippincott, 1975, p. 10.

[16] Robert C. Hilderbrand, *Power and the People: Executive Management of Public Opinion in Foreign Affairs, 1897–1921*. Chapel Hill: University of North Carolina Press, 1981.

[17] William Allen White, *A Puritan in Babylon: The Story of Calvin Coolidge*. New York: Macmillan, 1958, pp. 141, viii.

[18] HCHA, "President Reorg. – Roos.," Presidential Papers – Press Relations, January 12, 1933, Box 1176.

TABLE 6.1 *Summary of Editorial Comment on Election Results, November 8, 1930*

Topic	Number of Papers	Circulation
See result as rebuke to president	51	3,731,400
Outcome is rebuke to administration	53	3,971,700
See voters rebuking GOP leadership (national and/or state)	62	4,797,300
Result is a rebuke to congress	1	19,900
Chief factor believed to be depression	136	7,775,800
Wet-dry issue most important factor	140	9,320,100
Vote shows repudiation of "straddlers"	28	783,000
Forecast chaos in Congress	20	652,600
Expresses increasing independence of voters	22	695,700
See results as repudiation of "reaction and privilege"	9	556,300
See tariff as factor in results	16	1,549,600

Note: In total, editorials of 346 issues were analyzed confidentially over a four-year period.
Source: Herbert C. Hoover Archives, marked "CONFIDENTIAL," Presidential Papers – Press Relations, Box 1165. See Ibid., Boxes 1165–1177.

subscribed to each category were listed on a sheet of paper with a letter code (for example, Q, R) followed by the newspapers' circulation. Listings in these categories were mutually inclusive; a newspaper (such as the *Bangor* [Maine] *News*) was listed in several of these categories, indicating that the editorials were read with care and that the total circulation for each category was measured to reflect public opinion of newspaper readers, not the intensity with which the editorialists argued their respective positions. Total circulation was listed at the bottom of each page, providing an approximate number of readers who had read the editorial, and summaries of editorial content were tabulated for easy perusal (see Table 6.1). Despite his distrust of the press, Hoover recognized that the media narrated and reflected some aspects of public opinion. By totaling the circulation of each newspaper, his clerks confidentially quantified public opinion, as they implicitly defined it, as being reflected in newspaper editorials.[19] By sanitizing and to some degree objectifying editorials through quantification, Hoover reduced his dependency on the media as an institutional conduit of public opinion. Press Secretary Ted Joslin's published diary includes a reference to the Hoover

[19] The classified nature of these clippings was evidenced by the absence of memoranda from any of the Executive Clerks to President Hoover or his advisers, and by the reports' being marked in bold type as "CONFIDENTIAL." The number of these reports, and the time it would take to interpret, amass and tabulate the written data strongly suggest that they were of serious import to ascertain citizens' attitudes.

administration's "elaborate clipping bureau" that contained selected articles and editorials from 500 newspapers. "This gave him a thorough cross-
section," wrote Joslin. "It presented all shades of public opinion...I can
testify that he read them – and got more bad news than good."[20]

For Hoover and his advisers the media were comprised of Democratic
partisans. When editors praised the president, he was reluctant to coopt
them. His aide and confidante James MacLafferty once suggested that the
president visit with "republican [sic] editors all over the country." Hoover
neither approved nor rejected the idea, implicitly killing it with his silence.[21]
By secretly tabulating editorials, however, President Hoover revealed the
importance for the presidency to amass and interpret public opinion. The
tabulations, albeit crude, signify the roots of social scientific methodology
in the White House public opinion apparatus. By quantifying editorials,
Hoover's aides sought to create a systematic, ostensibly unbiased database
of public opinion.

ROOSEVELT

Although newspapers published Gallup polls showing Roosevelt's popularity, many newspaper editors thought the president and his wife were
egotistical socialists. Several scholars, including Barbara Houchin Winfield,
James David Barber, and Graham White have documented FDR's tense relations with the press. Media mogul Henry Luce, for example, used his *Time*
and *Life* magazines to propel the candidacy of Wendell Willkie against FDR
in 1936. FDR disdained certain newspaper editors and owners. According
to Barber, the feeling was mutual:

The *Washington Post* saw a 'Messianic complex' apparently 'possessing
Mr. Roosevelt even more firmly.' In 1937, the editorialists of the *New York Times* had
launched that paper's most intensive editorial attack ever, against Roosevelt's court-
packing plan, a series of fifty pieces running over six months. In 1940, with few exceptions, the columnists (fixed as a branch of newspaper journalism by Pulitzer's *New
York World*) had long been savaging Roosevelt. Pundit Walter Lippmann damned
his 'dictatorial tendencies'... Columnist David Lawrence even wrote a book accusing Roosevelt of *Stumbling into Socialism*. A rare supporter, columnist Dorothy
Thompson was eased off the pages of the *New York Herald-Tribune* when she put
out a column endorsing the President.[22]

FDR inherited these bellicose relations with some newspaper editors, publishers, and columnists from his predecessor, Herbert Hoover, who also was

---

[20] Joslin, *Hoover Off the Record*, p. 38.
[21] HCHA, MacLafferty Diary, January 18, 1932.
[22] Barber, *The Pulse of Politics: Electing Presidents in the Media Age*, pp. 139–140. Also see
Winfield, *FDR and the News Media*; and Graham J. White, *FDR and the Press*. Chicago:
University of Chicago Press, 1979.

exposed to the media's venom. FDR enjoyed the camaraderie of some reporters, but not their bosses. Publisher William Randolph Hearst antagonized FDR in 1932 by endorsing Speaker of the House John Garner for the presidency. To Roosevelt, certain editors, columnists, and business moguls were enemies of the New Deal and were not to be trusted as vehicles to measure public opinion.

The Republican Party further sought to discredit Roosevelt by generating press releases disseminating negative publicity about Roosevelt in mat, plate, and proof form.[23] The Republican Party's use of the news media, combined with the pundits' and editors' negative views of FDR, generated a political environment for Roosevelt that was conducive to seeking alternative gauges of public opinion.

Polls became Roosevelt's independent mechanism for measuring citizens' attitudes. Members of the FDR administration secretly met with Hadley Cantril. Richard Steele has noted that many of Hadley Cantril's poll reports concerned public relations matters, but he understates Cantril's role as a public relations adviser.[24] Hadley Cantril frequently accompanied his poll numbers with advice on how to market policies, including specific recommendations on how to advance the president's agenda by increasing FDR's exposure and popularity. Specifically, some of Cantril's reports explicitly were designed to assess public opinion as it related to the president's communicating with the public.[25] On September 17, 1941, for example, Cantril provided the administration with a report that compared "opinions of those who do and do not listen to the president's radio talks." Cantril concluded that radio listeners were wealthier, more interventionist, and more likely to believe that they would be personally affected by a German victory than nonlisteners, and therefore more likely to support FDR's wartime policies:

It is impossible to separate cause from effect in the data so far obtained . . . However, the fact that people in all economic groups who listen are more for aid to England and realize more the personal consequences than persons in comparable economic groups who do not listen, makes it seem safe to conclude that the President's talks do

---

[23] Ralph D. Casey, "Republican Propaganda in the 1936 Campaign," *Public Opinion Quarterly* 1 (1937): 27–44. Also see V.O. Key, Jr., *Politics, Parties, & Pressure Groups, Fifth Edition*. New York: Thomas Y. Crowell, 1964, p. 477.

[24] Steele, "The Pulse of the People."

[25] See, for example, Cantril memo [untitled], February 16, 1943 [Handwritten – "Information furnished by Mr. Niles' Office,"] in which Cantril recommended that poll data reflecting Americans' ignorance concerning the German army's cooperation with Hitler should result in Roosevelt's "explain[ing] briefly that the tradition and leadership of the German Army is as much of a menace to permanent peace as Nazism . . . ," FDRL 1943, Gallup Polls, Box 857; and September 30, 1944, Cantril to Rosenman, in which Cantril's postscript read, "Incidentally, I think it is a mistake to have major broadcasts on Saturday night. It's a poor night for coverage," FDRL 1944, Rosenman Files.

have some influence. If more effort were made to publicize these speeches in advance, especially among the lower income groups, the effect might be more noticeable.[26]

By discerning who was listening to the president's speeches, Cantril suggested ways of increasing listenership in order to advance the president's political agenda.[27] In a December 22, 1942 memorandum to FDR aide David Niles, Cantril criticized the administration's handling of gasoline rationing, recommending "a successful way to handle a public announcement" that included making a "public opinion survey in advance of the announcement to uncover reaction on the proposed statement. If survey is not possible, try to guess the state of mind."[28] Similarly in an April 14, 1944 letter to Niles, Cantril suggested that "if the plan [to establish refugee camps in the United States for those persecuted by the Nazis] is presented, <u>it is important</u> that the objections raised by those who disapprove of the proposal be met head-on in the announcement of the plan."[29] Cantril's advice signified both his willingness to provide poll data about policies not yet passed or discussed by Congress and his ability to include in these reports advice on how to market those potential policies in the media.

TRUMAN AND EISENHOWER

One cannot simply dismiss Truman's lack of polling to his being the victim of media polls that erroneously declared him a presidential loser. Truman, as a senator and chief executive, knew what he liked and was not likely to change campaign methods or decision-making models that had worked in the past. He distrusted image manufacturers and adulation seekers, accusing General MacArthur, among others, of harboring these negative characteristics. Truman did not watch television and showed no understanding of how

---

[26] FDRL 1941, P.O. Polls 35–41, Box 157.

[27] A one page note entitled "Princeton Public Opinion" contains what appears to be a title list of Cantril's poll reports. The memo reads as follows: "Public Opinion and the Returning Soldier; The NRPB Report and Social Security; Methods of building Confidence; Further Recommendations for President's message 12/22/42; Ban on Gasoline Sales; Manpower; Method of Peace Treaty Ratification; Possibility of Educating the People on Problem of Inflation; Suggestions on Speech – Conciliatory or independent 12/21/42; Use of Surveys to Anticipate Public Reaction; Do you approve or disapprove of way Roosevelt is handling his job as President today?; What People most criticize about President; Spy Trial; What people most like about the President; Keeping President's trips secret; Which party would handle best problems of country after war is won; Dewey and Willkie; Tone of Presidential talks; Are President's Talks interpreted as political?; Would people like to hear President more often?; Questions on post-war planning," FDRL, Rosenman Files. While it is difficult to determine if this (incomplete) list constitutes questions or report titles, this list symbolizes Cantril and Rosenman's keen interest in using public opinion poll data both for public relations and public policy purposes.

[28] FDRL 1942, Rosenman Files.

[29] Underline in original.

politicians used modern media or new technology for political advertising or campaigning. To use polls as aids in determining citizens' preferences was inconceivable to Truman, for campaigns were won and lost by parties and candidates, not by surveys that helped advertise public policies.

The Eisenhower administration recognized the integral role of television in shaping voter preferences and attitudes. Managed public relations, they believed, would result in increased popularity and the ability to shape and direct public opinion. Eisenhower actively used television commercials during his 1952 presidential campaign, spending over $800,000 to Adlai Stevenson's $77,000.[30] On January 19, 1955, President Eisenhower held the first televised news conference and in 1956 the National Academy of Arts and Sciences awarded President Eisenhower an Emmy for his contribution to television news. These facts attest to the explosive rise of television in the 1950s and suggest that the Eisenhower administration's interest in gauging public opinion stemmed in part from an understanding that television technology was an endemic part of the political landscape.

Eisenhower's advisers were interested in using the media to advance a going public strategy. Press Secretary Hagerty, for example, wrote in his diary that the objective of the televised news conference is to "go directly to the people." Oval Office Cabinet Liaison Maxwell Rabb suggested that holding fireside chats would help "present his message over the head of Congress directly to the people in a way that he cannot be criticized, and would help prepare public opinion."[31] Although the going public strategies promoted by Hagerty and Rabb were not systematically implemented, data from the Eisenhower archives reveal that the Eisenhower administration routinely used public polls as a means to gauge public opinion.

In 1952, the Republican National Committee hired the firm Batten, Barton, Durstein, and Osborn to coordinate advertising for the Eisenhower campaign, and after General Eisenhower's victory, the RNC signed a four-year retainer contract with BBD&O, which provided weekly tracking polls of about 100 persons. These tracking polls, according to Craig Allen, author of *Eisenhower and the Mass Media*, were circulated in the White House.[32]

[30] Kathleen Hall Jamieson, *Packaging the Presidency*. New York: Oxford University Press, 1984, p. 43.

[31] Craig Allen, *Eisenhower and the Mass Media: Peace, Prosperity, and Prime-Time TV*. Chapel Hill: University of North Carolina Press, 1993, pp. 21, 47–48. The Hagerty quotation is cited but not footnoted by Allen. The Rabb quotation can be found in ibid., 21, fn. 33, citing DDEL, Eisenhower Office File, Rabb to Adams, January 8, 1953, Box 415.

[32] Ibid., 38; Also see Stanley Kelley, Jr., *Public Relations and Political Power*. Baltimore, MD: Johns Hopkins University Press, 1956, p. 172; and David Halberstam, *The Fifties*. New York: Villard, 1993, pp. 224–236. BBD&O's polling for the RNC is documented in a September 29, 1956 memorandum from Chairman Leonard W. Hall to Sherman Adams, in which Hall states, "each week BBD&O is making telephone surveys for me on issues." DDEL, DDE Central General File 156-B, Polls, "1956 (2)," Box 1219.

As noted in Chapter 5, the administration's primary source for poll data was Sigurd "Sig" Larmon, president of the advertising firm Young and Rubicam, mentor of George Gallup and a friend of both Eisenhower and his chief of staff, Sherman Adams. By providing Eisenhower's advisers with Gallup poll data, Larmon simultaneously counseled the staffers with how to advance Eisenhower's image in the media.[33] One example of Larmon's advice was a suggestion to use a particular phrase for developing a presidential theme.

The playing up the phrase – 'a stronger America' – is significant. It seems to me that this is a better way to characterize the President's policy than 'middle of the road.' The phrase, 'a stronger America,' gives the President a theme that he could build around in every speech and statement. For example: Does McCarthyism and the continuing digging up of the past make for 'a stronger America?' Do the demands of various pressure groups make for 'a stronger America?' Should not every act and every note of every Congressman be dedicated to making 'America stronger?'[34]

Sherman Adams' response to Larmon revealed that he valued this advice and wanted to implement it.

Thank you for sending again the recent Gallup polls. More particularly, I liked your suggestion of playing up the phrase 'a stronger America.' In fact I liked it so much I am circulating your letter to the appropriate people here in the office. As you say, the applications of the phrase are myriad.[35]

Eisenhower repeatedly invited Larmon to join the administration, but Larmon declined, and as a result, Eisenhower's desire to coordinate public relations activities with a domestic board of strategy never materialized.[36] Nonetheless, Larmon's relationship with Eisenhower strengthened as the Citizens for Eisenhower campaign and White House advisers valued his advertising expertise and the Gallup poll releases he provided.

George Gallup also aided President Eisenhower in this regard by voluntarily sending the White House advance copies of his poll data. George Gallup

[33] For examples of the type of materials Larmon sent the Eisenhower campaign, see "Opinion Poll 1952 Presidential Race," in which trial heats against President Truman, and party breakdown were documented, DDEL, Staff Files: Committee for Eisenhower, Young and Rubicam 1952–61, Box 3; Young and Rubicam Files, "Correspondence of Sig Larmon," 1952, Box 1; and "Young and Rubicam," Box 5. Additional evidence of the Eisenhower campaign's gathering of poll data included an August 1952 confidential "Political Notebook" compiled by the pollster Claude Robinson, in which Mr. Robinson provided charts and graphs about party turnout, independent voters, and voter intentions, as well as a recommendation for using Gallup polls for future research. See DDEL, "Political Notebook 1952," Young and Rubicam Files, Box 5. Also see "Public Opinion Polls '52–'53 (Surveys) (2)," DDE Central General File 156-B, Box 1218, and "Polls" "1954 (1)," "1955 (1)," "1954 (2)," "1955 (3)," Box 1219.
[34] DDEL, "1954 (2)," Polls 156-B, Correspondence between Sig Larmon and Gov. Sherman Adams, January 13 and 26, 1954, Box 1219.
[35] Ibid.
[36] See Allen, *Eisenhower and the Mass Media*, p. 42.

periodically sent advance copies of his press releases to Adams and Hagerty. "I hope you don't mind if I send you an occasional release," Gallup wrote Hagerty early in the Eisenhower term. Hagerty replied, "I would like very much to receive your releases from time to time because I value them highly."[37]

In addition to collecting Gallup polls, Eisenhower's advisers also requested that other pollsters send them poll data. Early in the administration's first term, James M. Lambie, Jr., special assistant in the White House, wrote to Claude Robinson, president of the Opinion Research Corporation, requesting that he and other public pollsters provide the administration with poll data.

Before 'informing' or 'educating' the American people, it is desirable to have whatever specific knowledge or indication is available of what is presently in the public mind . . . This, of course, is where research experts come in. I shall be most grateful if you will let me have three things: 1) your general thoughts on the problem; 2) information as to recent surveys which throw light on the knowledge or information the public has on, and its attitude toward, various aspects of the problem; 3) guidance as to other quarters from which pertinent opinion might be had. (I am writing in the same vein to Ted Gallup and Elmo Roper.)[38]

The "problem" that concerned Lambie was the perception that the administration was weak and transitory in nature. While it is unclear if Lambie received the data he requested, his letter to Robinson, as well as Hagerty's correspondence with Gallup, both indicated that Eisenhower's White House advisers considered media pollsters to be "research experts" and their data to be potentially available for the administration's use.

The Eisenhower administration's appetite for using polls to gauge public opinion was further evidenced by their taking advantage of opportunities to receive poll data from friends in public service and the media who were conducting surveys. Ohio State Senator Fred W. Danner asked presidential adviser Wilton B. "Jerry" Persons if "he is interested in having any special questions asked" in an upcoming poll of Danner's Summit County constituents. Persons affirmatively responded to Danner's suggestion after receiving some recommendations from his White House colleague Jerry Morgan.

I'd like to pass along, for what they are worth, the following subjects which you might wish to include in your poll in addition to those as outlined in your letter. 1) Do you think that social security should cover everyone, or should any of the following groups be excluded: a) farm labor, b) doctors, c) lawyers, and d) state and municipal employees. 2) Do you think that the carelessness and laxity of a previous Administration in dealing with security risks in the Government should be brought

37 DDEL, "Polls '52–'53," Correspondence between Press Secretary J. Hagerty and George Gallup, May 8 and 13, 1953, 156-B, Box 1218.
38 DDEL, CHRON FILE May–June 1953, June 9, 1953, James M. Lambie, Box 3.

to public attention? 3) Are you in favor of the basic principles of the Taft-Hartley Act? Needless to say I shall look forward to receiving the results when you have completed the survey . . .[39]

Although the second question was worded to evoke criticisms of the Truman administration, the first and third questions indicate that Morgan and Persons were seriously interested in secretly using Danner's poll to ascertain public opinion on domestic policy issues.

Persons was not the only White House official to suggest that particular questions be included in outside surveys. Press Secretary Jim Hagerty was asked by an acquaintance, Fritz S. Updike, general manager of the Rome Sentinel Company, if the administration wished to include questions in a poll that was being conducted by the *Rome Daily Sentinel*. Hagerty seized at the opportunity.

I would like to suggest several questions. They are as follows: 1) Do you approve of the way the President is conducting the affairs of the Government? 2) Do you approve of the Administration's action on Korea? 3) Do you approve of the President meeting with the officials of Britain and France at Bermuda later this month? If I may, I would like to send you some other questions from time to time. It would be a great help to us here in getting the comments of the people on the street.[40]

Even though Updike warned Hagerty of the polls' dubious scientific validity, Hagerty wanted to use the local media poll to assess how Eisenhower's international actions would be perceived. Persons and Hagerty's interest in amassing poll data about political issues and policies, and their willingness to write poll questions to be included in survey instruments not commissioned for presidential use, indicates that for them, friends in the media aided them in measuring public opinion about issues of interest to the administration.

The relationship between Eisenhower's advisers and members of the private sector, including journalists and editors, enabled the White House to gain access to poll data from a variety of sources. Because of their previous friendships with Eisenhower and his staffers, some individuals provided key aides with advances of poll data. Eisenhower sought, in the words of Craig Allen, to "circumvent the press" as a means both to advance his policy agenda and to exploit the media (by using their polls) in order to avoid relying on members of Congress and political parties as regular sources for public opinion. In short, as media polls became more commonplace, they were read more frequently by presidents. By the 1950s, media polls served

---

[39] DDEL, "Public Opinion Polls '52–'53 (Surveys) (2)," Correspondence between State Senator Fred W. Danner and Deputy Assistant to the President Wilton B. Persons, October 30 and November 19, 1953, GF 156-B, Box 1218.

[40] DDEL, "Public Opinion Polls '52–'53 (Surveys) (1)," Central General Files, 156-B, GF 156, Box 1218. Updike and Hagerty knew each other because Hagerty previously served as New York Governor Thomas Dewey's Press Secretary.

as a key link between the president and the citizenry and they began to replace parties and Congress as institutional conduits of public opinion.

KENNEDY

President Kennedy's complicated relations with the media stemmed in part from his understanding of how television was transforming American politics. In 1959, Senator Kennedy wrote an article in *TV Guide* entitled "A Force That Has Changed The Political Scene," suggesting that television would enable citizens to form opinions about politicians in new and healthy ways:

The slick or bombastic orator, pounding the table and ringing the rafters, is not as welcome in the family living room as he was in the town square or party hall. In the old days, many a seasoned politician counted among his most highly developed and useful talents his ability to dodge a reporter's question, evade a 'hot' issue and avoid a definite stand. But today a vast viewing public is able to detect such deception and, in my opinion, willing to respect political honesty...Honesty, vigor, compassion, intelligence – the presence or lack of these and other qualities make up what is called the candidate's 'image' – and while they may in fact be based only on a candidate's TV impression, ignoring his record, views, and other appearances – my own conviction is that these images or impressions are likely to be uncannily correct.[41]

The net effect of television, Kennedy argued, "can definitely be for the better – the impact of TV on politics is tremendous."[42] To Kennedy, television enhanced democracy by preventing demagogues and party bosses from imposing their views and candidates on the public. Even at the heart of Kennedy's praise of television as a political medium lay the roots of his struggle with the media. Kennedy saw television both as a conduit between political elites and the public and as an arbiter that could distinguish between good and bad politicians. These conceptions necessitated that he (and others who shared this view) think of the media as both a friend and an adversary. Presidents needed the media to transmit their messages to the public; the media in turn needed the president for newsworthy information, but wanted to retain a sense of autonomy from the president so as not to be manipulated.

Kennedy conceded that voters would base their political decisions on the televised image of politicians, but he believed that television exposed politicians' characters and prevented politicians from avoiding questions, issues, and positions. In this regard, television stunted political deception by accurately revealing and reflecting candidates' moral core. The images of

[41] John F. Kennedy, "A Force That Has Changed the Political Scene" *TV Guide*, November 14, 1959.
[42] Ibid.

dishonest, demagogic, and callous politicians would be exposed by television, as would the images of honest, straightforward, and sensitive politicians.

Lou Harris shared Kennedy's view that television image was replacing party identification as a primary determinant in how voters chose candidates. In a December 9, 1957 letter from Harris to Kennedy aide Ted Sorensen, Harris discussed how his polls could help win elections.

From such [survey] research comes the sound basis on which to assess where Senator Kennedy stands today, where his sources of strength and weakness are, and how he can maximize his margin of victory on election day. [Polls could be used for] obtaining an accurate profile or image of the candidate . . . In an era when party regularity is at a relatively low ebb, when ticket splitting and switch-voting have reached unprecedented proportions, an enormous burden is placed on the individual candidate to connect directly with voters. There is strong evidence that for a variety of reasons, voters are casting their ballots more for the individual man than for any party or set of party principles he may stand for . . . The day is probably past when either party can take for granted that it will automatically win simply because it has a majority of the voters enrolled in its party, or because the voters produced a winner for the party in recent elections . . . [43]

Harris argued that because party-line voting had waned, candidates needed to know how to communicate and connect with voters without relying on the party's get-out-the-vote apparatus. As political parties no longer attracted citizens to vote for candidates, personalities and image would play a greater role in determining voter outcomes. Individuals might vote the party line, but the candidate's personality and style would primarily influence how citizens cast their ballots. Harris did not enumerate the causes of ticket splitting. Instead he claimed that voters responded best to candidates who could connect directly to the people.

Harris used polls to monitor reactions of citizens after each of the three presidential debates between Kennedy and Nixon. Respondents were asked within twenty-four hours after the debates, "Which candidate was most effective in the debate, or didn't you see much difference between them?," and in a section of the ensuing report titled "The Kennedy Image in the Debate," a table summarized respondents' comments about the candidate or about his positions. [44] The first debate report discussed the senator's "clean-cut manner" and mentioned how his intelligence had "shone through," concluding that the polls indicated that Kennedy's performance on television was better than Nixon's.

---

[43] JFKL, Letter from Harris to Sorensen, December 9, 1957, Sorensen Files, Box 17.

[44] JFKL, "An Analysis of the First Kennedy-Nixon Debate, 29 September 1960," "An Analysis of the Second Kennedy-Nixon Debate, 11 October 1960," and "An Analysis of the Third Kennedy-Nixon Debate, 19 October 1960," Poll #873, RFK Pre-Administration Papers, Political Files, Box 44. The second poll was a telephone poll taken within twelve hours after the debate's conclusion and the third poll was conducted the morning after the debate, which took place on a Friday in Los Angeles, California.

Kennedy exploited his talents in the media by holding live televised press conferences. The media did not fully appreciate Kennedy's maneuver and there was resistance among print reporters in recognizing the legitimacy of television reporters. A *Chicago Tribune* editorial referred to the administration as promoting "government by public relations."[45] Kennedy chose Pierre Salinger as his press secretary. Salinger, a former reporter with the *San Francisco Chronicle*, was thirty-five when Kennedy assumed the presidency; his youth was fodder for Washington insiders to conclude that, in the words of Louis Liebovich, author of *The Press and the Modern Presidency*, "the new administration was filled with neophytes."[46]

Harris' postelection analyses continued to focus on developing an image that was conducive to the television medium. Evidently, Harris believed that it was vitally important for the president to personalize his political agenda:

...His press conferences are widely acclaimed, but more as feats of incredible personal accomplishment and clarity of expression and response and fearlessness in calling a spade a spade, rather than as sharply focused expressions of understanding. His public appearances have been dramatic and simply cry out with the strength and purpose and dedication and seriousness of the man. But the small human concern, the genuine feeling for mankind in day-to-day terms, has not yet been registered profoundly.

This raises a central question of communication. It is perfectly apparent that the President has communicated the spirit of himself personally and of his Administration and even more the style that the American people can now grow accustomed to...he has not yet come face to face with the people in a frank and moving discussion of what all this means in terms of people...the P. must take care to explain that the role of government is not to be the beginning and ending of endeavor, but rather that marginal thread of difference to really help alleviate the plight of our fellow countrymen or those abroad. Perhaps even more important is to go before the people in 'face-to-face talks' via television, not so much to 'go over the head of Congress,' as to speak frankly about some of the problems confronting our citizens and what the federal government can do, along with state and local government and private sources, to meet these problems. The manner should be calm, the mood one of frankness, but the illustrations must always be human, the solution assisting legislation that is specific and concrete...

We would urge in the strongest possible terms that such 'face-to-face talks' be begun, for neither the press conferences nor speeches in Washington or around the country will substitute for this direct and personal communication through the most intimate medium our civilization possesses: television.

In short, the focus of the President's legislative program is not entirely sharp, certainly not as sharp as it can be made to be, and if there is a missing dimension in

[45] "Live Press Conferences," *Chicago Tribune*, editorial, January 2, 1961.
[46] Louis W. Liebovich, *The Press and the Modern Presidency: Myths and Mindsets from Kennedy to Clinton.* Westport, CT: Praeger, 1998, p. 17.

what is otherwise a truly phenomenal public imprint for only 60 days, it is the stress on the human side of the nation's problems and challenges.[47]

Harris supplemented his public opinion information with public relations advice. He concluded that the president's legislative program was unpopular even though he did not measure citizens' ostensible indifference toward President Kennedy's programs. The poll data neither supported or refuted Harris' claim, but his interpretation of the data suggested that it was a viable hypothesis. Harris recommended that television be used to develop a personalized "human" dimension to the presidency. Harris specifically recommended the method by which Kennedy should communicate on television (for example, televised "face-to-face talks"), and the style he should adopt in these talks ("calm, the mood one of frankness"). Harris also hypothesized that these televised talks served to establish a rapport with the American people that would ultimately manipulate public opinion. This point confirms a theme addressed in Chapter 2, namely that the perception of going public among White House advisers as a viable legislative strategy is a part of the presidential polling calculus.

According to Liebovich, Kennedy enjoyed the press. He ensured that reporters had stories, frequently granting interviews or appearing before the camera. Simultaneously, Kennedy sought to restrict the access given to journalists. For example, after receiving criticisms by editors after the Bay of Pigs invasion, Kennedy suggested that journalists voluntarily censor themselves when military operations were occurring. He developed personal friendships with editors and tried to spike newspaper stories that showed his administration in a poor light. In return, some members of the media sensed that they were being manipulated in order to generate or receive favorable media coverage.[48]

The Kennedy era denotes a significant change in presidential polling. Party politics was replaced by television and Harris' poll reports repeatedly emphasized how to market the Kennedy image. Harris continued in the mold of Hadley Cantril and Sig Larmon, serving as the primary provider of public opinion information to key White House officials. Harris' reports resembled Hadley Cantril's in two respects: They were easy to read, containing tables without mentioning margins of error or other measures of statistical significance that may have confused lay readers, and they provided extensive public relations advice. Just as Cantril advised Roosevelt about how to use the radio to disseminate his message to the American people, Harris articulated a similar message about television, stating that his polling would help create accurate profiles of candidates, and that television would help elect Kennedy to the presidency.

[47] JFKL, "Polls – Public Reaction to President Kennedy During the First 60 Days of Administration, 22 March 1961-A," POF, Box 105.
[48] Liebovich, *The Press and the Modern Presidency*, pp. 16–21, 27.

Harris' campaign reports elevated his status as a provider of important information about how to assess the views of the American public. He, not the Democratic Party, the media, nor members of Congress, gauged and interpreted public opinion. As citizens continued to ticket split, and as parties became less able to gauge public opinion, secret polls became the instrument by which President Kennedy's advisers attempted to assess citizens' attitudes.

Kennedy did not entirely abandon alternative means of measuring public opinion. Ted Sorensen contends that candidate and President Kennedy continued to receive nonprivate polls and newspaper articles as means to gauge public opinion. Polls, public and private, became an important instrument by which Kennedy attempted to ascertain citizens' opinions on personal images and public policies.[49]

JOHNSON

The symbiotic relationship between the press and the presidency that began during the Kennedy administration was further institutionalized in the Johnson administration. Johnson's vice president, Hubert Humphrey, generously said that Johnson was "hardly in love" with the media. After leaving office, Johnson stated that the media had too much power and repeatedly lambasted him when he was in office.[50] Johnson both respected and distrusted the media. He was an avid television viewer and newspaper column reader who, like his predecessors, frequently believed that the press treated him and his administration unfairly. The phrase "credibility gap" – used liberally by members of the media to describe the administration's Vietnam War policy – irked him. Walter Lippmann's critical columns also bothered him, probably because he knew how influential Lippmann was in shaping mass and elite opinions. Johnson actively responded to criticism, however, fueling more comments that he was overly sensitive, which in turn made Johnson believe that some members of the press were betraying him and his attempts to establish cordial relations.

Although Johnson masterfully wooed members of Congress, he was less successful in winning over the media. He made repeated overtures to befriend some of them, simultaneously berating others. Some reporters mocked his

[49] According to Sorensen, congressional contacts, tabulations of White House mail, reactions to events, and meetings with citizens' groups, and not polls, served as the primary vehicles for measuring public opinion. Fax from Sorensen to this author, July 28, 1994.

[50] See Vaughn Davis Bornet, *The Presidency of Lyndon Baines Johnson*. Lawrence: University Press of Kansas, 1983, pp. 147–162. The quotation by Humphrey is on p. 161. For more on tensions between Johnson and the press, see Branch, *Pillar of Fire: America in the King Years 1963–65*, pp. 532–533, 544; Johnson, *The Vantage Point*, p. 96; George Reedy, *Lyndon B. Johnson: A Memoir*. New York: Andrews & McKeel, 1982, pp. 51, 67; Liebovich, *The Press and the Modern Presidency*, pp. 43–45; and Dallek, *Flawed Giant*, pp. 286–287.

crude nature, such as when he revealed a scar on camera, or when he picked up his dog by the ears. Others found his candor refreshing, in part because he often spoke his mind, albeit sometimes off camera, using a rural, Texan vocabulary that some journalists found appealing. But the institutional function of the press prevailed – they were critical of him and his policies, especially Vietnam, in part because they recognized their role as skeptics of the administration. Johnson felt betrayed.

President Johnson's early polling operation was uncoordinated. Neither the White House nor the Democratic Party had a systematic method for amassing or interpreting poll data. After Johnson won reelection and as his administration matured, however, the method by which his administration obtained poll data acquired a degree of organization. The administration exploited certain members of the media, pollsters in particular, both to collect and to exercise influence over public opinion–related information.

Lawrence Jacobs and Robert Shapiro's study of Johnson's polls elegantly notes that the Johnson administration "used polling to evaluate and improve the White House's effectiveness in promoting themselves and their policies."[51] Similarly, Bruce Altschuler argues that the Johnson administration used polls to advance public relations purposes by routinely suppressing negative poll information.[52] Repeatedly, Johnson's advisers sought and received poll data from public pollsters. Louis Harris, among others, periodically aided the Johnson administration by including survey questions requested by them. "Attached are the results of the polls I mentioned to you last night," Press Secretary Bill Moyers once wrote President Johnson, "Lou Harris asks that we not let anyone know he did it for us."[53] In a July 15, 1966 letter to Marvin Watson, Moyers' assistant, Hayes Redmon wrote that he's "trying to get the lead sentence changed" of a Harris survey question.[54]

Harris also provided Panzer with campaign suggestions just one month before Johnson withdrew from the presidential race. Panzer wrote:

Here is his [Harris'] 'one big idea' for your speech tomorrow night. It is based on very sound and as yet unpublished data which will not be out for about two weeks and for which he asks to be protected.[55]

[51] Jacobs and Shapiro, "Disorganized Democracy," p. 16, fn. 47, citing LBJL, Letter from Bill Moyers to Jack Jacobsen, March 28, 1967, Marvin Watson Files, Box 27.
[52] Altschuler, *LBJ at the Polls.* Altschuler argues that the poll data given to LBJ were rose-colored snapshots of public opinion, not the gray or bleak images of a country in the midst of an increasingly unpopular war.
[53] LBJL, "10/29/64–5/19/65," Memorandum from Bill Moyers to the President, February 16, 1965, WH Central File PR16, Box 346.
[54] LBJL, Letter from Hayes Redmon to Marvin Watson, July 15, 1966, WH Central File PR16, Box 354.
[55] LBJL, "Public Opinion Polls 1967," Memorandum from Fred Panzer to the President, March 30, 1968, WH Central File PR16, Box 82.

Harris was not alone in quietly polling for the administration. In a June 10, 1965 letter to Assistant to the President Hayes Redmon, Irving Crespi of the Gallup organization told Redmon that the Gallup organization would poll for the White House.

Your letter with the questions on immigration has just arrived. We will pre-test them first thing next week, for inclusion on our next survey, scheduled for the week of June 22nd. Results should be available for publication in the early part of July, though I cannot give you a precise date as yet. As soon as pre-testing is completed I will let you know what re-wording, if any, is indicated. My immediate reaction is that making the wording more colloquial would help, but that the approach is sound and unbiased.[56]

The Gallup organization also provided poll information directly to the Democratic Party, whose finance chairman, Arthur Krim, then delivered the data to the White House. In a letter from Marvin Watson to President Johnson, Watson relayed a discussion he had with Arthur Krim:

Arthur Krim reports that Dr. Gallup is in the Bahamas and not available by phone. He therefore talked to Mr. Gallup, Jr., who handles polling for his father . . . Mr. Gallup would not give the specifics but did say the Gallup poll which would run Sunday, without Wallace in the poll, will show the President with a big lead over Reagan, Romney and Nixon and a six point lead over Rockefeller.[57]

The politicized nature of these data exemplify the sometimes obstreperous relationship between the Johnson White House and the media. Johnson's advisers surreptitiously asked media pollsters to supply poll data. They did, in secret. The advisers then attempted to use the data for political purposes – spinning public opinion in a certain direction consistent with the administration's views. By exploiting their relationship with public pollsters, Johnson's advisers were even able to write poll questions or obtain the answers before the media did.

Members of the Johnson White House understood that the media were also conduits through which public opinion was shaped. Fred Panzer in particular appreciated this concept and attempted to manipulate public opinion by artificially generating support for the administration. An October 7, 1967 memorandum from Panzer to President Johnson read, "Here are the five letters you asked me to prepare last night."[58] These letters, written to Dr. George Gallup, accused Gallup of using his October 4, 1967 poll to advance Governor Rockefeller's presidential candidacy. Each version of the

---

[56] LBJL, "4/27/65–7/31/65," Letter from Irving Crespi to Hayes Redmon, June 10, 1965, General PR16, Box 353.

[57] LBJL, "Arthur Krim," Letter from Watson to the President, January 17, 1968, Marvin Watson Files, Box 26.

[58] LBJL, "Fred Panzer Memos," Fred Panzer to the President, October 7, 1967, Marvin Watson Files, Box 28.

letter was slightly different, and on the Panzer memo was a handwritten note that appears to read, "Sent to Committee [,] Meeting in Hilton Head."[59] One can only speculate if these letters were eventually sent to members of the Democratic National Committee, which was meeting in Hilton Head, South Carolina at the time. At minimum, these letters to Gallup reveal that Panzer fabricated an anti-Gallup, letter-writing campaign.

Panzer also provided Watson with a list of radio shows in the Washington, D.C. metropolitan area "where our telephone talkers could be active."[60] By suggesting that these call-in shows could be infiltrated with pro-Johnson callers, Panzer tried to sway public opinion; disseminating pro-Johnson rhetoric on the radio, without divulging that the callers were Johnson supporters, served as a means by which Johnson's advisers sought to change the direction and intensity of public opinion.

Additional evidence that public opinion was scrutinized and shaped can be shown by a comparative analysis by Special Assistant to the President Walt Rostow of Quayle's poll of Vietnamese citizens, with a similar poll commissioned by CBS.[61] White House official William J. ("Bill") Jorden forwarded this analysis to Marvin Watson, who wrote a note to President Johnson concluding that "by and large, they show a similar portrait of public opinion."[62] In both studies, conclusions were made that many Vietnamese citizens wanted the U.S.'s bombing of villages to continue.[63] Quayle's poll, while purporting to represent the views of the Vietnamese, ignored numerous methodological sampling obstacles and instead served as an instrument to note support for the U.S. military policy in the region. Even though there were no public statements by the president or the secretary of defense about the Vietnam poll, the mere existence of the poll shows the White House's

[59] Ibid. The author of this note is unknown, but based on other handwritten notes, it was probably written by Marvin Watson.
[60] LBJL, "Fred Panzer Memos," Memo from Fred Panzer to Marvin Watson, March 28, 1968, Marvin Watson Files, Box 28.
[61] LBJL, "PR 16 3-1-67–4-20-67," Marvin Watson to the President, April 17, 1967, White House Central File PR 16, Box 348. The CBS poll was conducted from November 24, 1966 through February 1, 1967 by the Opinion Research Corporation and the Center for Vietnamese Studies.
[62] LBJL, April 17, 1967, Comparative Analysis of the Oliver Quayle and CBS Public Opinion Surveys in South Viet Nam, White House Central File, PR 16, Box 348. The exact wording of the two poll questions as noted in the report are, [CBS] "Should bombing of villages continue when necessary? Continue = 37%; Stop bombing and burning = 46%; No opinion, not reported = 17%. [Quayle] "The Americans should stop their bombing" Agree = 25%; Disagree = 46%; Not Sure = 29%, ibid., 4. Additional archival data about the usage of Quayle's Vietnam poll is limited to a May 25, 1966 note about the poll from Benjamin H. Read, Executive Secretary of the State Department, to Hayes Redmon, that reads, "Returned with thanks." Read's returning the poll to Redmon suggests that the poll was initiated by the White House, and not the State Department.
[63] Ibid.

keen interest in how public opinion about Vietnam was shaped by the media.[64]

These attempts to use the media, however, did not guarantee that the administration employed sophisticated techniques to conduct or interpret polls. Quayle's domestic polls were repeatedly misinterpreted by Johnson's advisers. For example, an August 1964 poll question tested who would be the best vice-presidential candidate to share the ticket with President Johnson. The results read that a Goldwater-Miller ticket would lose by a landslide to seven fictitious Democratic tickets as follows:

LBJ -Humphrey (70.0%) -McCarthy (69.0%) -Ribicoff (68.5%) -Muskie (68.0%) -Pell (68.0%) -Pastore (68.0%) -Wagner (67.0%)[65]

Although these numbers were virtually identical and statistically insignificant, Assistant to the President Fred Panzer interpreted the data as if the variance among these senators were meaningful:

We have no choice here but to point to the fact that Humphrey is slightly stronger than the others in New York. In the present situation, the President will win with any of the seven. In a suddenly close race, the ticket will be stronger with Hubert Humphrey in New York.[66]

Panzer was not alone in misinterpreting the nuances of polling. In March 1968, White House Chief of Staff James Jones decided to conduct a poll from the White House, as if his secretaries were professional poll interviewers:

My two secretaries will use a Watts line and they have phone books from small and large cities in every section of the country. They will make a sample poll too.[67]

On the same day, Jones wrote Watson to let him know that the secretaries had completed their interviewing:

Sally and Donna have completed their calls to citizens at random from Boston; New York City; Washington; Montgomery County, Maryland; Indianapolis; Chicago; Seattle; Pueblo, Colorado; Atlanta; Knoxville, Tennessee; and Houston. I have given their results to Fred Panzer to analyze and he will get them to you.[68]

Rather than speculate as to whether or how the White House secretaries employed random sampling or why the internal poll was being conducted, Jones, Watson, and Panzer implied that their internal poll conducted by

[64] More specifically, I could find no public statements about this poll after reviewing *The New York Times* Index.

[65] LBJL, "PAST (NY) 1 of 2," Study 181 New York State August 1964, Fred Panzer Files, Box 175.

[66] Ibid.

[67] LBJL, "PR16 3-6-68–4-4-68," Memorandum from James R. Jones to W. Marvin Watson, March 11,1968, White House Central File PR16, Box 350.

[68] Ibid.

White House secretaries was identical to polls conducted by a professional pollster. Senior White House officials dismissed or ignored survey methodology, assuming that randomization constituted methodological accuracy. As for Quayle's polls, Panzer and other senior advisers assumed that polls were sufficiently accurate because if they were not, then the pollster would not have proceeded with his poll analysis and report.[69]

The two episodes cited above demonstrate that the administration's strive for accuracy was occasionally replaced by haste or misinterpretation. In these cases, warnings about polling methodology were casually discussed or not mentioned at all.

While some of Johnson's advisers did not understand the nuances of polling methodology, one exception was Albert Cantril, who besides being the son of FDR's source of polling information, Hadley Cantril, served as an interpreter of polling data during his tenure in the LBJ administration. Cantril was hired to provide the Johnson administration with analyses of polls. For example, if two polls with two different sample sizes came to the White House, or if polls were received with differently worded questions, then Cantril would assess the polls, and write a memo to Redmon explaining to him the methodological obstacles and the polls' nuances. Cantril's role as in-house interpreter of poll data is novel, as previous administrations did not have someone in the Old Executive office building reviewing polls for this purpose.[70]

Cantril notes in one memo that Quayle's sample was too small:

Only 302 interviews were conducted. This means that the percentages reported here may vary as much as eight percentage points in either direction. The sample is too small for precise measures of opinion and inferences from these figures had best be cautious.[71]

Johnson received this information in his night reading; the president was not only concerned about the attitudes of the public, but he was also informed about misinterpretations of poll results.

For all their efforts to poll independently of the media, Johnson's advisers had a peculiar relationship with the media. Johnson himself claimed

---

[69] Quayle's analyses were sometimes confusing if not contradictory. See, for example, Study 204, October 1964 Maryland poll, especially Quayle's description of the typical white backlash voter. See LBJL, Fred Panzer Files, Box 171, 9. Gerald Hursh-Cesar, who worked for Vice President Humphrey, described Quayle's poll interpretations as frequently "meaningless" and "nonsense." Hursh-Cesar stated, "When I had access to Quayle's polls in 1968, after Johnson withdrew, I wouldn't even let people read the interpretations; I would take the numbers, copy them, and not let others see the full report." Conversation with Gerald Hursh-Cesar with this author, April 4, 1995.

[70] More on Cantril's job in the Johnson administration can be found in LBJL, Albert H. Cantril CHRON FILE.

[71] Ibid. Memo from Cantril to Redmon, Aug. 26, 1966 re: Quayle WI 6th C. D. Poll. In President's night reading Aug. 30, 1966.

that his administration's "most tragic error was our inability to establish a rapport and a confidence with press and television, the communication media."[72] President Nixon followed Johnson's pattern of conflating public relations and public opinion, in part because presidential polls served as a convenient, secret means to obtain advice about how to market policies and attack political opponents. But Nixon's relations with the media were less than sanguine, and as a result, his White House public opinion apparatus would become better organized, more secretive, and hence further institutionalized, than LBJ's.

NIXON

President Nixon and his advisers thought that the media treated them unfairly, so much so that it became a preoccupation among key advisers to monitor the press and their polls, and in some cases, consider attacking the pollsters' reputations.[73] According to William Safire, a former speechwriter for Nixon, the president personalized press criticism, repeatedly referring to the press as "the enemy."[74] Because they thought of the media as sabotaging them, President Nixon and his advisers attempted to manipulate public opinion by disseminating poll data showing the president in a positive light and by discrediting polls and pollsters when the president's polls were less than flattering.[75]

Lou Harris and his polls were considered particularly worthy of scrutiny by the White House. A June 22, 1970 memorandum from Dwight L. Chapin to Haldeman suggested that the White House encouraged members of Congress to investigate Harris.

In light of the black eye given the pollsters by the electorate in the British election last week, perhaps now is the time to have a select group of our people on the Hill launch an investigation of pollsters in the United States. Specifically, I think they could concentrate on the Harris organization – perhaps by name . . . We can tie the inaccuracies to their findings in England to those which are published in the United States. There is a good case to be made on the fraud of publishing inaccurate polls and attempts to mislead the public. Do you think this is a good idea? Can we assign [Lyn] Nofzinger the project of seeing that the Congressional group is pulled together and they launch their investigation?[76]

---

[72] Dallek, *Flawed Giant*, p. 592, citing LBJL, Diary Backup, Johnson meeting with Helen Thomas, November 22, 1968.

[73] RMNP@NA, Memorandum from Jeb S. Magruder to Chapin, Colson, Dent, et al., 20 January 1970, Dwight Chapin Files, Box 22.

[74] William Safire, *Before the Fall: An Insider View of the Pre-Watergate White House*. Garden City, NY: Doubleday, 1975, pp. 342–352.

[75] For more details on this subject, see Jacobs and Shapiro, "Presidential Manipulation of Polls and Public Opinion."

[76] RMNP@NA, "[CF] PR 15 Public Opinion Polls [1969–1970]," June 22, 1970 Memorandum re: Polls, Box 53.

Haldeman responded to the first question by writing, "Excellent! Even superb," but disapproved of using Nofzinger, writing, "get someone more buttoned up to move it – with Nofzinger as Hill contact. Maybe [Charles] Colson?"[77] Even as Nixon's advisers attempted to "cultivate" Harris by inviting him to social functions at the White House and by employing his firm to conduct polls for the Domestic Policy Council, Haldeman considered Harris' polls to be a product of the liberal, anti-Nixon media, and therefore an enemy of the administration.[78]

Soon after receiving Chapin's memo, Haldeman informed Colson about the project to attack Harris.

President Richard Nixon and advisers H.R. Haldeman, Dwight Chapin, and John D. Erhlichman, 3/13/70 (Courtesy of the White House Photo Office and the Richard M. Nixon Library at the National Archives, NLNP-WHPO-MPF-3144(04A))

Working with Lyn Nofzinger, will you please put together a group of Congressmen to take on this project which should be well publicized and we should make every effort to help them in any way possible. This project is considered to be a top priority,

---

[77] Handwritten comments by Haldeman, ibid.
[78] RMNP@NA, "Harris Poll questionnaire – Domestic Council," Harris to Edwin Harper, July 29, 1971, Charles Colson Files, Box 69.

and I am sure it will pay rich dividends. Needless to say, the White House in no way should become identified with this undertaking.[79]

A month later, Haldeman suggested another way to discredit Harris after reading a Roper poll that differed from a Harris poll. "Can we start a fight here between Roper and Harris and get Roper to take Harris on, on the basis of how far off he is," he wrote. "If Roper won't do it directly, can we get someone else to do it?"[80] Defaming Harris and his polls was a top-secret priority.

Obtaining media poll data became a preoccupation of Haldeman's assistants. An August 6, 1971 memorandum from Larry Higby to Gordon Strachan showed the extent to which White House officials tried to obtain "additional background data" on a July 27, Roper poll. The memo showed that they had been unsuccessful in getting their data via Tom Benham and Harry O'Neill, but that Derge would "try to obtain the material through his university contacts."[81] Handwritten comments by Higby noted that Jeb Magruder had worked for the Roper Organization at Williams College, that three phone calls had been placed to Roper, and that inquiries should be made to see if any (White House or ORC) staffers were friends with Roper.[82]

Haldeman and Nixon sought to attack the credibility of pollsters they believed were affiliated with the Democratic Party, as well as media pollsters whose data yielded uncomplimentary portraits of the administration. The following excerpts from a June 7, 1972 telephone memorandum from Haldeman to Colson highlighted Haldeman's assault strategy against Mervin Field and the Field poll.

We should launch an all-out attack on the Field Poll in California and try now to totally destroy their credibility. We have the golden opportunity. We should make the point that they were wrong in 1968 (you will have to check the facts on this), they were wrong on McGovern in 1972, they were wrong on Proposition No. 9 (where they said it would carry 3 to 1 and it lost 2 to 1); in other words, Field has an unblemished record of wrong predictions. We also should build from this that the media and the pollsters have combined in a conspiracy to get McGovern the nomination, which is obviously the case . . . there should be a series of letters to the editor of the LA Times regarding polls, they subscribe to Field. Maybe a mailing to prominent businessmen on the disgrace of the pollsters, particularly in California would also be worthwhile.[83]

[79] RMNP@NA, "[CF] PR 15 Public Opinion Polls [1969–70]," Undated memo from Haldeman to Colson, (undated), Box 53.
[80] RMNP@NA, "[CF] PR 15 Public Opinion Polls [1969–70]," Memorandum from Haldeman to Finch, July 13, 1970, Box 53.
[81] RMNP@NA, "Polls Chron 1971–72," Memorandum from Higby to Strachan, August 6 1971, HRH Files, Box 335.
[82] Ibid.
[83] RMNP@NA, "Field Poll," Telephone memorandum from Haldeman to Charles W. Colson, June 7, 1972, Charles Colson Files, Box 99.

By proposing a campaign against Field, Haldeman revealed his broader assumptions about the operation of polls in politics. To him, there were good, honest pollsters, and dishonest, Democrat pollsters and journalists who hated Republicans and conspired to advance a distorted point of view about America. To Haldeman, Field was a dishonest pollster who should have been publicly criticized for his ostensible conniving. This normative framework, no doubt shared by others in the White House, gave Haldeman a strong incentive to distance the White House from the media by replicating a number of their opinion-assessment functions within the executive branch.

Sampling techniques of the media pollsters were analyzed by Strachan, but unlike ORC and Gallup, Harris was reluctant to share his sampling techniques with the White House, further convincing Haldeman and his staffers that Harris was dishonest.[84] If some data were biased (as Haldeman was convinced Harris' data were), then the public had to be educated about this apparent conspiracy. Only then could Nixon's true, positive character be received by the citizenry.

In his diary, Haldeman suggests that the idea of using private poll data to counter the media poll data stemmed from the president himself:

We got into the polling question. The P[resident] is disturbed, obviously, by the Gallup Poll, which only shows him up 4 points while our poll shows an increase of 11. He's suggesting that we should probably build our own established poll, such as ORC (Opinion Research Corporation), on a continuing basis, so that we have a third poll that's taken regularly to counteract Gallup and Harris. He makes the point that the results of the polls directly affect our ability to govern, because their influence on Congressmen, foreign leaders, etc., and that it's important that we keep the published polls honest, and that we know ourselves exactly what the actual poll status is.[85]

Haldeman's suggestion that President Nixon initiate ORC as the White House's private polling outfit to "keep the published polls honest" is entirely conceivable given Nixon's own comments about the media. In his memoirs, Nixon spoke of "the decision to take on the TV network news organizations for the biased and distorted 'instant analysis' and coverage," because, he said, failing to do so would "make it impossible for a President to appeal directly to the people, something I considered to be of the essence of democracy." Nixon fervently believed that the media were hostile toward him and his politics. He harshly criticized *The New York Times* for publishing the Pentagon Papers, contending that their "decision to publish the documents was clearly the product of the paper's antiwar policy rather than a consistent attachment to principle." He similarly thought that the media was

---

[84] RMNP@NA, "Polls Chron May–June 1971 [I of II]," Memorandum from Higby to Strachan, March 18, 1971, and Memorandum from Strachan to Haldeman, March 24, 1971, HRH Files, Box 334.

[85] Haldeman, *Haldeman Diaries*, January 19, 1971.

infatuated with 1972 Democratic presidential contender Senator Edmund Muskie of Maine, and sympathetic toward Democratic nominee Senator Hubert Humphrey of Minnesota.[86] The result of Nixon's perspective was a desire, instigated by him and implemented by Haldeman, to use polls as an instrument to counter the media's biases.

Haldeman's assistant, Dwight Chapin periodically succeeded in obtaining Gallup data before they were publicly released. For example, an October 10, 1969 memorandum from Chapin to Haldeman outlined the contents of a Gallup poll to be published "this Sunday." A November 23, 1970 memo from Chapin to Haldeman also cited poll data "to be published this coming Sunday" and suggested how to "game plan the exploitation of the results of this poll."[87]

However by 1971 Haldeman and Strachan were dissatisfied when Chapin did not regularly receive Gallup data in advance of their public release. Strachan noted that "Chapin has had very limited success either in obtaining the results of polls in advance or in explaining our substantive complaints about some of the releases," and suggested to Haldeman that Chapin be replaced by Donald Rumsfeld as the Gallup contact.[88] Haldeman approved Strachan's recommendation that Rumsfeld replace Chapin as the pointman with Gallup "to acquire interesting results early."[89]

Haldeman thought that disseminating poll data which showed a popular President Nixon would further strengthen the president's ability to govern. White House staffers therefore showed ORC poll data in order to steer the media toward discussing positive elements of the Nixon administration. A May 24, 1971 memorandum from Charles Colson to Gordon Strachan accentuated the merits of this strategy. "The ORC polls have been getting good publicity considering that they are not syndicated polls," Colson wrote. "As you know, the ORC polls last week hit the network news and are always on the wires – sometimes after a little extra nudge . . . In short, it is the people we are trying to influence. They hear the poll results and that makes an impact on them."[90]

The ORC poll press releases were widely distributed to members of the press, and White House advisers sometimes cowrote the ORC press

[86] Nixon, *RN*, pp. 411, 509. Also see pp. 320, 329–330, 412–413, 420, 542, 623.

[87] RMNP@NA, "[CF] PR 15 Public Opinion Polls [1969–70]," Memorandum from Chapin to Haldeman, October 10, 1969, Box 53; "Polls [3 of 4]," Memorandum from Chapin to Haldeman, November 23, 1970, Dwight L. Chapin Files, Box 22.

[88] RMNP@NA, "Polls September–October 1971 (Continued)," Memorandum from Gordon Strachan to H.R. Haldeman, September 20, 1971, Box 335.

[89] Ibid. Also see "Polls 1971 (Continued)," September 20, 1971 Memorandum Subject: George Gallup, Jr. – Rumsfeld Meeting, HRH Files, Box 335; and "[CF] PR 15 Public Opinion Polls [1969–70]," October 10, 1969 Memorandum Re: Gallup Polls, Box 53.

[90] RMNP@NA, Memorandum from Charles Colson to Gordon Strachan, May 24, 1971, "ORC Polls," Charles Colson Files, Box 102.

releases.[91] O'Neill remembers Strachan, Higby, and Haldeman as active players in writing the ORC press releases. "We amended and approved the press releases," O'Neill said.[92] Sections of a May 1, 1972 memo from Strachan to Haldeman exemplify the importance they placed on distributing ORC press releases.

The ORC Vietnam Release was hand-delivered today before 3:30 P.M. to Ken Clawsen's contacts at ABC, CBS, NBC, UPI, and AP. Reuters, the Booth Newspapers, the Copley News Service, the *Post, New York Times*, and the magazines (*Life, Time, Newsweek*, and *U.S. News and World Report*) also received copies hand-delivered this afternoon from ORC's Washington office... ORC at Princeton today mailed the release to the 186 individual contacts at newspapers, wires, radio, and TV stations supplied by [Assistant to the Director of Communications DeVan L.] Van Shumway... Colson believes that to protect ORC's credibility while assuring maximum usage, mass distribution of the release through mailings, speech inserts, etc., we should await media pickup. The release can be attached to the wire copy or newspaper story.[93]

Press releases of their private polls were a vital component of the Nixon administration's political strategy, but it was important for them not to look like they were manipulating public opinion even as they were trying to do so. ORC polls were distributed to White House speechwriters, members of the cabinet, certain members of the House and Senate, state chairmen of Nixon's reelection campaign, Philadelphia Mayor Frank Rizzo and Los Angeles Mayor Sam Yorty [both Democrats], "Prominent Democrats (i.e., Connally)," and *Roll Call*, a Capitol Hill newspaper, with instructions that the polls should be delivered personally, perhaps via an intermediary, and not anonymously from the White House.[94]

Nixon's private polls were also used to help determine his schedule. On one occasion, Under Secretary of the Interior John Whitaker concluded after reading an ORC poll that the public was unimpressed with the president's domestic accomplishments. Whitaker suggested that Nixon change his schedule to demonstrate his focus on domestic affairs.

There has to be a radical change in the President's scheduling so he does events concentrating on the economy, drugs/crime, and pollution – and by concentrate, I mean this in an extreme way – by following one basic rule – that never a week goes by that the President doesn't himself get on the tube – not Mitchell or Richardson on drugs; not Train, Morton, or Ruckelshaus on pollution; not Schultz, McCracken on the economy; but the President. The objective is therefore simple: each week the

[91] Ibid.
[92] O'Neill interview.
[93] RMNP@NA, "ORC Polls," Memorandum from Strachan to Haldeman, May 1, 1972, Charles Colson Files, Box 102.
[94] RMNP@NA, "ORC Polls," ORC Poll Distribution memo from Kathleen Balsdon to Dick Howard, May 5, 1972, Charles Colson Files, Box 102.

President does one event that features the economy, drugs/crime, or pollution. This way, even with slippage, we have one TV event a month on each of these three big issues ... The only issue is to get the President on the tube and involved.[95]

Whitaker was not alone in using poll data to plan political events. Robert Teeter also envisioned polls as devices for determining where and how the president should be seen. Teeter recommended that one poll, "used in conjunction with the ticket-splitting maps we went over this morning should be of assistance to you in scheduling the President and the First Family."[96]

Haldeman echoed this theme of polls as instruments of political planning in his diary log, in which he explicitly linked a discussion about polls to a discussion about scheduling.

Some more on Kevin Phillips to analyze Senate races and the Derge poll. Also very interested in Roper poll about student unrest, exactly the opposite findings from those of Harris poll Heard is peddling. More emphasis on basing all scheduling and other decisions on political grounds. Especially emphasize Italians, Poles, Elks, and Rotarians, eliminate Jews, blacks, youth. Covered some more detailed notes he had made about Derge poll, and gave me a copy back, with a lot of notes.[97]

To many of Nixon's advisers, polls were needed to shape the president's image, legislative strategy, and reelection campaign. All of these were intertwined through what President Nixon did, with whom he did it, and how he and his agenda were presented in the media. Polls determined which constituencies needed wooing and which ones could be ignored.

Similar to the Hoover administration, which tracked newspaper editorials, the Nixon pollsters tracked the media feedback of their poll press releases. ORC counted how many newspapers published press releases of polls they conducted for the Nixon White House. But the media were not to be trusted. They infringed on presidential autonomy, disrupted the president's agenda, and therefore restricted presidential power.

Gauging public opinion was done not only to find out what people were thinking, but to market an agenda once supporters of that agenda had been identified. Marketing the president required exploiting public opinion information. Presidential polls were not vehicles for gauging public opinion as much as they were instruments to manipulate it. This manipulation strategy was a complex affair. First, it required a private polling operation separate from other political institutions. Second, it entailed broadcasting poll data that aided the President's standing, and discrediting polls that showed the

---

95 RMNP@NA, "Polls [From CFOA 762 [3 of 4]]," Memorandum from Whitaker to Ehrlichman, June 14, 1971, John Whitaker Files, Box 92. Underlining is in original document.
96 RMNP@NA, "Polls 1972," Memorandum from Teeter to Strachan through Chapin, July 25, 1972, Egil Krogh Files, Box 18.
97 Haldeman, *Haldeman Diaries*, July 13, 1970.

president in an unfavorable light. Third, the strategy included receiving public polls (favorable or unfavorable) in advance of their publication date, in order to highlight the positive data or downplay the negative poll data. Fourth and finally, this strategy attempted to coopt public pollsters, perhaps without their knowledge. One memorandum describes White House advisers' employing "loaded questions, using Gallup, Harris, and Sindlinger," suggesting that the media pollsters were being asked to word questions in such a way as to aid the president.[98] Media poll data were trustworthy if they came from an ally – otherwise they were biased and needed to be refuted. Nixon argued that he was taking a "constant pounding from the media and our critics in Congress," and that going public was the only way to counter his critics. Private polls, therefore, became vehicles to shape public opinion. Poll data were not only analyzed in-house, but they then were disseminated to the national press, in the hope that the media would print and broadcast the poll data that already had been interpreted by the White House.

CONCLUSION

Nixon's presidency marked exceptionally tense relations between the White House and the media, but a tradition of adversarial linkages between the two institutions can be traced back to Hoover. These tensions gave a reason for presidents to employ private polls, resulting in increased tensions between the two institutions. As presidents grew to distrust the investigative mandate of the press and television media, they turned to private pollsters to help present themselves through the media. These private pollsters, however, were partisan in nature. President Nixon, for example, envisioned the media as biased against him; hiring a Republican pollster was not biased to him; rather, it merely enabled him to gauge public opinion independently of the ostensibly biased media pollsters.

The polling presidents played the media card in various ways to measure and manipulate public opinion. President Hoover's positive relations with the press stemmed from his days as a cabinet secretary. As president, however, his cordial relations with reporters dwindled. FDR's polling sources created surveys to measure the public's reaction to various media and public policy strategies. Presidents Eisenhower and Kennedy learned to use television to reach out to the public and take their message directly to the voter. Finally, Nixon leaked survey data to the press in an attempt to inundate the news with positive coverage of his presidency.

[98] Haldeman, *Haldeman Diaries*, February 7, 1973. Also Jacobs and Shapiro, "Presidential Manipulation," fn. 45.

Polling presidents no longer had to rely solely on newspaper editorials to gauge the public's inclinations toward policy options or presidential contenders. By addressing questions directly to the masses, the post-Hoover presidents (except Truman) snatched the powerful tool of public opinion assessment away from a potential adversary – the media – and into their own hands. In turn these hands soon grasped the reins of presidential power with more autonomy.

7

Counting the People

The Evolution of Quantification and Its Effects on Presidential Polling

> The more enthusiastic observers of the polls see in them a device for the imple-
> mentation of a theory of pure democracy; the governor need no longer be much
> more than a rubber stamp for *vox populi* [voice of the people] as evidenced by
> the poll. The representative, harassed by the raucous demands of lobbyists and
> letter writers, need only consult the oracle to determine the status of public
> opinion. At the other extreme there are those who are skeptical of the wisdom
> of following public opinion, even if it be granted that the polls measure that
> opinion with accuracy. They regard the suggestion that poll findings should
> guide public opinion as destructive to orderly government.[1]

The previous chapters have shown that the evolution and trajectory of presidential polling are by-products of politics. By using polls, presidents no
longer have had to rely on Congress, parties, or the media to gauge public
opinion. An alternative explanation also may explain the rise of presidential polling. Namely, technological advances may have made polls more
attractive than their public opinion–gauging alternatives. That is, it is possible that the allure of private polls by presidents may not have arisen because
they circumvented other political institutions that obstruct the president's
agenda, but rather that polls were just better indicators of the public mood
than their alternatives. This chapter analyzes this counterargument. As evidenced in the previous chapters, the rise of polls corresponds to the advances
in polling technologies, but this coincidence insufficiently explains the rise of
presidential polls. Politics, not improvements in how polls were conducted,
appear to account for the rise of presidential polls. While the art and science
of polling continue to strengthen polls' place as a legitimate means to gauge
public opinion, these advances complement, but do not appear to explain
fully, why presidents have been so eager to use them.

---

[1] V.O. Key, Jr., *Politics, Parties, and Pressure Groups, Third Edition.* New York: Thomas
Y. Crowell, 1952, p. 677.

A BRIEF HISTORY OF QUANTIFICATION
AND OPINION MEASUREMENT

Paul Lazarsfeld argued that Adolphe Quetelet served as a central figure in the development of quantification in the social sciences. Quetelet, a Belgian, believed that probability explained social phenomena and that intellectual and "moral" characteristics – tendencies (*penchant*) – could be measured by employing scientific techniques.[2] At about the same time Quetelet was trying to measure *penchant*, Frederic LePlay was studying social structures and families in France. LePlay introduced the family budget as a social measure, spoke of constructing a "scientific mechanism" to study mankind's happiness, and of reaching conclusions that were "logically derived."[3] His charismatic personality generated a political following and his protégés were political reformers who created a journal titled *La Science Sociale*, which combined methodological and political interests. LePlay and his disciples were ideologues who sought to measure society systematically in order to advance their academic and sometimes undemocratic political agendas. Changing the world for the better, LePlay believed, demanded that one rigorously study society and its structural elements.

In the mid-nineteenth century, the Englishman, Charles Booth, linked the humanitarian efforts of urban reform with the quantitative efforts espoused by LePlay and Quetelet. Booth's *Life and Labour of the People in London 1892–1897* is a seventeen-volume treatise that incorporated personal observations, secondary sources, and interviews. Mark Abrams, writing about the history of social surveys, notes that "Booth's principal contribution was not the discovery of particular facts, but the elaboration of an adequate technique for expressing the qualitative concepts and arguments about society in precise numerical terms."[4]

As Englanders were developing empirical sociology, so were Germans, in part by using techniques developed by Booth and Quetelet. Anthony Oberschall's comprehensive study of the empirical sociological tradition in Germany delineates how empirical research conducted by Max Weber and Ferdinand Tönnies initially was unappreciated by the German academy. Oberschall argues that empirical social research was not institutionalized in Germany partly because of "the suspicion of the state authorities for an

---

[2] Paul F. Lazarsfeld, "Notes on the History of Quantification in Sociology – Trends, Sources and Problems," *Isis* 52 (1961): 297.

[3] Ibid., 314.

[4] Mark Abrams, *Social Surveys and Social Action*. London: William Heinemann, 1951, p. 41. Further reading about how statistical developments shape British society, especially those of Francis Galton, Karl Pearson, and R.A. Fisher, can be found in Donald A. MacKensie, *Statistics in Britain 1865–1930: The Social Construction of Scientific Knowledge*. Edinburgh: Edinburgh University Press, 1981.

intellectual discipline which was so closely identified with 'leftist' political sympathies."[5]

The merging of empirical research and politics was advanced further in the 1880s by the American sociologist Lester Frank Ward, who maintained that an intellectual alternative to laissez-faire capitalism and social Darwinism required an educated citizenry that would seek out answers to puzzles plaguing society. Ward believed that there existed a correct answer about all political matters. For example, citizens may disagree about whether or not there should be reforms to labor laws, but to Ward, there was an appropriate answer not borne from compromise, but from the Truth. Disagreements among the populace inhibited society's betterment; rather, humankind's advancement would be hastened if one listened to differences and debates between opposing ideological viewpoints. What was needed was a means other than deliberation to ascertain the True and Correct Opinion.

Opinions are only settled at great expense of intellectual energy. Discussion, debates, dissensions, and disputes cost society heavily in its most important commodity... It therefore becomes the highest duty of mankind and society to see to it, with the least possible delay, that all questions capable of complete settlement be immediately put in the way of such settlement.[6]

To Ward, societal dilemmas arose partly because misguided, unscientific debates perpetuated the dissemination of erroneous points of view. Opinions therefore should not be emotionally driven, but rather should be made based on objective facts. Scientific education could save society because it apparently viewed and studied concepts objectively.

One great barrier to the attainment of correct opinions lies in the undue preponderance of subjective influences... A truly healthy state of public opinion can never be reached until it becomes impossible to determine the personal bias of a speaker when expressing his opinion on questions of fact... The great remedy for this deplorable condition of things [the subjective view of objective facts] must come, if at all, from the gradual extension of the exact, or scientific, method to every department of human thought and opinion. Politics, law, business, morals, and even religion, must fall under this *régime*, and every question, from the success of an enterprise to the hope of salvation, must be made to yield to the logic of fact, evidence, and statistics.

[5] Anthony Oberschall, *Empirical Social Research in Germany 1848–1914*. Paris: Mouton & Co., 1965, p. 140. Oberschall's book is highly recommended for readers interested in investigating the history of German social research. Additional summaries of social surveys can be found in Mildred Parten, *Surveys, Polls, and Samples: Practical Procedures* (esp. Chapter One). New York: Harper & Brothers, 1950, and Martin Bulmer, et al., *The Social Survey in Historical Perspective 1880–1940*. Cambridge: Cambridge University Press, 1990.
[6] Lester Frank Ward, *Dynamic Sociology, Vol. II. Dynamic Sociology, or Applied Social Science, As Based upon Statistical Sociology and the Less Complex Sciences, in Two Volumes*. New York: Appleton, 1968 [1883], New York: Johnson Reprint, pp. 406–407.

Opinions resting upon any other basis are worse than worthless, and to cling to them is suicidal.[7]

By embracing a philosophy that had the scientific assessment of public opinion as its core, Ward helped advance public opinion research even before polls had been invented. While Ward's aversion for deliberation is antithetical both to democratic tenets and to the ability to derive facts, his eagerness to employ scientific methods in social research contributed toward accepting public opinion as something that can and should be quantified.

As quantification of public opinion, and in the social sciences more generally, was slowly being accepted and advanced, so too was the concept of representative sampling.[8] While early sampling techniques at the turn of the century were not used by the U.S. government for political purposes, the academic use of surveying populations in the 1920s was borne largely from normative concerns. Frustrated with the deleterious effects of urbanism, Paul Kellogg and Shelby Harrison conducted systematic social surveys to study urban areas. While these surveys did not employ representative sampling methods, they frequently amassed variables about social and political issues such as poverty rates and racial composition.[9]

Harrison in particular thought that his surveys had "the correcting power of facts, which must be gathered as carefully and faithfully as the truth-loving

---

[7] Ibid., *Vol. II*, pp. 408–410.

[8] The term "representative sampling" appears to have emerged in 1895 by A.N. Kiaer at the Berne meeting of the International Statistical Institute (ISI). Its use and study in the United States began two years later by Cressy L. Wilbur, who suggested that "small representative areas" be chosen for the amassing of vital statistical data. Similarly, in 1901 at the Budapest meeting of the ISI, Carroll D. Wright wrote about his positive "sampling experiences" for the U.S. Department of Labor. See William Kruskal and Frederick Mosteller, "Representative Sampling, IV: the History of the Concept in Statistics, 1895–1939," *International Statistical Review* 48 (1980): 169–195, esp. p. 172. To Wright and other statisticians at the turn of the century, sampling meant studying a substantial portion of a population. According to Kruskal and Mosteller, Wright's views about representative sampling are naively optimistic, as they do not include his method of sampling or more than a superficial discussion about errors. The authors also cite how Karl Pearson, Adolph Jensen, and Jerzy Neyman's studies were instrumental in the advancement of sampling in the political and academic spheres. Neyman's 1934 demands for specific sampling procedures are considered a turning point in the development of using representative samples.

[9] Bulmer, et al., *The Social Survey in Historical Perspective 1880–1940*, remains the authoritative text that provides excellent in-depth analyses of the emergence of social surveys, including those works conducted by Harrison and Kellogg. I do not wish to dismiss the contributions of these social surveys, as they also contribute to the appreciation for and legitimation of empirical research. I limit discussion about them so as not to digress beyond the focus of discussing the emergence and institutionalization of presidential polling. For more discussion about social surveys, also see Converse, *Survey Research in the United States*, Chapter One.

scientists in any field gather them."[10] Harrison's studies advanced the notion of quantification in the academic and political spheres, but it was not until the late 1920s when L.L. Thurstone attempted to quantify attitudes by stating that opinions were the accessible portion or external expression of attitudes. To Thurstone, ascertaining peoples' attitudes involved asking a series of questions that enabled respondents to reveal their opinions.[11] Thanks in part to financial support from the Rockefeller family, social scientists including Thurstone gathered at Dartmouth College for what became known as the annual Hanover Conference. These meetings were designed to begin developing ways to measure social attitudes. Dismissing arguments that attitude measurement was an ersatz enterprise, Thurstone contended that determining people's attitudes was no different than measuring physical concepts such as volume and weight:

The question has been raised whether the concept of attitude as here used and as measured by an attitude scale is not hypothetical rather than 'real.' It is just as hypothetical as the concept of intelligence which is measured by what it supposedly does. But these concepts are hypothetical in the same sense that the concepts force, momentum, volume, are hypothetical in physical science. No one has ever seen or touched a force or a momentum or a volume. They are measured by what they supposedly do.[12]

By 1929, Thurstone had created attitude scales, in which respondents were asked a series of questions about a topic, and from those answers, indexes were created to assess the intensity of one's attitude toward that topic. Thurstone saw opinion measurement as a "scientific problem" that, when untangled, would make it possible to "apply the methods of quantitative scientific thinking to the study of feeling and emotion, to esthetics, and to social phenomena."[13]

Thurstone's work advanced public opinion research in innumerable, and perhaps in immeasurable ways; Gordon Allport, writing in 1935 in *The Handbook of Social Psychology*, described Thurstone's creation of psychophysical scales and his work on opinion measurement as revolutionary. "The success achieved in the past ten years in the field of the measurement of attitudes," Allport wrote, "may be regarded as one of the major accomplishments of social psychology of America."[14]

[10] Shelby M. Harrison, *Community Action through Surveys*. New York: Russell Sage Foundation, 1916, p. 27.
[11] L. L. Thurstone, "The Measurement of Social Attitudes," *Journal of Abnormal and Social Psychology* 26 (1932): 262–263.
[12] Ibid., 265.
[13] Ibid., 268–269.
[14] Gordon W. Allport, "Attitudes." In *A Handbook of Social Psychology*, edited by Carl Murchison. Worcester, MA: Clark University Press, 1935, pp. 831, 832. Also see Jensen, "History and the Social Scientist," p. 5.

As Thurstone was creating his scales, the United States Department of Agriculture (USDA) (specifically the Bureau of Agricultural Economics) was using social surveys to study rural and farm life. The USDA pioneering work on probability sampling and open-ended questions was so success- ful that it expanded during World War II beyond agricultural issues to a variety of topics under the newly organized Division of Special Surveys.[15] Jean Converse notes that the USDA found surveys to be so beneficial, that they expressed an interest in expanding their polling operation. Converse cites economist Howard Tolley: "The public opinion polls were a develop- ment in the social sciences as important to us in Agriculture as if a chemist had found a new compound like DDT. If it worked for Gallup, why would it not work for us? We wanted a try at it."[16]

GEORGE GALLUP, THE *LITERARY DIGEST* AND FOUNDING OF AAPOR

It was not always the case that properly administered polls were considered reliable and valid measures of public opinion. In 1936, when the *Literary Digest* poll that showed Alf Landon defeated Franklin Roosevelt differed significantly from George Gallup's poll showing the opposite, a public dis- cussion emerged about the accuracy of polls. This dispute ensued in *The New York Times*, and Gallup ultimately was proven correct when FDR defeated Landon in a landslide.[17]

[15] Jean M. Converse provides a cogent description of the USDA surveys in *History of Survey Research in the United States*.
[16] Converse, p. 52, citing Tolley in Thelma A. Dreis, 'The Department of Agriculture's Sample Interview Survey as a Tool of Administration,' Ph.D. dissertation, American University, Washington, DC, 1950, p. 30.
[17] Jean M. Converse provides a detailed description of Gallup's criticism of the 1936 *Literary Digest* poll in *History of Survey Research in the United States*, pp. 114–117. It should be noted that Gallup was not the first person publicly to denounce the *Literary Digest*'s polling methods. Cornell University Professor Walter Wilcox's paper delivered at the Ninety-Second Annual Meeting of the American Statistical Association, December 30, 1930, and subse- quently published in the *Journal of the American Statistical Association* in 1931, objects to the "representative character" of the *Digest*'s large samples. See Walter F. Wilcox, "An Attempt to Measure Public Opinion about Repealing the Eighteenth Century Amendment," *Journal of the American Statistical Association* 26 (1931 New Series): 243–261, esp. 245. A January 1936 article in *The American Criterion* also questioned the nonpartisanship of the *Digest* polls. See Paul Harris, "What's Behind the 'Digest' Poll?" *The American Criterion* 1 (January 1936): 4–7. Also see Hadley Cantril, "Straw Votes This Year Show Contrary Winds," *The New York Times*, October 25, 1936, p. 3, in which Cantril distinguishes between polls he considers scientific, and the *Literary Digest* polls, which he labels as "practical"; "Dr. Gallup Chided by Digest Editor," *The New York Times*, July 19, 1936, p. 21; Fabian F. Levy, "Forecasting the Election," Letter to the Editor, *The New York Times*, October 16, 1936, p. 24; Fabian Franklin, "Refiguring the Digest Poll," *The New York Times*, October 28, 1936, p. 24; and Amateur Statistician, "The Literary Digest Poll," *The New York Times*, Letter to the Editor, October 31, 1936, p. 18.

Much of the reason why polls are now considered accurate indicators of the public mood stems from Gallup himself. Gallup actively promoted polls as a positive influence in democracy and forged positive relations with President Franklin Delano Roosevelt, even though he (Gallup) was friends with Republican Thomas Dewey.[18] In response to a letter Gallup wrote to FDR on January 15, 1940, Secretary to the President Stephen Early, wrote that the president "has appreciated your thoughtfulness in sending him from time to time advance proofs of polls and other material of interest to him."[19] At about the same time, Gallup and Saul Forbes Rae coauthored *The Pulse of Democracy: The Public Opinion Poll and How It Works*, in which they argued that polls, while still in their incipient and experimental stages, nonetheless provided more accurate information than alternative means of gauging public opinion, most notably newspapers and interest groups.[20]

The meteoric rise of Gallup and his polls, combined with his belief that polls were an integral part of advancing representative democracy, cannot be overlooked as a factor contributing to FDR's interest in employing polls. Soon after Gallup's successful presidential election prediction of 1936, the first issue of *Public Opinion Quarterly* (*POQ*) was published, in which it was declared that "for the first time in history, we are confronted nearly everywhere by mass opinion as the final determinant of political and economic action."[21] In the *POQ* inaugural issue, Archibald Crossley described polls as a vehicle to aid democracy and an antidote to the biased measures of public opinion provided by pressure groups.[22] Measuring public opinion was more than novel; it was invaluable to democracy.

The fervent belief by leading academics that polls were an antidote to democracy's woes, combined with Gallup's successful election predictions and Hadley Cantril's association with Gallup, influenced the Roosevelt administration's adoption of polls as a means to measure public opinion. These factors should not be misconstrued however as an argument that advances in polling technology *determined* the use of polls among FDR's White House advisers, or that Cantril's polls replaced other means by which the administration gauged public opinion. In fact, according to James MacGregor Burns, FDR feared that Gallup might have been trying to manipulate poll results against the Democrats. This, combined with Gallup's being an acquaintance of Thomas Dewey, did not endear him to FDR New Dealers. Daniel Robinson reveals how concern that Gallup's polls were partisan culminated in a congressional investigation by the House Committee to Investigate Campaign Expenditures. They visited Gallup's Princeton offices

---

[18] Lambert, *All Out Of Step*, pp. 251–262.
[19] FDRL 1940, Gallup Polls, Box 857.
[20] Gallup and Rae, *The Pulse of Democracy*.
[21] "A New Situation," Forward, *Public Opinion Quarterly* 1 (1937): 3.
[22] Crossley, "Straw Polls in 1936."

and he in turn visited the committee in Washington. The committee's report, written by Rensis Likert among others, concluded that Gallup's American Institute of Public Opinion (AIPO) polls' undercounting of Democrats was due to his quota sampling methods.[23]

Had polls not been invented and financial resources been unavailable, Roosevelt and his aides could not and would not have employed surveys. But available resources and advances in polling technology only partly explain FDR's poll usage. Roosevelt's desire to assess the citizens' views without relying on major media organizations is better explained because prominent columnists and newspaper owners described him as a dangerous socialist.[24] The confidentiality of Hadley Cantril's meetings with FDR's advisers suggests the sensitivity of the subject matter and that they were discussing political, not statistical, jewels of information. Emil Hurja's connections to the Democratic Party and the executive branch, Cantril's lack of partisanship, and the lack of communication between key White House advisers and other divisions of the executive branch administering polls (for example, USDA), all fortify the argument that FDR's yearning for a stronger, more autonomous executive greatly launched the trajectory of presidential polling.

If 1936 served as an important year for the advancement of polls, so did 1948. Just a few years prior to the 1948 election, the American Association of Public Opinion Research (AAPOR) was formed. Media pollsters such as Gallup collaborated with his former advertising colleague at Young and Rubicam, Harry Field, to discuss the future of opinion research. They were joined by Cantril, who would ultimately serve with Gallup on the AAPOR Board of Directors. These fathers of survey research met in 1947 at Williams College along with other leaders in the field of survey research. The Williamstown Conference, and a previous conference in Central City, Colorado, served as the beginnings of AAPOR's annual conferences. These conferences were fun excursions for the pollsters, but the creation of AAPOR and its meetings also helped to advance survey research.[25] At AAPOR conferences, standards were discussed, methodologies were improved, and the belief that polls were valid, reliable instruments of measuring public opinion further gained academic credence. Commercial market researchers, government employees, and social scientists collectively changed the nature of polling itself as the enterprise of polling was no longer solely considered a marketing technique or an instrument for journalists or bureaucrats. Instead,

[23] Burns, *The Lion and the Fox*, p. 445; Daniel J. Robinson, *The Measure of Democracy: Polling, Market Research, and Public Life, 1930–1945*. Toronto: University of Toronto Press, 1999, pp. 60–61.

[24] See James David Barber, *The Pulse of Politics: Electing Presidents in the Media Age.*

[25] For an excellent discussion about the formation and development of AAPOR, see Paul B. Sheatsley and Warren J. Mitovsky, eds. *A Meeting Place: The History of the American Association for Public Opinion Research*. Ann Arbor, MI: AAPOR, 1992.

AAPOR created a pleasant environment where practitioners and academics interacted with one another and learned about the latest polling techniques, dilemmas, and technologies.

Polling suffered a second public relations disaster in 1948 when Gallup's election polls showed New York Governor Thomas Dewey as a victor over Harry Truman. This blunder resulted in criticisms that polls were spurious inventions that both distorted and manipulated public opinion. Survey researchers retorted that the absence of polls would generate a pernicious effect on democracy. Polling was nonetheless discredited and one author, Lindsay Rogers, coined the term "pollster" to rhyme with huckster.[26] AAPORites responded by holding conferences, writing papers, discussing standards, and ultimately creating an academic subfield – survey research. Having already established *Public Opinion Quarterly*, scholars of public opinion debated the role of polls in politics, further legitimizing polls as part of the American political vocabulary.

POLITICS TRUMPS TECHNOLOGY

Statisticians and empirical sociologists indirectly affected why modern presidents have trusted polls, but the underlying cause for secret polling by presidents is politics – that is, autonomy from public opinion–gauging institutions – and not a recognition that the polls were scientific measures of the public mood. The archival data from the previous chapters indicate that politics drove and continues to actuate private polling by presidents. Without technological and academic advances, polling could not have attained its primacy as the presidency's chief measure of public opinion. But such improvements in how to poll do not explain the evolution of presidential polls. When presidential advisers seek out public opinion data in relative secrecy from Congress, the parties and the media, and from sources that parallel partisan identifications, something is at work besides simple technical conveniences.

Why? First, the reliability and validity of polls did not result in FDR's abandoning alternative measures of public opinion. FDR found both Hurja's surveys and Cantril's polls of great interest, but he also continued to read White House mail as a means to gauge public opinion.[27] While polls' accuracy attracted FDR to surveys, their accuracy did not replace other gauges of public opinion.

Second, FDR's poll usage did not occur within a political vacuum. Hurja's relationship with Democratic Party boss James Farley makes Hurja's work appear to be less of a contribution to the science of survey research than

---

[26] The most famous post-1948 criticisms of polls is Lindsay Rogers' *The Pollsters: Public Opinion, Politics, and Democratic Leadership*. New York: Knopf, 1949.

[27] Sussman, "FDR and the White House Mail."

a facet of partisan politics. Furthermore, the nature of Cantril's polls intimates political savvy; public opinion data were a treasured and powerful commodity to be guarded carefully and shared selectively. These circumstances surrounding FDR's public opinion inquiries suggest that political and social scientific forces propelled these advances in presidential polling.

Third, despite the improvements in polling methods during the 1940s and 1950s, Presidents Truman and Eisenhower barely used polls. Truman didn't use private polling, instead opting to rely on less scientific methods of measuring citizens' views. His reluctance to believe that polls measured public opinion may be a product of the 1948 polls that predicted he would lose to Dewey. Truman publicly stated that he found them to be unreliable and invalid: "I did not believe that the major components of our society, such as agriculture, management, and labor, were adequately sampled. I also know that the polls did not represent facts but mere speculation, and I have always placed my faith in the known facts."[28] To Truman, polls did not accurately count Democrats, and therefore were not to be trusted. Gallup's friendship with Republican opponent Thomas Dewey further distanced Truman from believing Gallup's surveys were polling key Democratic constituents, and when Truman won, he had good reason to believe that polls were inaccurate tools designed by the Republican establishment.

President Eisenhower's polling was sparse, but congressional hearings about secret State Department polls reveal that the executive branch hid polls from the legislative branch. To Eisenhower and his advisers, polls were by and large political instruments to be used by the GOP, not directly by the White House's advisers.[29] Although his administration commissioned a few polls, it was the State Department, not his key advisers, that largely employed the polls. Nonetheless, Congress found private polling by the executive branch unacceptable.

This phenomenon of polls being used as political instruments, even as they were gaining academic credence, was further catapulted in the 1960s when John Kennedy hired Lou Harris and LBJ brought on Oliver Quayle. Harris was a partisan – loyal to the Democrats and Kennedy in particular. By seeking poll data from partisan sources, Kennedy (and later LBJ with Oliver Quayle's polls) implicitly acknowledged that their polls were political devices and not merely objective gauges of citizens' views.

Quayle, like Harris, perpetuated presidential polls as political vehicles, as he too was a partisan who largely polled for Democrats. His poll reports were

[28] Harry S. Truman, *Memoirs by Harry S. Truman, Volume Two: Years of Trial and Hope*, pp. 177, 196.
[29] Stanley Kelley notes in his landmark work, *Public Relations and Political Power*, that advertising agencies were hired by the Eisenhower campaign to conduct polls. Stanley Kelley, Jr., *Public Relations and Political Power*. Baltimore, MD: Johns Hopkins University Press, 1956.

also personalized, as if he were assessing the political tone of the region he had polled. Quayle frequently sampled one congressional district and interpreted the results through a qualitative lens. Additionally, his poll summaries often included lengthy verbatim comments from survey respondents. One example of Quayle's personalized commentary is cited below:

We talked with the wife of a Supervisor of the electrical department in a manufacturing plant. She, too, was of Japanese extraction and in her forties. She was a Republican with a solid Republican voting record. She plans to vote for Goldwater and Fong this year: The unemployment situation is getting worse – the unemployed boys have nothing to do and get into all kinds of trouble. The government should make more work projects like roads and then hire the unemployed at some of the jobs. The government should also provide more funds to build more roads and highways because there's [sic] so many cars and not enough roads. The traffic problem is terrible.[30]

By including qualitative information in his reports, Quayle produced a homespun document that highlighted his understanding of the region and its residents, much like a party boss. Public opinion was not merely the aggregation of numbers; it had a human pitch and depth to which advisers keenly listened.[31] Chapter 8 will show that recent presidents have continued this trend of using quantitative and qualitative methods to gauge the public's pulse. Presidential polling of the 1970s, 1980s, and 1990s remained a viable political practice, in large part because of the autonomy that presidents gained by polling privately.

[30] LBJL, Study 169 Hawaii August 1964, "Past (HAWAII)," Fred Panzer Files, Box 169.
[31] As recently as the Clinton presidency, focus groups were being used frequently to help discern how citizens understood policies and issues. Stan Greenberg, Clinton's former pollster remarked how he often visited the focus group sessions that his firm was conducting for the White House in order to see how people grappled with the questions they were being asked. Telephone conversation with Greenberg, June 6, 2000.

8

White House Polling in the Post-Watergate Era

coauthored with Andrew Zahler

I do not think a President should run the country on the basis of the polls. The public in so many cases does not have a full comprehension of the problem. A President ought to listen to the people, but he cannot make hard decisions just by reading the polls once a week. It just does not work and what the President ought to do is make the hard decision and then go out and educate the people on why a decision that was necessarily unpopular was made.[1]

[i]t took some persuasion to convince P of the importance of getting this information on a regular continuing basis in order to keep in close touch with general public reaction to events.[2]

The post-Watergate presidencies warrant special attention. Watergate enervated citizens' trust in government and struck a political nerve; if politicians were not to be trusted, then the people were. Public opinion not only deserved monitoring – the people necessitated that politicians hear them. Party bosses were soon replaced by primaries in which activist citizens elected presidential candidates. Polls gauging attitudes toward President Nixon, his advisers, Republicans, Democrats, and the press became common fixtures of the evening news, and another chapter in the evolution of presidential polling had been born.

After Richard Nixon resigned in 1974, his successor, Gerald Ford, soon found himself trying to assuage the nation as he simultaneously sought election. Watergate had transformed the national mood. Citizens were skeptical that their leaders were worthy of honor; politics was now an integral part of the presidency and, more broadly, the American political landscape.

---

[1] Gerald R. Ford, "Imperiled, Not Imperial," *Time*, November 10, 1980, p. 31.

[2] Haldeman, 1994 addition to his April 14, 1969 diary entry, *Haldeman Diaries*. Haldeman's edits are italicized in his CD-ROM diary, enabling the reader to decipher what was written at the time of the entry, and what has been added.

The surge of White House polling over the past twenty-five years merits discussion. Why? Because recent presidents' relationships with Congress, parties, and the media have ebbed and flowed, yet they continue to conduct private polls in order to gain political autonomy. The remainder of this chapter seeks to identify changes in presidential polling briefly and chronologically. This discussion is not intended to be a comprehensive analysis of recent presidential polling; rather it is designed to reveal how the arguments addressed in the previous six chapters are supported by recent political and social scientific developments.

THE FORD PRESIDENCY

As early as one month after Ford took office as president, his advisers received poll data from Robert Teeter of Market Opinion Research (MOR). Teeter worked for the Nixon reelection campaign in 1972 and in the ensuing administration, and so his work for the Nixon White House made him a natural selection for Ford's private pollster. While his role in the Nixon White House was limited to analyzing poll data, Teeter's spectrum of influence broadened during Ford's abbreviated term.[3] Teeter's consultations were formalized when Ford's election campaign, entitled the President Ford Committee (PFC), hired Teeter and MOR to conduct surveys for the 1976 presidential election.[4]

During Ford's presidential tenure and election bid, Teeter became both the president's pollster and informal political adviser. Following the mold of Cantril and Harris, Teeter's advice concerned polling, issue development, elections, and politics. In a December 24, 1975 memo to Chief of Staff Dick Cheney, Teeter revealed that his political advice included telling Cheney what Ford should discuss in his State of the Union address.[5] Teeter peppered his memo with opinion data from his private polling for Ford. "Interestingly," Teeter wrote in his section about addressing inflation, "only 7% of them [the public] think that the Ford Administration is the leading cause of the

---

[3] David W. Moore, *The Super Pollsters: How They Measure and Manipulate Public Opinion in America*. New York: Four Walls Eight Windows, 1992, p. 225.

[4] The decision to choose Teeter as President Ford's pollster for his election bid was based partly on Richard Wirthlin's commitment to join Ronald Reagan's presidential campaign. According to Jerry Jones, Wirthlin's decision to work for Reagan was based on financial and personality reasons: "Wirthland [sic] is a supporter of the President and would have preferred to conduct President Ford's survey research. However, he was in desperate financial straits and [Bo] Callaway was non-commital [sic] as to his plans for survey research. In addition, RNC operatives have been telling Wirthland that he was distrusted by the Rumsfeld people because he had previously done work for [Robert] Hartmann." GRFL, September 17, 1975 memorandum from Jerry Jones to Don Rumsfeld and Dick Cheney, "Polling," Richard Cheney Files, Box 17.

[5] GRFL, December 24, 1975 memo from Teeter to Cheney, "Teeter (3)," Foster Chanock Files, Box 3.

Market Opinion Research Corporation Vice President Robert M. Teeter presents information to President Ford and some of his staff at a Camp David meeting to discuss campaign strategy, 8/6/76 (clockwise from President Ford – his son Jack Ford, Counselor John Marsh, Robert M. Teeter, President Ford Committee Chairman for Political Organization Stuart Spencer, Chief of Staff Dick Cheney, and Counselor/ Speechwriter Robert Hartmann) (Courtesy of the Gerald R. Ford Library)

inflation but an overwhelming majority think the administration is not doing anything or enough to solve the problem." Additionally, Teeter's comments to Cheney included advice about how to market President Ford after his State of the Union address. Teeter noted that the president must not be perceived as indecisive and that one person should be in charge of "orchestrating the program" of getting people outside the administration to support the president publicly.[6] Noting that the public did not think the Ford administration was doing enough to combat inflation, Teeter advised action; a decisive president, he believed, would be an elected president.

[6] GRFL, "Teeter (3)," December 24, 1975 Memorandum from Teeter to Cheney, Foster Channock Files, Box 3.

Teeter played this role of a key presidential adviser throughout Ford's tenure. In an October 18, 1976 memo about the last presidential debate between Ford and Democratic opponent Jimmy Carter, Mike Duval, a senior Ford adviser, summarized to Ford the views of the president's senior advisers, including Teeter:

Bob Teeter advises that you should attempt to reach the following audiences during your last debate...To summarize, your advisers (principally Carruthers, Gergen, Teeter, Baily [sic] and Deardourff), have two general recommendations concerning style...Bob Hartmann makes the additional point that it would be very useful if you can answer just one question with a simple yes or no. Teeter agrees with this but feels a brief sentence or two in explanation might be appropriate...Our review of the analysis developed by Bob Teeter...shows that you scored most heavily in the first debate with your statements concerning tax cuts.[7]

Teeter concretely suggested ways to improve the president's style. The president's ability to get elected was partly dependent on using polls to help shape an electable image. For Teeter, shaping that image included supplementing polls with qualitative methods. Already having used multidimensional scaling for President Nixon's 1972 campaign polls, Teeter began to employ daily tracking polls and response meters (sometimes known as dials) during Ford's campaign. When asked if he used the latest methods available to him, Teeter replied:

As an industry, marketing research operates on very small margins and does not generate many resources for R&D [research and development] work. Also, most clients will conduct one, or maybe two, surveys in a year using relatively small (300 to 800) sample sizes. These numbers do not provide much reliability for developing new technology or methods. In a presidential campaign, however, you usually find the size, breadth and need for developing and/or refining new techniques.[8]

Dials were provided to focus group participants in preparation for and during the presidential debate between President Ford and Democratic candidate Jimmy Carter. Participants held dials with knobs and were asked to respond to the debate by turning the dial in a certain direction to denote a positive or negative reaction to comments made by the debaters. Using results from respondents' dials, Teeter recommended that Ford highlight some issues and downplay others. Yet politics – not technological innovation – drove Teeter's use of response meters, for these meters were invented in the late 1930s by Paul Lazarsfeld and Frank Stanton.[9]

---

[7] GRFL, October 18, 1976, Mike Duval to The President, "Third Debate-Memos from Duval," White House Special Files, Box 3.

[8] Letter from Robert M. Teeter, June 20, 1996.

[9] Teeter appears to be the first pollster to employ them for presidents. For brief descriptions of the invention of these dials, see Sally Bedell Smith, *In All His Glory: William S. Paley: The Legendary Tycoon and His Brilliant Circle.* New York: Simon and Schuster, 1991, pp. 153–155; and Michael X. Delli Carpini and Bruce Williams, "The Method is the Message: Focus Groups as a Method of Social, Psychological, and Political Inquiry," *Research in Micropolitics: New*

Teeter also used focus groups to ascertain how and why citizens arrived at certain opinions. According to one poll report, focus group participants (Democrats from Wayne County, Michigan; Republicans from Columbus, Ohio; Democrats from Atlanta, Georgia; and Democratic ticket-splitters also from Wayne County) helped determine which questions should be asked in a national survey.

The major purpose of the focus groups was to provide information for the development of the questionnaire for the national survey. Various subject areas were tested as to their importance to the group subjects and their relevance to political attitudes. On this basis, the worth of each subject area for inclusion in the questionnaire was evaluated.[10]

Teeter's research initially paid more heed to the president's party than had many presidential pollsters in years. "We very much appreciate the opportunity to share this information with senior White House officials and look forward to developing strong channels of coordination in the future," wrote Dick Thaxton of the RNC to Chuck Lichenstein, Special Assistant to the President.[11] Thaxton's comments suggest that the party was sharing the polls with the president and not vice versa. Teeter was initially hired and paid by the RNC, and in some instances, the RNC's proprietorship of Teeter's poll data showed up in his survey summaries. The lines of ownership for Teeter's polls between president and party, however, were blurred by President Ford's election bid. In the 1976 presidential campaign, Teeter's work responded to a shift in national electoral politics and mirrored the disappearing power of the parties. The Democratic Party's McGovern-Fraser Commission also affected the GOP, as primaries and open caucuses were increasingly popular among Republicans, creating more of a need to determine who primary voters were and what they believed. Because of these reforms, public opinion data were needed to test themes and track immediate responses to comments made by Ford and Carter. Gauging public opinion was no longer limited to measuring the attitudes of a representative public, but rather entailed test-marketing ideas (through focus groups and dial research, if necessary) to assess how specific segments of the public would react to speeches, campaign ads, and policy proposals.

By the fall of 1975, Teeter polled in key primary states with large numbers of electoral votes and as he did so his polls became more focused toward a particular region of electoral importance.[12] In October 1975 MOR

Directions in Political Psychology, edited by Michael X. Delli Carpini, Leonie Huddy, and Robert Y. Shapiro. Greenwich, CT: JAI Press, 1994, pp. 57–85.

[10] GRFL, Forward and Overview (1), U.S. National Study, 2/1975, Robert Teeter Papers, Box 51.

[11] GRFL, September 6, 1974 Memorandum from Thaxton to Lichenstein (on RNC letterhead), Robert Hartmann Vertical Files.

[12] State polls were conducted in Alabama, California, Florida, Illinois, Indiana, Iowa, Maryland, Michigan, Missouri, New Jersey, New York, North Carolina, Ohio, Oklahoma,

conducted polls in New Hampshire and Illinois. A month later, Floridians were polled, even though the Florida primary was over five months away.[13] The purpose of these polls was to "measure the relative ballot strength" of Ford and Reagan, "describe the voters' awareness and perceptions" of the candidates, and assess what issues most concerned the electorate.[14]

There was great similarity among Teeter's state polls, but he amended them to adapt to the political tenor of the region. The New Hampshire poll asked about perceptions of the *Manchester Union Leader* newspaper, Vice President Rockefeller, and New Hampshire Governor Meldrim Thomson, Jr. The Florida poll added questions about Senator Lawton Chiles and Cuba. Teeter also conducted two separate polls over a two-week span in Texas before that state's 1976 primary election; whereas the first Texas poll sought to identify likely voters, the second Texas poll probed them about potential endorsers, personal images, and perceptions of issue positions.[15] Having learned from the first poll that agriculture and foreign policy were issues of interest to Texans, Teeter investigated their concerns by asking several questions about their views in the context of issue positions taken by President Ford and Ronald Reagan. By amending his poll to Texans, Teeter was able to ask likely voters what most concerned them and then used those answers to measure differences between Ford and Reagan.[16] By tailoring polls by region and by state, Teeter's MOR polls recognized the importance of key primaries and attempted to gauge Ford's support accordingly. More importantly, Teeter's polls had become political organs designed to help Ford win election.

Oregon, Pennsylvania, Rhode Island, South Carolina, Tennessee, Texas, Vermont, Virginia, and Wisconsin. Some of these states were polled repeatedly – in August, late September, and late October.

[13] GRFL, FL Primary Study 11/1975 #5691, "10/75–11/75 Florida Primary Study Analysis (1)"; Illinois Primary Study 11/1975 #5728, "10/1975–11/1975 Illinois Primary Study (1)"; New Hampshire Primary Study 10/1975 #5690, "NH Primary Election Study Analysis," PFC Records 1975–76, Box H1. Archival data also show that a poll was conducted in January 1976. I have not included discussion of this poll because the other examples adequately served as illustrations of the MOR polls. See GRFL, NC Primary Study January 1976 #6701, "1/1976 NC Primary Study," PFC Records, Box H3.

[14] Ibid. In these state polls, Teeter would ask if endorsements by local and national political figures would increase the likelihood of voting for President Ford.

[15] GRFL, 3/76–4/76 Texas Registered Voters, "3/76–4/76 Texas Registered Voters," PFC Records, Box H5, and GRFL. Texas Statewide Study, 4/1976 #6708, "4/76 Texas Statewide," PFC Records, Box H6.

[16] Teeter also changed his poll questions in a state poll to Wisconsin residents. The poll before the April 6 primary asked respondents if the primary would be close, if 1976 would be economically prosperous or difficult, and a bevy of questions about milk price supports. The postelection poll conducted on April 3 and 4 asked respondents if inflation and unemployment were worsening or improving, if they saw Ronald Reagan's national television address, and what impressions they had about Reagan and his speech. See GRFL, 4/76 Wisconsin Post-Election Study #6711, "4/76 WI Post Election Study, Analysis (1)," PFC Records, Box H6.

After Ford officially became the Republican nominee at the Republican convention in August, Teeter's polls changed focus from questions about Reagan to questions about Carter. "Because you must come from behind, and are subject to many constraints," Teeter wrote, "no strategy can be developed which allows for any substantial error."[17] His poll questions remained focused on one strategy – winning enough delegates in the electoral college to elect President Ford. From Labor Day to the election, Teeter continued to tailor his state polls to the region, adding or subtracting an occasional question. For example, the questions, "Are you aware or not aware of a recent increase in the price of natural gas," and if so, "Who do you think is responsible for this?" were only included in an Oklahoma state poll. Only Iowans were asked if any member of one's family was involved in farming, and New Yorkers were asked their impressions of Nelson Rockefeller, Jacob Javits, and Joint Chiefs of Staff Chairman General George Brown's remarks concerning Israel.[18] Teeter astutely recognized that national electoral politics was what mattered and his poll questions were therefore regionalized, reflecting an electoral strategy designed to win the White House.

Other players besides Teeter factored prominently into the Ford polling operations. Once Teeter was hired, he worked closely with White House Chief of Staff Richard Cheney. Cheney and Teeter worked well together, so much so that Cheney felt comfortable proposing to Teeter ideas for and amendments to specific poll questions.[19] Cheney's pivotal role as poll reader and interpreter for the Ford presidency and election campaign entailed understanding subtle details about question wording. The White House chief of staff followed Haldeman's lead, serving as the point man for the development of a polling operation aimed directly at the president's election.

Cheney's assistant, Foster Chanock, also played a key role in providing analyses to Cheney. Chanock, a twenty-three-year-old University of Chicago graduate, reviewed media and public polls throughout the Ford presidency, especially during the latter stages of the 1976 campaign. What was significant about Chanock's perusal of the media polls was how he described them in relation to Teeter's private polls. One memo entitled "Polling Information on Foreign Policy/National Defense," first discussed Teeter's MOR polls and then mentioned polls conducted by Daniel Yankelovich and Potomac

---

[17] GRFL, Memorandum, August 1976, "National Surveys – Strategy Book," Teeter Papers.

[18] In one instance, computer sheets were tabulated to questions not seen in any of the MOR poll reports. Labeled under "Louisiana," the sheet was a computerized breakdown to questions concerning President Carter's comments in a *Playboy* magazine interview. There were questions about whether or not the respondent had read, seen, or heard about the statements in *Playboy*, whether or not the statements made one more or less favorable toward Carter, and whether or not the respondent knew what was in the interview. See GRFL, Louisiana, "Vol. III, Aug–Oct. 1976," Teeter Papers, Box 58.

[19] GRFL, October 29, 1975 memorandum from Bo Callaway, Stu Spencer, and Fred Slight to Dick Cheney, "Teeter, Robert, Memo and Polling Data (1)," Foster Chanock Files, Box 4.

Associates. Chanock intertwined all the poll data to make recommendations on how to "be strong enough to keep the peace" and "face the fact that it is a hostile and difficult world where we must often settle for less than perfection to protect the safety of our nation."[20] Although Teeter's polls were first mentioned in the memo, Chanock lent credence to the other polls by citing them and by employing them in his analysis. About a year earlier, Chanock provided Cheney with his views on the "status of the presidency." Chanock argued that the public's "generalized loss of faith and respect" for the presidency could be explained by the economy and the timing of Ford's taking office, and that President Ford should develop a coherent philosophy by making a speech that emphasized the growth of government and faith in the free market. Ford never delivered the speech, but Chanock's advice underscored how institutionalized presidential polling had become; it was now proper for an assistant to the chief of staff whose job entailed reading polls to recommend that a president deliver a major speech.

Unlike the Johnson or Nixon administration, media polls did not appear to weigh heavily in the daily operations of Ford's senior staff. Chanock read them, but unlike Haldeman, Cheney and Chanock did not systematically provide updates of media polls. Four months into Ford's presidential tenure, Special Assistant to the President Jerry Jones noted that the RNC had paid for presidential polls at least since 1969, but that there was no one in the Ford White House with personal contacts to the Harris, Sindlinger, or Gallup organizations.[21] Perhaps due to the lack of personal contacts with media poll organizations, there was little evidence that Ford's advisers tried to court media pollsters for poll data. This is not to say that media polls were ignored. After a U.S. cargo ship returned safely after being seized by the Cambodian government in May 1975, Jones wrote Dick Cheney a memorandum informing him about NBC poll data and letting him know that Harris and Gallup polls would be published shortly.[22] President Ford read some media polls as evidenced by a few handwritten notes to Cheney. Still, media polls were not systematically collected, organized, or regularly interpreted by the Ford White House and the president himself was not an avid poll reader as Johnson or Nixon were. Rather, poll information – mostly from MOR – was filtered to Chanock or Cheney. Polling had become a central function of the presidency and the president's pollster became the center of the institution.

Ford's presidency adopted a model for interpreting internal polls that was highly centralized and institutionalized. Teeter used technology and techniques not previously used for politicians, including the use of dials for

[20] GRFL, October 1, 1976, Chanock to Duval, "Second Debate-Polling Information," Papers of Gerald R. Ford, Special Files, Box 2.
[21] GRFL, January 7, 1975 memorandum from Jerry Jones to John T. Calkins, "Polls-General (1)," Foster Chanock Files.
[22] GRFL, May 27, 1975 memorandum from Jones to Cheney, Chanock Files.

immediate responses to presidential debates. But more importantly, Teeter had a keen sense of the political purposes underlying his polls. He tailored his early primary polls to current events and by the region where the poll took place. He targeted and prioritized states, aiming to win both presidential challenges from Ronald Reagan in the Republican primary and Jimmy Carter in the national election. Primaries and the electoral college were factored into Teeter's strategy as he limited his national polls to the end of the primary season when Ford had defeated Reagan. After the nomination was sealed, Teeter strategized by using his polls to gauge public sentiment about Jimmy Carter and the Democrats.

While Chief of Staff Cheney served as the director of receiving and interpreting Teeter's polls, there was no formal or systematic operation of receiving or interpreting non-Teeter polls. Why? Whereas Haldeman ensured that Nixon's polls were interpreted in closed circles, Vice President Ford and his senior staff were not part of Nixon's poll interpreters. Once catapulted into the presidency, the transition to adapt to the new job probably absorbed Ford's senior staff. Rather than combat poll data from a potentially hostile press, Teeter's poll data satisfied President Ford's senior advisers' demand for public opinion information; media polls would be read as they became available.

Ford's private presidential polls were financed by the Republican National Committee and it is therefore difficult to argue that the polls were completely independent of the party that funded them. Rather, at first glance, it appears that Teeter served as the conduit between the GOP and the White House. But if the GOP played an important role in financing the polls, it played virtually no role in conducting or interpreting them.

Teeter's polls for President Ford also remained independent of any congressional interference. They were not used in conjunction with or against members of Congress. Ford, a former House leader, did not contact individual members of Congress to tell them that their views were popular or unpopular according to internal polls. Going public based on the polls was not a part of President Ford's modus operandi. Ford's unique position as a nonelected president, his experience as a former member of Congress, and perhaps his personal style all may account for why Ford's polls were not instruments for going public. Rather, the MOR polls were designed to help the president, not his former GOP congressional colleagues, get elected.

Two overriding themes dominate President Ford's private polling. First, the role of the president's pollster had become institutionalized. Teeter met thirty-eight times with Ford in 1976, and it was considered commonplace for White House Chief of Staff Cheney or his assistant, Foster Chanock, to review Teeter's private polls.[23] Such events were normal functions of the president, his pollster, and his senior advisers; a White House bureaucracy

---

[23] GRFL, Presidential Daily Diary Card Catalog.

had evolved to ensconce polling in the presidency. Second, presidents' private polls were now unadulterated political vehicles designed to help the president get elected. The maturation of presidents' private polling operations meant that gauging public opinion had increasingly become a political endeavor. Questions were asked about issues and personality characteristics. Underlying these questions was a common goal – identifying how people wanted to vote for their political preferences. In this sense, the line between public opinion and public relations was blurred as polls became an important vehicle from which the president marketed himself.

PAT CADDELL AND PRESIDENT CARTER: THE WUNDERKIND GOES TO 1600 PENNSYLVANIA AVENUE

Jimmy Carter found an eager and energetic young pollster in Patrick Caddell. Caddell worked on George McGovern's 1972 presidential campaign, where he befriended McGovern's campaign manager, Gary Hart. During the McGovern campaign, Caddell accompanied his candidate to the governor's mansion in Georgia to visit Democrat Jimmy Carter. Caddell, who had studied Southern politics at Harvard, made a quick and amicable acquaintance with Carter; by 1975, at the age of twenty-five, he had become Carter's campaign pollster.[24]

President Carter's White House polling can be summarized along the following lines. First, Caddell conducted national surveys first for Carter's presidential campaign, then, once Carter was elected, for the administration, and then again for the Carter reelection campaign. Caddell sent summaries of his polls to various White House officials, including the president. The information was not uniformly spread amongst Carter's advisers, suggesting that politics still necessitated a careful distribution of precious information. Second, Caddell rose to prominent stature within Carter's circle of advisers shortly after the 1976 election. Caddell enjoyed unprecedented access to the president and attended frequent meetings at the White House. Third, Caddell's lengthy poll summaries often arrived at the White House immersed in strategy and advice to the president. At times these included outright suggestions for policies, and in one case, Caddell composed a memo based almost entirely upon theories about leadership. In this regard, Caddell functioned as a confidante and political consultant who employed both quantitative poll data and abstract reasoning to counsel and engage the president. Finally, while the use of private polls continued to set the presidency apart from other institutions of public opinion measurement, politics did not preclude collaboration with Congress or other methods of public opinion assessment.

[24] Moore, *The Superpollsters*, p. 136.

President Jimmy Carter and Pat Caddell (Courtesy of the Jimmy Carter Library)

Various Carter officials reviewed Caddell's data. For example, National Security Adviser Zbigniew Brzezinski read foreign policy–related research, as evidenced by an October 21, 1977 memo from Caddell to Carter: "Enclosed is some foreign policy information from our September field survey that Zbig wanted you to have immediately."[25] On another occasion, Caddell wrote a sixty-page memo to Assistant to the President for Domestic Affairs and Policy Stuart Eizenstat containing poll data and analysis.[26] The circulation of Caddell's survey research, however, stopped short of certain offices. Associate Director of the Domestic Policy Staff Orin Kramer wrote to Eizenstat on June 12, 1978 to request a meeting with Caddell and mentioned "we are in a fairly insulated environment and generally rely upon limited sources of information," suggesting that Caddell's data were typically out of reach for the domestic policy staffers.[27]

Many of Caddell's polls went directly to the president. Press Secretary Jody Powell received a Caddell memo in February 1977 forwarded to him by Carter. A July 15, 1977 memo to the president from Caddell contained

[25] Jimmy Carter Library [JCL], "Patrick Caddell (1) (Confidential)," October 21, 1977 Memorandum from Pat Caddell to Jimmy Carter, Chief of Staff Jordan Files, Box 33.

[26] JCL, "Pat Caddell Files, 7/77–3/80," August 9, 1977 Memorandum from Patrick Caddell to Stuart Eizenstat, CF O/A 743, Box 1 of 3.

[27] JCL, "PR 15, 6/1/78–12/31/78 Confidential File," June 12, 1978 Memorandum from Orin Kramer to Stu Eizenstat, Public Relations Files, Box PR-75.

responses to surveys on Jewish attitudes toward Carter and American opinions about the Middle East.[28] In addition to sending poll data to the president, Caddell had personal access to the president. The White House diary from January 1, 1977 to December 9, 1980 records 144 entries pertaining to Caddell. Forty-one of the entries represent phone calls Caddell made to the president. The remainder were in-person meetings. Caddell was a regular attendant of Carter's 1980 campaign committee meetings, press briefings, cabinet meetings, and frequently joined the president on Air Force One and Marine One.

Before and after Caddell conducted a poll, he would request to meet with the president. In a June 17, 1977 letter to the president, sent to the attention of Assistant to the President for Appointments Tim Kraft, Caddell announced he would be going into the field and wanted to meet with Carter. The president made a note on the top right-hand corner to acknowledge his approval of the meeting: "Tim – OK – brief (15 [minutes])."[29]

Caddell used his access to make political arguments, including some that were not entirely based on the poll data he had amassed. On the issue of inflation, for example, Caddell mixed economics and politics to outline potential reactions to rising price levels. In a March 1, 1980 memo he wrote, "I think we have to do something – my concerns, however, are rooted in the substance, timing and exposure of this issue ... I hope you would be open for discussion on the idea of <u>not</u> doing a prime time television speech to announce the program."[30] This memo, like so much of Caddell's correspondence to the White House, contained some poll data, but also contained advice rooted in theories not easily discerned from poll numbers.

The crowning jewel of Caddell's advice to Carter was an April 23, 1979 seventy-five page essay titled, "Of Crisis and Opportunity," in which Caddell elevated his role of presidential pollster to a new level. Caddell elucidated his perception of growing pessimism and dwindling confidence in the American body politic. He quoted liberally from James MacGregor Burns' book, *Leadership*, and offered inspiring words about the president's opportunity to join the ranks of Lincoln, FDR, and Woodrow Wilson. Marked by a dearth of poll numbers and an overflowing of theory and narrative, this essay represented a departure from the presidential pollster's traditional role as analyst and informal adviser. Press Secretary Powell treated it as such, attaching the following handwritten note before forwarding the memo to

[28] JCL, "Pres. Handwriting File 2/24/77," February 24, 1977 Memorandum from Rick Hutcheson to Jody Powell, Staff Offices Files, Office of Staff Secretary Handwriting File, Box 10; "Pat Caddell, 7/77–3/80," July 15, 1977 Memorandum from Pat Caddell to Jimmy Carter, CF, Oversize/Attachment #743, Box 1 of 3.

[29] JCL, "PR 15, 1/20/77–8/31/77 Executive File," June 17, 1977 letter from Pat Caddell to Jimmy Carter, Public Relations Files, Box PR-75.

[30] JCL, "Pat Caddell Files, 7/77–3/80," March 1, 1980 Memorandum from Patrick Caddell to Jimmy Carter, CF O/A 743, Box 1 of 3. [Underline in original.]

Carter: "If you have time, you may want to read the sections underlined before we see you tomorrow. Pat also suggested that you take a look at sections of Burns [sic] new book on leadership. I have not given you the book because I don't think it is necessary at this point – particularly given your schedule this week." Carter ultimately gave what is now known as the malaise speech, in which he articulated many of the same ideas that Caddell had espoused.[31] Among many opinion elites, the speech was considered a disaster, prompting Ronald Reagan's pollster Richard Wirthlin, among others, to think that the White House could be won by a Republican.[32] Whether or not Carter read Burns' book or the entire memo, Caddell's theorizing marked a novel foray into the presidency. Caddell, accepted into Carter's official family to assess the public mood with polls, had now framed his version of public opinion by expressing his own political ideas and ideals to the president.

Caddell's affinity for infusing academics into his correspondence surfaced when he forwarded a report to the Carter campaign written at his firm Cambridge Survey Research with Professors Samuel Popkin of the University of California and Robert Abelson of Yale, who were responsible for the Simulmatics project during the Kennedy election: "I've given Jody [Powell] a copy of the Popkin/Abelson memo on 'Ambiguity and Conviction'...I urge you to read it."[33] Instead of letting the numbers alone tell Carter that he had an image of evasiveness and ambiguity, Caddell let the writing of two academics send the message home.

For all of Caddell's advice and polls, White House advisers continued to peruse other poll data. Poll statistics from *The New York Times*/CBS, NBC/Associated Press, Dan Yankelovich, Roper, Gallup, ORC, and Harris were compiled from May 1976 to March 1978 on Americans' perceptions of the Panama Canal. Concerning energy, Yankelovich sent a summary in June 1977 of an energy poll. Vice President Walter Mondale's administrative assistant, Gail Harrison, summarized the results of a Harris poll on inflation and energy for the vice president. Harrison, however, wasn't merely recapping published poll data; Lou Harris had phoned the results directly to the White House.[34]

---

[31] JCL, "Memoranda: President Carter 1/10/79–4/23/79." Memorandum from Jody Powell to Jimmy Carter CF O/A 519, Box 40. "Transcript of President's Address to Country on Energy Problems," *The New York Times*, July 16, 1979, A10.

[32] Moore, *The Superpollsters*, p. 205.

[33] JCL, "Patrick Caddell Memoranda," September 11, 1976 Memorandum from Patrick Caddell to Jimmy Carter, Jody Powell/Press Offices Files, Box 4.

[34] JCL, "Polling Data – Polls (1)," Compilation of Media Polls, George D. Moffett Collection, Box 9, JCL, "PR 15, 1/20/77–8/31/77 Executive File," June 10, 1977 Memorandum from Rick Hutcheson to Jimmy Carter, Public Relations Files, Box PR 75; "PR 15, 1/1/79–12/31/79," March 17, 1979 Memorandum from Gail Harrison to Walter Mondale, Public Relations Files, Box PR-75.

Carter's advisers infrequently received poll data from members of Congress. On at least two occasions, congressional Democrats volunteered to send Carter poll data from their states and districts. In a memo to Assistant to the President for Communications Gerald Rafshoon, Hubert Harris, Jr., Assistant Director of the Office of Management and Budget for Congressional Relations, explained that South Carolina Representative Ken Holland "would be happy to share his poll with you."[35] On another occasion, Stuart Eizenstat and Frank Moore wrote to the president that Delaware Senator Joseph Biden had called in data from his own statewide poll.[36] The collaboration between White House and Capitol Hill displayed by the Holland and Biden polls is rarely present in the evolution of presidential polling, one characteristic of which has been the growing autonomy of the presidency from Congress. Biden's offering to show his poll, however, should not be mistaken as presidential-congressional comity among Democrats. Caddell had polled for Biden's 1972 senate campaign, engendering a political connection that endured until 1987 and Biden's short-lived run for the presidency. In 1986 Caddell announced that he was leaving the world of political polling, but identified Biden and his 1988 presidential campaign as a final commitment he intended to keep.[37]

On occasion, White House officials dismissed polls entirely and turned to alternative means of gauging public opinion. By monitoring incoming phone calls, Carter's officials departed from relying entirely on a public opinion machine built solely around Caddell's polls. Two memos point to a phone and mail tallying operation within the Carter White House. Special Assistant to the President for Administration Hugh Carter received phone call tallies in a February 10, 1978 memo.[38] In addition, a September 10, 1979 memo from Chief of Correspondence in the Office of White House Operations Dan Chew to Hugh Carter contained tabulations of phone calls and mail after a few of Jimmy Carter's recent speeches.[39] By keeping track of phone calls and disseminating the numbers through the White House, the Carter presidency showed that polls had not yet universally usurped other, more traditional measures of the public mood.

White House officials provided input to Caddell's operation from time to time, but the extent of their influence was limited by politics: Caddell

[35] JCL, "Poll Information," August 8, 1978 Memorandum from Hubert Harris to Gerald Rafshoon, Greg Schneiders Files, Box 30.

[36] JCL, "PR 15, 6/1/78–12/31/78," September 27, 1978 Memorandum from Stuart Eizenstat and Frank Moore to Jimmy Carter, Public Relations Files, Box PR-75.

[37] Moore, *The Superpollsters*, pp. 131, 133.

[38] JCL, "Rex Granum," February 10, 1978 memorandum from Jane Simpson to Hugh Carter, Staff Offices – Press Files, Box 17.

[39] JCL, "Correspondence Office – Caddell Data," September 10, 1979 Memorandum from Dan Chew to Hugh Carter, Staff Offices – Malachuk Files, Box 2.

liked to maintain control over his operation. In a November 27, 1978 memo, Domestic Policy Staff Assistant Director Steve Simmons wrote to Alan [Scotty] Campbell, Chairman of the Civil Service Commission, and Wayne Granquist, Associate Director of the Office of Management and Budget for Management and Regulatory Policy, about the possibility of including their own questions on civil service reform on the next Cambridge poll. He passed on the advice of Dottie Lynch, Caddell's vice president: "Generally it is helpful to give us a list of topics (in order of priority) and let us write the questions. However, if you have some specific question [sic] in mind we will try to incorporate them." By requesting input in the form of topics, Lynch's instructions showed that Caddell was open to suggestions on survey content, even as he maintained autonomy over his polls. A September 1980 memo on Cambridge letterhead to the White House on horse-race questions exhibited an even stronger sense of propriety over Caddell's polls: "It is absolutely essential that there be no further disclosure of this information – other than principals."[40]

Pat Caddell is now considered a critical figure in the development of presidential polling. The power and access he achieved in the Carter White House, particularly at such a young age, made him a target of criticism as the Carter presidency's popularity ebbed. Critics noted before he won the White House, Carter appreciated Caddell's insights: "It's a marriage made in purgatory," an anonymous commentator said in a *New York Times* article about Caddell. "Jimmy and Pat both think in themes and the themes are almost identical."[41] As a result of this close relationship that grew during the Carter presidency, Carter's reading of public opinion became personally identified with Caddell. Such identification was not a creation of the press; President Carter acknowledged Caddell's importance, expressing in a holiday card that Caddell was "a member of our official family. We have relied on you greatly, and you have never let us down."[42] After Carter left 1600 Pennsylvania Avenue in defeat, Caddell's imprints on White House polling, specifically the role of the pollster as a key adviser, endured. As will be shown in the next section about President Reagan and his pollster Richard Wirthlin, the post-Carter presidency institutionalized private polling as a means to gauge public opinion and to market policies and agendas before Congress.

---

[40] JCL, "PR 15, 6/1/78–12/31/78," November 27, 1978 Memorandum from Steve Simmons to Scotty Campbell and Wayne Granquist, Public Relations Files, Box PR-75; "Misc. [Including Cambridge Research Reports] 7/16/80–10/8/80," September 23, 1980 report from Cambridge Survey Research to the White House, Press – Powell Files, CF O/A 745, Box 10.

[41] Charles Mohr, "A Young Pollster Plays a Key Role for Carter," *The New York Times*, August 1, 1976, 28.

[42] JCL, "Caddell, Patrick," Undated note from Jimmy Carter to Pat Caddell, WHCF.

RICHARD WIRTHLIN AND PRESIDENT REAGAN: PRESIDENTIAL
POLLING IN THE 1980S

Richard Wirthlin, head of the polling firm Decision/Making/Information
(DMI), conducted polls for the Reagan White House. He earned his
doctorate in economics at the University of California at Berkeley, where he
served as a teaching assistant in economics and statistics. Later, he taught
at Brigham Young University, where he served as the economics department
chairman for five years. Wirthlin emerged from academia to conduct polls
for Ronald Reagan's 1970 gubernatorial reelection bid, his 1976 and 1980
presidential campaigns, and during the Reagan presidency.[43] Beginning in
1978, Wirthlin developed a political information system (PINS) based on
the experience of the 1976 unsuccessful Reagan bid for the presidency.
Wirthlin observed that the most serious shortcoming of the campaign was
providing relevant, timely, and actionable data. The PINS system not only
used polling data, but integrated historical vote data, demographic data,
and used modeling and simulation to preaccess strategic positioning.[44] In
February 1980 Reagan asked Wirthlin to assume one of the roles formerly
filled by campaign strategist John Sears. Wirthlin helped develop the formal
strategy for the 1980 presidential campaign. After the 1980 election,
Wirthlin also directed the planning and strategy unit of the presidential
transition.[45]

Like his predecessor Pat Caddell, Wirthlin filled several roles as the president's pollster. First, Wirthlin had direct access to the president. While many
poll reports were sent to senior White House officials (for example, chiefs of
staff, national security advisers), several memoranda were written to and for
President Reagan. Wirthlin did not have an official position in the Reagan
White House, but he led the White House polling operation by interpreting
the polls and disseminating them to the appropriate advisers. Wirthlin set up
a new White House unit, the Office of Planning and Evaluation, to provide
him with an "inside" source and a mechanism to access the wide variety
of government sponsored studies and census analysis that could impinge on
White House policy. Dr. Richard Beal, who ran the polling activities of the
1980 campaign, served as the director of the new office.[46]

Second, Wirthlin played the part of an informal adviser to the president
and his staff, giving recommendations for and analyses of major speeches and
issues. Wirthlin frequently met with President Reagan, by his account once
every three to four weeks, and assumed a prominent role in deciding not only

---

[43] Moore, *The Super Pollsters*, pp. 194, 197–198.
[44] Letter from Richard Wirthlin, July 15, 2000.
[45] Ibid.
[46] Ibid.

which questions should be asked in certain surveys and who should receive what poll data, but also how to strategize politics based on the poll data he had amassed.[47] Third, Wirthlin's extensive polling for the Reagan administration was complemented by his perusal of media polls. David Chew, Staff Secretary and Deputy Assistant to the President, often received summaries of media polls about a whole host of policy issues and current events.[48] As the deficit rose and scandal erupted over the Iran-Contra affair, Wirthlin watched the media carefully, trying to understand how Reagan was being portrayed to the American public. In this regard, Wirthlin appreciated the importance of merging polls and public relations in order to advance the president's agenda.

Wirthlin conducted polling for both the RNC and White House advisers.[49] Wirthlin would often send his poll reports or overviews of the reports to RNC senior staff (such as Chairman Frank Fahrenkopf) and to senior White House officials. Other times, he would send poll reports or memos citing poll data directly to the president.[50] Whether or not polls were prepared officially for the president or his staff, nearly all to most of Wirthlin's data reached the White House. Having arrived, however, the poll data were not uniformly read among Reagan's senior staff. Evidence of this can be found in a handwritten memo from Chew to Chief of Staff Don Regan. "Bud [McFarlane] has the foreign policy stuff only."[51] In another instance, Chew wrote Regan a memo indicating "this is what [National Security Adviser] John Poindexter will get as the foreign policy summary of Wirthlin's latest polls," suggesting that Poindexter would not

---

[47] Moore, *The Super Pollsters*, p. 215.

[48] See Ronald Reagan Presidential Library [RRPL], PR 015, Boxes 7–9.

[49] Examples of poll titles include: Social Security – An In-Depth Look (August 1981); Nuclear Power (May 1986); President Reagan's Economic Program (January 1983); Strategic Defense Initiative (July 1985); Farm States Panel (August 1985); Sanctions against South Africa (September 1985; June 1986); Young Voters (April–May 1986); Supply and Demand for Drugs (June 1986); Mandatory Drug Testing (July 1986); Anti-Drug Crusade (September 1986); Iran (for RNC – December 1986); Pre-State of the Union Survey (December 1986); Pulseline (tm) Speech Analysis of Address on the Venice Summit and Budget Issues (June, 1987). RRPL, PR 015, Boxes 2, 5, 9, 10, 12, 14, 15.

[50] Regular White House recipients included David Chew, Donald Regan, Edwin Meese, James Baker, and Michael Deaver. RRPL, February 7, 1985 Memorandum from Richard Wirthlin, Jr., to Frank Fahrenkopf and Donald Regan, PR 015, Box 8, Folder Title 358566, 5 of 5; June 10, 1986 Memorandum from Richard Wirthlin, Jr., to RNC Senior Staff (cc: to Don Regan and David Chew), PR 015, Box 9, Folder Title 401081-401100; April 2, 1986 Memorandum from Richard Wirthlin, Jr., to Donald T. Regan, PR 015, Box 9, Folder Title 383501-392000. Also see January 24, 1986 Memorandum from Richard Wirthlin, Jr. to Ronald Reagan, PR 015, Box 8, Folder Title 366001-377000; and February 14, 1986 Memorandum from Richard Wirthlin, Jr., to Ronald Reagan, PR 015, Box 8, Folder Title 366001-377000.

[51] RRPL, November 14, 1985 Memorandum from David Chew to Donald Regan, PR 015, Box 6, Folder Title 351511-353539.

President Ronald Reagan and Richard Wirthlin (Courtesy of Richard Wirthlin)

receive a complete poll summary.[52] When poll data reached Reagan, it was usually by indirect paths. After Chew received a Wirthlin report in January 1987, he asked Regan if he should forward a copy to the president.[53]

Many White House officials were involved in receiving, interpreting, and disseminating poll data. Wirthlin described how he shared information as follows:

I would almost always present to the President first. Sometimes I would give the Councilor to the President or the Chief of Staff a verbal heads-up. It was customary that the Councilor and the Chief of Staff would be in the Oval Office when I reviewed the political environment with the President. On some occasions, when the information was particularly sensitive, I briefed the President alone... Then when there were some key issues that might pertain to the Director of Communication, a member of the cabinet, etc., I would give follow up briefings. Simultaneously, I would present most of the results to the Chairman of the Republican National Committee and his key staff. I also addressed virtually every gathering of the RNC and the Republican Governor's Association. On more than one occasion I briefed the entire cabinet. I frequently, both before the 1980 election, during, and after the election, gave briefings to the Republican Congressional leadership, some of the members of key committees, and after the 1980, 1982, 1984, and 1986 elections I briefed the

---

[52] RRPL, April 2, 1986 Memorandum from David Chew to Donald Regan, PR 015, Box 9, Folder Title 383501-392000.
[53] RRPL, January 9, 1987 Memorandum from David Chew to Donald T. Regan, PR 015, Box 14, Folder Title 469001-4703333.

newly elected congresspersons. During this period many of the Republicans running for office were our clients. If a major speech was being prepared on a specific topic that I had reviewed I would present that data to the White House speech writers. The data would then be separated by topic and I would prepare a memo on each topic that had fairly wide distribution in the White House and the RNC. These memos were drafted against the criterion that nothing should be put in these writings that would cause embarrassment to the White House or the Republican Party.[54]

Wirthlin had virtually unlimited access to President Reagan and his senior advisers. While he also briefed GOP party leaders, governors, and members of Congress, he presented, in his words, "most of the results" to them. In short, Wirthlin served as a critical nexus of public opinion and public relations, with his allegiance first and foremost to the presidency. The president's pollster was now gauging public opinion for institutions that a century ago had been assessing citizens' views for the presidency.

In 1984, Wirthlin sent his campaign poll data to Jim Baker, White House Chief of Staff; Mike Deaver, Deputy Chief of Staff; RNC Chairmen Dick Richards and Frank Fahrenkopf; Paul Laxalt, Campaign Chairman for Reagan-Bush '84; Ed Rollins, Campaign Director for Reagan-Bush '84; and Stuart Spencer, who also worked on the campaign. On July 26, 1985, Director of Communications Pat Buchanan, Counsel to the President Fred Fielding, Legislative Strategy Coordinator Max Friedersdorf, Assistant to the President for National Security Affairs Bud McFarlane, Assistant to the President for Legislative Affairs M.B. Oglesby, Principal Deputy Press Secretary Larry Speakes, Assistant to the President for Policy Development Jack Svahn, and Executive Assistant to the White House Chief of Staff Dennis Thomas received the following message from Chew and Rollins: "Dick Wirthlin will be providing an update on current public attitudes on Tuesday, July, 30th at 1:00 P.M. in the Roosevelt Room."[55]

In sharing his data with the White House, Wirthlin would almost always meet directly with the president. In Wirthlin's words, "There was never a time when I requested a meeting with the President that it was not granted."[56] A December 9, 1981 memo from Wirthlin to Deputy Chief of Staff Mike Deaver contained a request to meet Reagan and even suggested dates for the meeting: "If possible, Mike, I would like to make a 35 to 40 minute presentation to the President on December 16, 17 or 18."[57] Wirthlin continued to meet with Reagan throughout his presidency, even after the 1988 election. A November 29, 1988 scheduling memo to the president from Frederick Ryan, Jr., Director of Presidential Appointments and Scheduling, reminded Reagan

[54] Letter from Richard Wirthlin, July 15, 2000.
[55] RRPL, PR 015, Box 5, Folder Title 292001-307000.
[56] Wirthlin letter.
[57] RRPL, December 9, 1981 Memorandum from Richard Wirthlin to Michael Deaver, PR 015, Box 1, Folder Title 050001-056000.

of his "periodic meeting with Richard Wirthlin to see the results of his latest poll."[58]

Wirthlin's access to the president allowed him to take on the role of an informal adviser. One handwritten memorandum from Chew to Regan substantiates how broad Wirthlin's political tentacles were: "[H]e [Wirthlin] now feels the opening statement falls short of what is need [sic]."[59] On April 10, 1985, Wirthlin wrote Reagan a three-page, single-spaced letter, advising the president how to win a vote on aid to Nicaragua:

By raising the political stakes and the public salience of this particular issue, you would not only put into jeopardy the favorable job approval you now enjoy, but, more importantly, you will generate more public and congressional opposition than support ... I, thus, strongly recommend, Mr. President, that you not take your case concerning aid to the Contras to the public in some dramatic and/or symbolic fashion.[60]

Wirthlin offered political strategizing on other issues, such as reducing the deficit and fighting for a balanced budget amendment, as shown in an October 1983 DMI summary sent to the White House.

If this analysis is correct ... an aggressive program of presidential events, statements and surrogate support for a balanced budget amendment would improve the approval rating for the President's handling of the deficit, restore the conviction that he will follow through on his campaign promises and renew confidence in his handling of the economy.[61]

In making suggestions to the president's advisers on how to handle the deficit issue, Wirthlin analyzed the public mood, suggested a course of action, and forecasted public reaction to that strategy. In memos and meetings, Wirthlin's role entailed amassing poll data, interpreting it, and converting his analysis into advice.

According to Wirthlin, while the RNC paid for the White House polls, their influence in Wirthlin's operation did not stop at the pocketbook.[62] On one occasion, Wirthlin teamed with the RNC to identify how to attract women to the GOP. After studying the gender gap, Wirthlin's firm amassed a database of approximately 100,000 interviews. "Working with RNC Chairman Dick Richards and Bill Greener, communications director of the RNC, we designed TV ads specifically to impact that segment [older,

---

[58] RRPL, November 28, 1988 Memorandum from Frederick Ryan, Jr., to Ronald Reagan, PR 015, Box 25, Folder Title 618000-630402.

[59] RRPL, PR 015, Box 12, Folder Title 464525.

[60] Ibid., Folder Title 307001-318000.

[61] RRPL, October 19, 1983 DMI Summary, PR 015, Box 4, Folder Title 208001-222000.

[62] A memo from Chew to Regan reads in part, "Key questions start on page 7. Most of the other questions coming out of RNC budgets and not ours." RRPL, PR 015, Box 11, Folder Title 439788-459000.

nonworking women], and placed those ads on morning television on programs appealing to older women . . ."[63]

On occasion, at Wirthlin's invitation, White House officials involved
themselves in ordering and designing questionnaires. In January 1986,
Assistant to the President and Office of Intergovernmental Affairs Director
Mitchell [Mitch] Daniels requested that Wirthlin include a battery of questions about Central America and the judicial system in his poll. Daniels
provided detailed questions, including various formats and hypothetical
vignettes and scenarios for the questionnaire design. In a March 31, 1982
memo to Office of Management and Budget Director David Stockman,
Edwin Harper, Assistant to the President for Policy Development, alerted
Stockman that Wirthlin would be "going into the field" in the next week and
had called to ask if Reagan's staff had "any particular items that [they] would
like to have included." Harper wrote Wirthlin later that week with a slew
of suggestions from various Office of Policy Development staffers, including
the following question from Danny Boggs, Special Assistant to the President
for Policy Development: "In your opinion, is the energy situation for the
United States better or worse than it was a year ago?"[64] Wirthlin's
next survey included a reworded version of this same question, asking:
"Compared to a year ago, do you think the national energy situation has
gotten better, gotten worse, or stayed the same?"[65] Unlike the Nixon administration, in which Haldeman held an exclusive rein on who should
see White House polls, it was Wirthlin who controlled Reagan's polling
operation.

Wirthlin also recognized that polls were news and that interpreting the
polls to the media and the mass electorate required that the administration
articulate to the press what the polls were showing. On June 4, 1982, for
example, Wirthlin provided talking points to Chief of Staff James Baker,
presumably for an interview or press conference. Rather than have the media
misconstrue poll data, Wirthlin preferred to interpret it for them, recognizing
that they would seek alternative interpretations. By elucidating what the
poll data meant, Wirthlin had submitted one version of events that were
likely to get some air time, or at minimum, some pondering by journalists,
reporters, and their editors. Simultaneously, by providing talking points to
Baker, Wirthlin understood that poll data needed to be digested in a way
that the press (and the mass public) could understand.

[63] Wirthlin letter.
[64] RRPL, January 29, 1986 Memorandum from Mitchell E. Daniels, Jr., to Richard Wirthlin,
PR 015, Box 9, Folder Title 382001-383500; March 31, 1982 Memorandum from Edwin
Harper to Dave Stockman, PR 015, Box 1, Folder Title 066000-068000; April 2, 1982
Memorandum from Danny Boggs to Edwin Harper, PR 015, Box 1, Folder Title 066000-
068000.
[65] RRPL, April 29, 1982 Memorandum from Richard Wirthlin to Edwin Meese, James Baker,
and Michael Deaver, PR 015, Box 1, Folder Title 068001-073000.

As the White House poll data were being interpreted to and for the press, Wirthlin occasionally used focus groups in order to understand citizens' opinions on issues and politics. In June 1985, for example, DMI assembled three groups of blue collar Philadelphians to test market Reagan's tax proposal. On another occasion, focus group participants registered their opinions of Reagan's State of the Union address by dialing a handheld computer.[66] Focus groups added a qualitative element to his polls, supplementing the quantitative exactitude that Reagan's advisers sought. In addition, archival data also show at least one occasion in which senior officials studied incoming phone calls to the White House. In the midst of the Iran-Contra hearings, Assistant to the President for Operations Rhett Dawson forwarded a memo to Reagan showing how incoming phone calls to the White House about Oliver North on July 21, 1987 were disproportionately positive.[67] There is no evidence that this information was taken seriously or ignored entirely. That the phone calls were being monitored at all suggests that nonscientific means of gauging public opinion had not been abandoned, even as private polls had become an integral part of the presidency.

As with previous administrations, the Reagan White House put distance between its public opinion measurements and those in the media, even while trying to doctor the president's image in the press. Senior White House officials frequently dieted on outside media polling, often taking a close and critical eye to how the media portrayed the president. Two memos regarding Reagan's public opinion ratings in 1986 contain summaries of outside media polls, including data from *Wall Street Journal*/NBC, *Washington Post*/ABC, *New York Times*/CBS, Gallup, Harris, and Robert Teeter's Market Opinion Research (MOR), as well as DMI.[68] One memo to National Security Adviser John Poindexter from Rod McDaniel, Executive Secretary of the National Security Council, reported that in assessing public opinion on security issues, "major media polls and private sector polls have been used."[69] Another October 31, 1985 memo from McDaniel to Poindexter indicated outright dissatisfaction with the administration's image on security issues in the media and referred to upcoming analysis of multiple media sources: "The Washington Post regularly peppers us with its polls on various national security issues (30 October was the most recent example). I asked [Director, Special Studies Staff, Crisis Management Center (CMC), National Security

[66] RRPL, June 1985, "Qualitative Focus Group Research Concerning President Reagan's 'Fair-Share Tax,'" PR 015, Box 7, Folder Title 358566, 1 of 5; February 14, 1986 Memorandum from Richard Wirthlin to Ronald Reagan, PR 015, Box 8, Folder Title 366001-378000.

[67] RRPL, July 21, 1987 Memorandum from Rhett Dawson to Ronald Reagan, PR 015, Box 16, Folder Title 497401-500827.

[68] RRPL, February 26, 1986 Memorandum from William Lacy to David Chew, PR 015, Box 9, Folder Title 378001-382000.

[69] RRPL, January 15, 1986 Memorandum from Rod McDaniel to John Poindexter, PR 015, Box 9 Folder Title 392501-398000.

Council (NSC)] Ron Hinckley to analyze public opinion from more than one source to provide us with a sharper picture of U.S. attitudes on some of these issues."[70]

Attention to the media showed up in Wirthlin's questionnaires as well, especially during the Iran-Contra scandal. A DMI survey in the summer of 1987 added a new twist to Wirthlin's typical assortment of approve/ disapprove questions. In the midst of Iran-Contra congressional hearings, the poll included a "thermometer" question asking respondents to rate their approval of certain political figures and institutions, such as Reagan, Oliver North, and the national political parties. Although this was a standard item in Wirthlin's polls, this time his firm also asked respondents to rank television news anchors Tom Brokaw, Peter Jennings, and Dan Rather (all three of whom, it may be noted, received higher ratings than parties and politicians).[71] A special DMI tracking presentation in December 1986 titled "American Attitudes toward the Iranian Situation" contained a section of questions asking, "Does the public trust the media?" In a follow-up survey, Wirthlin asked interviewees if they thought the news media had exaggerated how important the Iran-Contra arms deals were. Reagan White House advisers, including Wirthlin, closely monitored the news and attempted to assess its credibility in the public eye.

On a few occasions Reagan officials and Wirthlin went on the offensive, criticizing pollsters for methodological and partisan reasons. In an August 3, 1987 memo to Tommy Griscom, Assistant to the President for Policy Development, Wirthlin critiqued a Harris poll for poor wording and design. He noted survey responses that showed "how a pollster can get the results he wants by careful wording and sequence of questions."[72] Democratic pollster Pat Caddell fared no better against this critique. When Reagan's advisers learned that Caddell's firm, the Cambridge Group, had obtained a lucrative polling contract for the Social Security Administration, they seized the opportunity to criticize and cease the deal on grounds of federal contract procedure violations.[73]

Like their predecessors, Reagan's White House advisers saw their private polls as vehicles to secure more autonomy for the presidency. The Reagans

[70] RRPL. October 31, 1985 Memorandum from Rod McDaniel to John Poindexter, PR 015, Box 7, Folder Title 353540-356999.

[71] RRPL, July 29–August 2, 1987 DMI Survey of Public Attitudes, PR 015, Box 18, Folder Title 513548, 1 of 4.

[72] RRPL, December 1, 1986, "American Attitudes Toward the Iranian Situation," PR 015, Box 12, Folder Title 464525, 6 of 8, 4 of 6; January 14, 1987, "Iranian Tracking – Flash Results," PR 015, Box 11, Folder Title 459001-459047; August 3, 1987 Memorandum from Richard Wirthlin to Tommy Griscom, PR 015, Box 17, Folder Title 504001-512000.

[73] RRPL, September 17, 1985 Memorandum from Alfred Kingon to Donald Regan, PR 015, Box 6, Folder Title 335300-339260.

and their advisers trusted Wirthlin and his analyses; in turn, he gave them unprecedented access and adopted the mantle of presidential adviser. To optimize the polling operation, Wirthlin and White House officials paid attention to how poll data were presented to the media, how the media reported the poll data and how the public perceived the media and media elites. Wirthlin's attention to political expediency showed up in his poll designs, which changed to reflect key issues and events.[74] The White House pollster had become an integral part of the modern presidency and the political efficacy of private presidential polling had, in a sense, redefined its operation.

CONCLUSION

The private polling operations of Presidents Ford, Carter, and Reagan indicate a reliance on in-house assessments of public opinion. These presidents sought independent gauges of public opinion, not merely because of tensions with Congress, their respective party leaders, or the media, but because presidential autonomy concerning public opinion had already begun to be institutionalized. As Diane Heith has noted in her work on staffing of the White House polling apparatus, Presidents Ford, Carter, and Reagan aided in "routinizing the incorporation of public opinion data and analysis in the office of the presidency."[75]

While these presidents never matched the enormity of Nixon's polling operation, they continued advancing and enhancing the role of their pollsters, both in the campaign and once elected to office.[76] Not only were their data important to the presidency, their insights about how to interpret the data were as well. As a result, the pollsters became important political players

---

[74] A sampling of Wirthlin's survey questions from 1987 to 1988 illustrates his adaptation of poll design: September 1987 – Bork nomination to Supreme Court; November 1987 – summit with Mikael Gorbachaev; February 1988 – drugs and AIDS; April, 1988 – trial heats between Bush v. Dukakis, and Bush v. Jackson; May 1988 – Manuel Noriega; June 1988 – pardoning Oliver North and Admiral John Poindexter; July 1988 – Michael Dukakis' acceptance speech at the Democratic convention, feeling thermometer questions about Jesse Jackson and George Bush; October 1988 – feeling thermometer questions for Bush, Quayle, Dukakis, and Bentsen, and questions about Dukakis' issue stances.

[75] Diane J. Heith, "Staffing the White House Public Opinion Apparatus: 1969–1988," *Public Opinion Quarterly* 62 (1988): 165–189.

[76] E.J. Dionne, Jr., "The Business of Pollsters," *The New York Times*, June 29, 1980, Sec. 3, 1; Robert G. Kaiser, "White House Pulse-Taking Pollster," *Washington Post*, February 24, 1982, A1; Lois Romano, "Wirthlin, The Optimist," *Washington Post*, January 15, 1984, C12; "Carter's Outside Insiders," *Business Week*, June 27, 1977, 94; William J. Lanouette, "When a Presidential Candidate Moves, a Pollster May Be Pulling the Strings," *National Journal* 11 (December 15, 1979): 2092.

and the focus of media attention. This evolution from the pollster as a quiet but trusted outsider, to that of the pollster as a trusted advising insider jibes after reviewing the history of the presidency. FDR created federal bureaucracies that replaced if not displaced many of the functions of party bosses. Modern presidential polling can be seen as a natural extension of the strains between the president and his own party. Theodore Lowi's description of a personalized presidency also dovetails well with the history of recent presidential polling. According to Lowi, citizens now expect presidents to be plebiscitary; private polling, and in particular, enhancing the role of their pollsters as key advisers to interpret public opinion, can be seen as a response to citizens' desires for presidents to be responsive to their needs.[77]

As the pollsters became increasingly employed in the White House, so too did other key advisers. Nixon's Chief of Staff Haldeman exemplified the White House adviser who devoted much of his day to assessing public opinion. As Diane Heith argues, the number of senior advisers who became part of the public opinion apparatus increased during the Ford, Carter, and Reagan presidencies.[78] What is revealing in this regard is not the mere increase in White House personnel associated with measuring the public's mood, but the high status of these advisers. Just as FDR recognized that public opinion was worthy of his personal attention, as well as that of his trusted adviser Sam Rosenman, modern presidencies to post-FDR presidencies elevated the importance of monitoring and distributing polls to senior advisers such as Messrs. Cheney, Powell, Eizenstat, Baker, Deaver, Regan, and Meese.

The presidents' pollsters gained increased access to the president. Simultaneously, the pollsters' influence permeated the president's close advisers. Stan Greenberg, President Clinton's former pollster, noted that he routinely sent memoranda to a myriad of persons in the White House, including Hillary Rodham Clinton and Tipper Gore.[79] A consequence of this process of sending poll data to so many advisers extends beyond the growth of the president's public opinion apparatus and into the nature of what role it plays in shaping policies. As advisers, particularly senior advisers, pay close attention to the nation's pulse via polls, their roles extend beyond interpreters of public opinion, to shapers of it. Lawrence Jacobs and Robert Shapiro note in *Politicians Don't Pander* that contrary to the notion that presidents react to public opinion, there is evidence showing that presidential advisers devote much time and energy trying to *direct* public opinion.[80]

[77] Lowi, *The Personal President*, p. 151.
[78] Heith, "Staffing the White House Public Opinion Apparatus."
[79] Telephone conversation with Stan Greenberg, June 6, 2000.
[80] Lawrence R. Jacobs and Robert Y. Shapiro, *Politicians Don't Pander: Political Manipulation and the Loss of Democratic Responsiveness*. Chicago: University of Chicago Press, 2000.

Explaining the evolution of presidential polling – first from FDR through Nixon, and then beyond to Reagan – also explains how trying to direct public opinion has been facilitated by key advisers. By creating a bureaucratic apparatus that used polls as the primary means to assess attitudes, recent presidents employed polls as vehicles for helping them market policies and shape public opinion. As will be shown in Chapter 9, using polls has transformed the presidency and how we perceive it.

9

Presidential Polling in the Post-Reagan Era

Consequences and Implications of Presidential Polling

Presidential polling has reached a new era. The foundations provided by previous presidents have made it viable for today's chief executives to use polls, so much so that citizens expect private polls to be part of a president's arsenal. This chapter evaluates the private polling of Presidents Bush and Clinton, with an eye toward the future. Much of the Bush administration's archival data remain closed to the public and none of the Clinton polling data is currently available to analyze. Still, the perusable data from the Bush presidential library, combined with interviews with interested parties and a nascent literature about Clinton's poll use reveal that both presidents and their advisers were keenly interested in monitoring public opinion polls. As George Edwards has accurately noted, the Clinton administration exemplifies the public presidency.[1] After evaluating how the Bush presidency conducted its private polling operation, I will then review the existing literature that has begun to speculate about the Clinton administration's use of private polls. While the journalists and scholars correctly note that the Clinton presidency extensively used polls, some of their claims about how the Clinton administration marks a radical departure from his predecessors may be overstated and exaggerated. This chapter concludes with an evaluation of the implications of past, present, and future presidential polling. Conservatives may be disappointed that I do not condemn Clinton's extensive polling; similarly, liberals equally may be disheartened to learn that Republican presidents of the past are commended for their keen sense of what the public should not decide. Rather than think of presidential polling along conventional ideological divides, I will argue that presidential polling has resulted in increased autonomy "at the margins" by allowing presidents to gauge public opinion independently of Congress, political parties, or the media.

---

[1] George C. Edwards, III, "Frustration and Folly: Bill Clinton and the Public Presidency." In *The Clinton Presidency: First Appraisals*, edited by Colin Campbell and Bert A. Rockman. Chatham, MA: Chatham House, 1996, pp. 234–261.

As vice president, George Bush contemplated succeeding Ronald Reagan after Reagan's second term was to expire. Not surprisingly, one of Robert Teeter's 1985 Market Opinion Research poll questions asked about a possible George Bush presidency. Bush was not yet a candidate for the presidency (he formally declared on October 12, 1987), but the mere asking of questions about a Bush presidential bid stoked many legal and journalistic fires. The RNC, which was subsidizing the MOR polls, did not endorse a Bush candidacy, especially one that did not yet exist, nor had they authorized questions to be asked about Bush, in part because political parties paid for polls, but did not control their composition. Affidavits were required by Bush's Chief of Staff Craig Fuller, his future campaign consultant Lee Atwater, and Robert Teeter, all of whom documented who requested which questions, and why the poll was paid for by several groups, including the Fund for America's Future, a group for which Atwater was serving as an unpaid political adviser. Bush himself wrote a letter to the Federal Election Commission in March 1986, noting that he was not a candidate for any public office, and that while he "was aware that the Republican National Committee was conducting a poll, I did not request or authorize any polling relating to the 1988 election or any possible candidacy."[2]

Teeter ultimately assumed the role of the candidate's pollster after Bush formally declared himself a presidential candidate. Teeter's poll questions initially sought to distinguish Bush from his competitors. Respondents were asked what they liked and disliked about Bush and Senator Robert Dole who also was running for president. Respondents were also asked if they thought Bush had "supported President Reagan too much, not enough, or about the right amount?" Also, the poll asked which candidate (Bush, Dole, duPont, Haig, Kemp, Robertson) could be trusted to do the right thing when making a difficult decision, was personally likeable, understood and was concerned about the problems of the average person, would be effective in getting results, and was a strong leader.[3]

Bob Teeter's experience as a GOP pollster helped ease a transition from the Reagan-Bush polling operation to a Bush-Quayle operation that he ran. The Wirthlin Group retained a contract polling for the RNC as Teeter's MOR prepared poll analyses for the Bush-Quayle White House. Yet according to RNC Chief of Staff Mary Matalin, the RNC 1989 polling budget was "less than half of the previous annual polling allocation."[4] While Teeter's expertise provided the impetus for most of the president's polls, the

[2] Vice President Bush to Federal Election Commission, March 13, 1986, in Craig Fuller Files, Polls, [OA/ID 14283] [3 of 4]. Unless otherwise noted, all data in this section are from the George Herbert Walker Bush Library [GHWBL].
[3] 99-0098-F, Craig Fuller "Polls" and Thomas Collarmore Files "Teeter Polls," [OA/ID 14284 and 14444].
[4] Mary Matalin to Jim Wray, August 4, 1989, 066009 PR 013-08.

RNC also "tagged-on" poll questions to other surveys conducted by GOP pollsters.

White House officials sometimes recommended questions to be asked in the MOR surveys. On November 27, 1990, Ed Goldstein, Senior Policy Analyst in the Office of Policy Development [OPD], informed Roger Porter, Assistant to the President for Economic and Domestic Policy, that Market Opinion Research [MOR] "has offered to occasionally run in the survey questions of interest to OPD, such as the tree questions I suggested to him last July . . . If you have any questions you would like to see in a future poll, I would be happy to pass them along."[5]

Repeatedly, Bush's advisers believed that good publicity in the media could and would influence public opinion and that it was the president's responsibility to understand what the public thought about major policy issues. President Bush's advisers frequently received polls from outside organizations, lobbies, and interest groups. Rather than read any or all poll data, President Bush's senior advisers Ed Rogers and Roger Porter, much like their predecessors Messrs. MacLafferty, Watson, and Haldeman, served as public opinion filters. These men, combined with President Bush's pollster, friend, and confidante Bob Teeter, functioned as conduits between the president and much of the poll data that the president received.[6] Sometimes the data were read; at other times, it appears from terse responses that these data were received but not consumed or digested in any substantive way. On one occasion, for example, Chief of Staff Sununu wrote Lou Harris a three sentence letter, thanking him for the "note and information" and ending, "I appreciate your help."[7] President Bush's advisers understood not only that public opinion mattered, but that the White House received a myriad of poll data, and so it was important to filter only relevant public opinion–related information to the president. In this regard, private polling had become well integrated in the White House.

[5] The tree question to which Goldstein refers is as follows: "President Bush has been urging Americans to make tree planting an important activity. Were you aware or not aware of his support for tree planting?" Also included was a question asking the likelihood that the respondent would plant a tree. In developing these questions, Goldstein consulted with several people, including Emily Mead, Senior Staff member of the OPD, Jim Pinkerton, Deputy Assistant to the President for Policy Planning, and Teresa A. Gorman, Special Assistant to the President for Policy Development, in developing (99-0098-F, Ed Goldstein Files, September 28, 1990, Goldstein to Porter, OA/ID 06673).

[6] For evidence of Porter's receiving unsolicited polls, see, for example, 99-098-F, "Public Opinion 91" [OA/ID 06681 [1 of 2]]. Several staff members ranging in seniority read or reviewed poll data, as evidenced by the names on memoranda sent to the president. Some of these include: Ed Rogers (July 12, 1990; April 26, 1990), G. Gregg Petersmeyer, Deputy Assistant to the President and Director, Office of National Service (May 3, 1990), Bob Grady (May 14, 1992), Judy Smith, Deputy Press Secretary (Jan 23, 1992), James Wray (Aug 6, 1989), Ron Kaufman (July 21, 1992).

[7] John Sununu to Lou Harris, July 19, 1990, 158792 PR 014.

The prevailing notion that public events could influence poll numbers is best exemplified by Sig Rogich, who, as assistant to the President for Public Events and Initiatives, scribbled a note to the president, informing him that Pete Wilson's poll numbers were up, "and probably a result of our trip."[8] On another occasion, Agriculture Secretary Clayton Yeutter writes to Chief of Staff Sam Skinner that Bob Teeter should be informed that October is the month for "red ribbon events on drug control/prevention activities." Yeutter suggests that Teeter and Office of National Drug Control and Policy Director ["Drug Czar"] Bob Martinez be appraised of "our then list of key states... [to] look for an attractive possibility in one of those locations."[9] Presidential polling was an integral part of policy making, not in the conventionally understood sense of polls shaping policy or as presidents allegedly being beholden to poll results. Instead, polls and pollsters were to be exploited for their ability to market existing policies. The president's staff understood that a drug policy had to be inaugurated somewhere. Why not introduce, unveil, or highlight it in a vulnerable state or region where the president could benefit from good publicity? As was the case with their recent predecessors, private polls provided the presidential advisers with a means to gauge and to sway public opinion. If the Bush administration sought to advance a legislative or political agenda, they had to do so by constantly marketing themselves to the American people. Failure to do so would result in waning public approval, further inhibiting their ability to advance their policy agenda.

Bush's policy advisers regularly received MOR's monthly survey of Americans. The 1990 surveys included questions about the president's approval rating, whether the respondent thought the country was headed in the right direction or wrong track, and expectations of the economy. Each month, questions about current events and policies were asked, including questions about clean air legislation, hostages in Lebanon, the U.S. policy toward China, and major league baseball games on cable television.[10] Teeter, Steeper, and other pollsters warned President Bush and his advisers that his high approval ratings were encouraging, but still not an accurate indicator that Americans were overly sanguine about the Bush presidency. As early as 1989, White House advisers received warning signs that President Bush's

---

[8] October 30, 1990, Sig Rogich Files [OA/ID 04732] [1 of 2].

[9] Clayton Yeutter to Bob Teeter, July 9, 1992, 99-0163-F, WHORM, Teeter, Robert.

[10] Exact wordings: "Do you feel things in this country are going in the right direction or do you feel things have pretty seriously gotten off on the wrong track?" and "1990 will be the first year most major league baseball games will be shown on cable television instead of regular network television. Of the following two statements about this issue, which comes closest to your opinion: There is enough baseball on TV and those who want to see more games can subscribe to cable, or, it is unfair to show most games on cable because many households do not have access to cable or cannot afford it." "Public Opinion Polls" [OA/ID 06777].

high approval ratings may enervate over time. While Bush had "placate[d] potentially hostile voters, the support of these voters will be conditional. They could disappear from the favorable column as quickly as they appeared there." In July of 1990, Bush advisers read of the "confidence disparity" in Wirthlin's polls; 71% of Americans approved of Bush, but only 36% thought the country was on the right track. In December of 1991, Teeter provided President Bush, Vice President Quayle, and Chief of Staff Samuel Skinner with a detailed analysis of public opinion, showing that only 23% of the respondents thought the country was on the right track, compared to 70% who thought that the country was headed in the wrong direction. Another graph tracked Bush's approval ratings to consumer confidence; not surprisingly, as consumer confidence ebbed, the approval ratings followed.[11]

George Bush often read the poll-related information he received and was frequently informed by his senior advisers of a whole host of poll data. For example, when James Wray, Director of the Office of Political Affairs, sent a note to Andrew Card, Deputy Chief of Staff, about a new Wirthlin Group poll showing Democratic Pennsylvania Governor Bob Casey was electorally vulnerable, and that the president had a high approval rating in Pennsylvania, President Bush handwrote "Nice!!" with his initials.[12] After reading poll data indicating favorable responses to his Points of Light volunteer initiative, Bush wrote to C. Gregg Petersmeyer, Director, Office of National Service, and Assistant to the President for Public Events and Initiatives Sig Rogich, "I was thrilled to see this. Keep up the great work."[13] On another occasion, Bush wrote "fascinating report" on a memo about the 1990 Texas gubernatorial race.[14] After reading a compilation of poll reports showing his favorability ratings trailing Democratic presidential nominee Governor Bill Clinton, Bush tersely handwrote "Ugh!" in the margins.[15]

Senators and members of Congress occasionally sent the Bush administration poll data. Congressman Bob McEwen (R-OH) provided Frederick McClure, assistant to the President for Legislative Affairs, with favorable poll results about Bush sent to McEwen by Dave Disher, President of Marketing Research Services, which is located in McEwen's Cincinnati congressional district. Disher wrote McEwen, asking him for "immediate help in conveying this message to the White House by the most expedient means." McClure replied to Congressman McEwen, thanking him for the poll data, and assuring the congressman that he "shared the results with several of the

---

[11] See April,1989 MOR Survey, 080581 PR 014; July 12, 1990 Memorandum,157401SS PR 014; December 10, 1991 (meeting with POTUS, VP and Skinner), 297070 PR 014.

[12] PR 014, WHORM, 055572SS.

[13] May 3, 1990 Memorandum to the president, 138105SS PR 014.

[14] February 22, 1990, 123193SS PR 014.

[15] Ron Kaufman to the president, July 21, 1992, 339149SS PR 014.

President's foreign policy and national security advisors so that they, too, have the benefit of this information."[16]

Similarly, Senator Strom Thurmond sent Sununu a newspaper article that showed strong support for Bush's military actions in the Persian Gulf. "I would appreciate your sharing this poll with the President. I believe that it is important that he know that the majority of the citizens of South Carolina and the United States stand behind him during this difficult time."[17]

In return, Bush's advisers occasionally provided members of Congress with poll data. Congressman Chuck Douglas (R-NH) wrote Chief of Staff John Sununu on June 13, 1989, thanking him "for sending over the Public Opinion Survey concerning the recent proposals of George Bush at NATO." Douglas responded, informing Sununu that a cursory form letter written by a Bush aide angered elementary school students in Douglas' district, and resulted in an unflattering story in the *Concord Monitor*.[18]

Perhaps the most convincing evidence that White House advisers procured poll data exclusively for its own purview is revealed by a 1987 memo that discussed when Republican candidates should not receive poll questions from the RNC:

Exceptions: There may be particular questions that are researched at the specific request of the White House with the results going only to the White House; in these cases, the RNC would inform each candidate representative that the question is being asked, but the Wirthlin Group would not share the information with any campaign organization without the express consent of the White House and then each organization would be informed.[19]

Also of note is how this memo advised how "overt disclosure" of poll questions or analysis by any campaign would "jeopardize further participation by the candidate's organization in the information sharing effort." The memo was written when President Reagan was still in office, but there is no evidence that this process was reversed in the Bush administration. To the contrary, RNC Chief of Staff Matalin's memo discussing how polling was conducted by the RNC strongly suggests that the Bush advisers could "tag-on" questions to polls conducted by RNC pollsters. The result was an administration that understood both the political value of polls and the negative ramifications of being considered beholden to polls. Bush White House aide Ed Rogers confirms that the Bush administration failed to create a central White House polling operation like Presidents Nixon or Reagan. "We never

[16] 99-0163-F, WHORM, ND016 [209792]. Other members of Congress sending Bush advisers poll-related data include Republican Congressmen Larry Combest and Lawrence Coughlin (PR 014 047540), and Senator Charles Grassley (ibid., 083389).
[17] 99-0163-F, WHORM, ND016 [212337].
[18] 99-0163-F, WHORM, IT067 [046323].
[19] Points on RNC Polling, October 10, 1987, Craig Fuller Files, "Polls" [OA/ID 14283][1 of 4].

had a central polling strategy. If you were preaching about polls, then you were suspected of not being a good steward of the President's statesmanship qualities."[20] A *National Journal* article notes that in Bush's first year in office, Fred Steeper conducted "only three national polls and a smattering of focus groups."[21] This might explain why Bush appears to have met with Teeter and Fred Steeper directly in the Oval Office, but sparingly. Bush appeared to be keenly interested in the polls that he saw, but hesitant to request their repeated use.

THE CLINTON ERA: POLLING AND COMMUNICATION STRATEGIES INTERTWINE

If many citizens think that President Clinton's private poll usage significantly differs from his predecessors, they can probably blame or thank Dick Morris. While the Clinton presidential library is not even built (and hence the data not available for analysis), scholars and journalists alike have been speculating about how the Clinton administration used polls, in large part because of Morris' claim that he conducted a poll about how citizens would react toward President Clinton's relationship with White House intern Monica Lewinsky. Morris – a former adviser to Clinton, candidly asserted how the president employed polls about a whole host of issues, including some that are not policy related. In his book *Behind the Oval Office*, Morris describes how he thought President Clinton used polls:

For Bill Clinton, positive poll results are not just tools – they are vindication, ratification, and approval – whereas negative poll results are a learning process in which the pain of the rebuff to his self-image forces deep introspection. Intellectually, polls offer Clinton an insight into how people think. He uses polls to adjust not just his thinking on one issue but his frame of reference so that it is always as close to congruent with that of the country as possible.[22]

One could speculate about whether or not Morris' unique relationship with Clinton make his comments especially prescient or whether they should be discounted. In *Politicians Don't Pander*, Lawrence Jacobs and Robert Shapiro contend that the Clinton administration's polling on health care was designed to market their agenda, not to succumb to the whims of the electorate. Morris, while claiming that the Clinton administration polled extensively, also has suggested that it did so to help figure out how to make policy arguments more persuasive and not to make policy.[23]

---

[20] James A. Barnes, "Polls Apart," *National Journal* (July 10, 1993): 1753.
[21] Ibid.
[22] Dick Morris, *Behind the Oval Office: Winning the Presidency in the Nineties*. New York: Random House, 1997, p. 11.
[23] Ibid., 10.

President Bill Clinton and Stan Greenberg (Courtesy of Stan Greenberg)

Similarly, works by White House adviser George Stephanopoulos, journalist Bob Woodward, and others appear to confirm both that polls were used extensively and that polls were primarily used to market agendas and lead the public, rather than to follow it.[24]

About fourteen months into President Clinton's tenure, a *Wall Street Journal* article reported that almost two million dollars had been spent on polling-related work in 1993 compared to about $200,000 spent by President Bush in 1989 and 1990.[25] President Clinton's pollster at the time, Stan Greenberg, noted that presidential private polls were being used to help the president familiarize himself both with citizens' attitudes and with the language common folk used to express their attitudes. According to the article, Greenberg met with Clinton once a week. Greenberg also mentioned in personal interviews and a subsequent article how focus groups were used to assist in appreciating the vernacular of the mass public; focus groups, he said, are "very important to listen to." Greenberg used dial groups, much like Bob Teeter and Richard Wirthlin had done for Presidents Ford

---

[24] George Stephanopoulos, *All Too Human: A Political Education*. Boston: Little Brown, 2000; Bob Woodward, *The Agenda: Inside the Clinton White House*. New York: Simon and Schuster, 1994.

[25] James M. Perry, "Clinton Relies Heavily on White House Pollster to Take Words Right Out of the Public's Mouth," *Wall Street Journal*, March 23, 1994, A16.

and Reagan. Viewers who watched a speech would turn a dial on a scale from zero to one hundred. According to the *National Journal* article, these responses helped Greenberg "see people's 'gut' reactions to particular phrases or explanations."[26] Greenberg also remarked that President Clinton had an astute sense of public opinion, so much so that he would comment about changing moods of the electorate after conversing with individuals, delivering speeches, or shaking their hands.[27] Just like Oliver Quayle sought to add some texture and qualitative dimension to his poll reports, Greenberg's analysis had expanded beyond polls to include subtle analyses of public opinion.

What is most important for understanding the evolution of presidential polling is not who polled, or even how much was spent on polling, but rather how the polls were used and why. Whereas the *Wall Street Journal* and comments made later by Morris implied that the Clinton administration depended on polls as an instrument of governing, such criticisms fail to acknowledge that previous administrations (for example, Nixon and Reagan) behaved similarly, albeit arguably to a lesser degree. In July of 1993, Greenberg acknowledged that polls were used to keep pressure on Congress, stating in a *National Journal* article that, "We need popular support to keep the pressure on Congress to vote for change . . . I view my role as how to keep the people with us through some very tough decisions."[28]

By helping the president frame his message, Greenberg was following a trend begun by Messrs. Cantril, Harris, Quayle, O'Neill, and Wirthlin. If Greenberg and his successors are to be faulted, it is not for conducting many polls and focus groups, but rather, as Bob Teeter in the *Wall Street Journal* article writes, for amassing so much data that they could not see the forest through the trees. That putting pressure on Congress was explicitly stated as a reason to use polls and focus groups underscores how presidents seek autonomy from institutions that could gauge and sway public opinion. As data from the Bush and forthcoming Clinton Library become more available, scholars and journalists will learn the extent to which these two presidents used polls with the intent of gaining autonomy and power from potentially competitive institutions such as Congress, the media, and their respective parties. The limited, available data strongly suggest that President Clinton advanced polling and public opinion analyses, much like many of his predecessors did. Clinton's pollsters used more focus groups and one should expect future presidential pollsters – Republican and Democrat alike – to follow Greenberg's lead by conducting focus groups that allow respondents to explain their views and policy preferences.

---

[26] Barnes, "Polls Apart," pp. 1751, 1753.

[27] Greenberg was deposed of his duties after the 1994 midterm elections, and was replaced by Dick Morris, Mark Penn, and Doug Schoen.

[28] Barnes, "Polls Apart," p. 1750.

CONCLUSION

A Burgeoning Presidency or Simply More Autonomy?

According to Sidney Milkis, Roosevelt replaced the Democratic Party with his alphabet programs as the political institutions that linked government with the citizenry. The result was a weakened Democratic Party and a concentration of presidential power now located in the executive branch, resulting in "a distressing deterioration of representative democracy."[29] Milkis contends that this transformation toward a strong presidency was intentionally designed and intended to weaken parties' role as the principal institutional conduit encouraging political participation among the mass electorate.

[T]he New Deal did not simply replace constitutional government with an administrative state; rather, the programmatic rights of the New Deal constituted the beginning of an administrative constitution, which was shielded from the uncertainties of public opinion, political parties, and elections.[30]

The history and evolution of presidential polling confirms Milkis' analysis. Developments in the field of public opinion research utilized in the FDR administration coincide with the growth of the federal government and the presidential branch in particular.[31] By using polls, FDR avoided isolation from the public, even as he shaped the Democratic Party to his liking.

Milkis' assertion that institutional changes in the presidency helped debilitate parties also must be reviewed in light of the data concerning the unique relationship between parties and presidents as it relates to presidential polls. Parties have paid for polls in the post-Kennedy era, but their role in the presidential polling process has been generally limited to that of financier. During the Nixon administration, for example, polls were sanitized for party elites. In this sense, presidents were dependent on parties, for without them, they could not privately poll. By retaining a sense of confidentiality about public opinion data, presidents have been able to maintain their private polls as proprietary information not to be shared with others. As a result, it is now considered commonplace and acceptable for presidents to conduct private polls, even as the poll results are interpreted in secret.

---

[29] Milkis, *The President and the Parties*, p. 255.
[30] Ibid., 145.
[31] Paid civilian employment in the federal government has grown threefold from 1935 to 1970. *Historical Statistics of the United States: Colonial Times to 1970, Part 2.* Washington, DC: U.S. Bureau of the Census, Series Y 308–317, p. 1102.

The President as Representative

As presidents use polls to measure public opinion, the concept of the president as representative demands reevaluation.[32] While Alexander Hamilton contended that "energy in the executive is a leading character in the definition of good government," both Federalists and anti-Federalists thought that legislators were to represent the citizens; presidents would execute the laws of the nation. Fast forward to the 1950s, when Congress learned of secret State Department polls. Legislators objected vehemently, exclaiming that the executive branch used funds that had not been appropriated for polls and that the executive branch was usurping a function of Congress. By secretly polling, the executive branch had deemed Congress irrelevant in the process of measuring public opinion.

Independence from Congress has had its costs, especially as it relates to executive-legislative relations. Charles Jones argues that public support is an elusive variable in analyzing presidential power and that presidents are often unsuccessful in fostering good relations with Congress.[33] When the executive branch began to measure public opinion without the aid of the legislative branch, tensions flared between White House advisers and members of Congress. Rather than accept the conventional wisdom that "gridlock" often explains executive-legislative tensions, this study suggests that independent polling by presidents was part of a strategy to boost the popularity of presidents and their programs, even at the expense of alienating members of Congress in the process. George Edwards underscores this point:

[T]here are very real limits to what public support can do for the president. The impact of public approval or disapproval on the support the president receives in Congress occurs at the margins of the effort to build coalitions behind proposed polices. No matter how low presidential standing dips, the president will still receive support from a substantial number of senators and representatives. Similarly, no matter how high approval levels climb, a significant portion of Congress will still oppose certain presidential policies... Public approval gives the president leverage, not control.[34]

Some individual members of Congress have come to expect poor treatment from the White House, especially those of a different party than the president.

[32] See Gary L. Gregg, II, *The Presidential Republic: Executive Management and Deliberative Democracy*. Lanham, MD: Rowman & Littlefield, 1997; Karen Hoffman, "The President as Representative: The Founders' Intent." M.A. thesis, unpublished, University of Chicago, 1992.

[33] Charles O. Jones, *The Presidency in a Separated System*. Washington, DC: The Brookings Institute, 1992, pp. 25, 112–146.

[34] Edwards, "Frustration and Folly," p. 254.

As Ric Uslaner notes in his book about the decline of congressional comity, those expectations are often fulfilled.[35]

Whether or not presidential polling has been a critical factor in exacerbating bad executive-legislative relations deserves further analysis, especially by those who argue, as Mark Peterson does, that the legislative successes of both branches have depended on their working in tandem with one another.[36] Presidents' success in usurping public opinion–measuring from Congress, parties, and the media bolster Peterson, Jones, and Lowi's arguments that the American government has become presidency centered, and that the presidency has become increasingly personalized and legislative.[37] By allowing the presidency to perform this function without question, Congress may be further abdicating its responsibility to represent the citizenry. As the relationship between Congress and the presidency continues to evolve, the role of gauging public opinion should be advanced into the current scholarly discussion.[38]

As presidential polling has proliferated in the past thirty years, members of Congress have twice sought to implement a national public opinion data bank. In the 1970s, Congressman Morgan F. Murphy (D-IL) sought to create an Office of Congressional Polling. The bill was tabled and never signed into law. Twenty years later, in 1994, Congressman Ron Klink (D-PA) and Congresswoman Cynthia McKinney (D-GA) offered a similar bill. It too was tabled and died in committee. That both of these bills died an unnewsworthy death suggests that a federally funded congressional polling operation is unlikely to resurrect itself, and if it does, it is not likely to become law. Congress will continue to receive polls from their party caucuses, and individual congresspersons will poll as they choose, leaving presidents ample opportunity to conduct private polls and function as the nation's executive representative.

Deliberation, Public Opinion, and Public Relations

Benjamin Ginsberg and Christopher Hitchens have described polls as potentially debilitating forces in democracy. To them, polling enervates the citizenry by mollifying it to accept the predispositions of the state. Susan Herbst argues that polls may have another deleterious effect:

[P]olls encourage a structured, reactive sort of participation, making it unnecessary to generate our own forms of public expression... There is some evidence that

35 Eric M. Uslaner, *The Decline of Comity in Congress*. Ann Arbor: University of Michigan Press, 1993.
36 See Peterson, *Legislating Together*.
37 See ibid.; Jones, *The Presidency in a Separated System*; and Lowi, *The Personal President*.
38 See, for example, Louis Fisher, *The Politics of Shared Power: Congress and the Executive*, 4th ed. College Station: Texas A&M University Press, 1998.

polling may discourage certain forms of political participation by instigating bandwagons . . . I contend that the rigid, structured nature of polling may narrow the range of public discourse by defining the boundaries for public debate, and by influencing the ways journalists report on politics.[39]

Hitchens takes this point to another level, arguing that, "Pollsters, in effect, wield the gavel at the town meeting – framing a question to limit, warp, or actually guarantee the answer."[40] The evolution of presidential polling complicates the contention that polls debilitate representative government, even as public opinion increasingly has become defined as poll data. Presidents now trust polls as scientific instruments to tell them what the American people are thinking. However presidents and their advisers do not envision themselves either as Burkean trustees or as plebiscitarians who decide what to do based on the views of the electorate. To the contrary, ample evidence indicates that presidents use polls to tailor agendas and market policies, not to reverse their policy preferences, or to preserve them regardless of citizens' views.[41] No doubt, presidents vary in how they interpret their polls. LBJ's polls, for example, showed that his advisers sometimes used polls to confirm their political predilections. But one can argue that they employed their methods at their own peril, as LBJ's administration's policies concerning Vietnam ultimately clashed over time with public opinion; similarly, Nixon's White House ultimately became a bunker of clandestine activity and distrust.

The evolution of presidential polls has enhanced accountability, for their absence may result in presidents' relying on unscientific means of gauging public opinion. In this regard, the argument that polls debilitate deliberation is tempered by data from the presidential archives. Despite the protestations of Hitchens, Ginsberg, Herbst, and others, presidential polls have provided political elites with a reliable means to ascertain what concerns the mass citizenry.

If presidential polls aid representative democracy in one sense, they attenuate it in another. By equating polls and public opinion, some presidential advisers appear to have downplayed the deliberative nature of public opinion.[42] Polls are wonderful instruments to monitor the public's mood, but they are difficult tools to calibrate intensity of attitude, or to understand why particular views are held. It is not surprising, therefore, to see the Reagan and Clinton administrations using focus groups, in part, to assess the underlying "whys" behind certain poll responses. One should expect

---

[39] Herbst, *Numbered Voices*, p. 166.
[40] Hitchens, "Voting in the Passive Voice," p. 46.
[41] Jacobs and Shapiro, *Politicians Don't Pander*.
[42] Daniel Yankelovich, *Coming to Public Judgment: Making Democracy Work in a Complex World*. Syracuse, NY: Syracuse University Press, 1991; James S. Fishkin, *Democracy and Deliberation: New Directions for Democratic Reform*. New Haven, CT: Yale University Press, 1991; Elisabeth Noelle-Neumann, *The Spiral of Silence: Our Social Skin, Third Edition*. Chicago: University of Chicago Press, 1998.

presidential polling to include more sophisticated and elaborate focus group usage, in order to understand the vocabulary of the mass public and to incorporate their vernacular to gain public approval and, ultimately, congressional support.

Here again, the qualitative analysis of public opinion has both benefits and costs. While the textured analysis provided depth beyond the mere numbers which can be interpreted in multiple ways, what is also noticeable has been the personal and politicized nature of presidential poll reports over time. On several occasions, presidential pollsters invoked broader themes into their poll analyses and summaries. Harris and Quayle infused their poll reports with theories about religion and race respectively, even though their polls did not readily determine the extent to which these topics were a factor in voters' preferences. Caddell regularly infused his ideas and theories in his poll reports. These pollsters assumed that their theories were valid and included them in their respective analyses. The failure of presidential advisers to question these theories underscores how powerful the presidential pollster has become in American politics. That these advisers accepted pollsters' interpretations of polls even when they were sometimes loosely linked to raw numbers, suggests that White House advisers sought and trusted the pollsters' thematic interpretations of polls. By using focus groups, the unelected presidential pollster must be keenly aware of their nonrepresentativeness. But presidential advisers may not, and if they mistakenly assume that a dozen housewives speak for the nation, then gross miscalculations will be made about what and when the public desires and needs.

The rise of presidential polling also reveals how the relationship between public relations and public opinion gathering has become increasingly intertwined. When Presidents Johnson and Nixon instructed their speech writers to note trends in poll data, one learns that both presidents valued polls for purposes beyond gauging public opinion. When Eisenhower attempted to hire his primary dispatcher of polls, Sig Larmon, he did so to streamline a White House public relations office. Stan Greenberg, President Clinton's pollster, spoke about a prevailing suspicion in the White House that the press may not provide a favorable climate for the president, and how he, as the White House pollster, served as a conduit between the president and the media.[43] Here is where this historical analysis is particularly fruitful. While John Harris suggests that the Clinton administration's "reliance" on polls played a "central role" in the policy-making process, the evolution of presidential polling suggests that the Clinton era continued a path paved by his predecessors.[44] Since FDR, polls frequently were used for public relations purposes,

---

[43] Telephone conversation with Stan Greenberg, June 6, 2000.

[44] John F. Harris, "A Clouded Mirror: Bill Clinton, Polls, and the Politics of Survival." In *The Post-Modern Presidency: Bill Clinton's Legacy in U.S. Politics*, edited by Steven E. Schier. Pittsburgh: University of Pittsburgh Press, 2000, p. 93.

often as a direct link between measuring public opinion and marketing an idea or policy. While the Clinton presidential archival data ultimately will substantiate or refute Harris' claim of the "primacy" of Clinton's pollsters, the evolution of presidential polling reveals a blurring of the lines between public opinion and public relations. There is every indication that the future will be even fuzzier, especially if old-fashioned arm twisting is met with congressional resistance.

Haldeman, Polls, and Propaganda

It is only apt to return to the Nixon presidency, which in many ways represents an extreme in letting politics guide polling operations and using polling operations to influence politics. Haldeman's experience with surveys from his work in advertising enabled him to organize and administer a complex polling operation in the Nixon White House. But Haldeman's expertise did not temper his political passions. For example, one Nixon poll question read "Should the government give financial aid to parochial schools so their students won't be dumped into the public school system?"[45] This question is worded to evoke a particular answer and not to assess genuine public opinion about financial aid to parochial schools. Can polls be misused in this regard? Surely. But blaming presidential polling for creating an ersatz response is both misguided and illogical. President Nixon's staff also kept tabs on the amount and type of mail being sent to the White House, and used the mail as a means of manipulating public opinion.

> Now that we are well into the school year, the Children's Mail is also on the increase and we are taking a closer look at this to see if we can get a little more mileage out of it in terms of its human interest value.[46]

Additionally, the White House Office of Communications asked ORC to track the "feedback" of an ORC press release about Nixon's proposed trip to Mainland China. "[Newspaper] [c]lippings are still coming in at a substantial rate per week," wrote Leonard Milchuk, director of Communications at ORC. "We have 93 clippings on the story that represent a circulation factor of 11,796,218. This exceeds our previous best release by 2,401,494."[47] In short, if a president desires to manipulate or fabricate public opinion, he need not use polls to do so.

While the mail and phone calls indicate that some advisers found all measures of public opinion worthy of tracking, Haldeman's background in

---

45 Gerald Ford Library [GRFL], ORC Poll, January 3–20, 1972, Question 22–14, Teeter Files.
46 RMNP@NA, "President's Handwriting October 1 thru October 15, 1971," Memorandum from Roland Elliott to Ray Price, October 14, 1971, President's Office File – President's Handwriting File, 10/71–11/15/71, Box 14.
47 RMNP@NA, "Polls Chron July–August 1971," Leonard C. Milchuk, Jr., to DeVan L. Shumay, assistant to the Director of Communications, August 23, 1971, HRH Files, Box 335.

marketing and advertising helped him understand the interconnectedness of elections, policies, and public opinion. To Haldeman, polls were essential to market the president. Lengthy, thematic interpretations of poll data were replaced by press releases, for brief poll summaries were for dissemination – to the media, to members of Congress, cabinet officials, speechwriters, and schedulers.[48] Haldeman's tight leash on who could access poll data, the secrecy underlying the internal polls, the multiple attempts to discredit media pollsters, the use of polls to alter schedules, and the constant drumbeat of publicity that surrounded poll data reveal how Nixon's polling operation surpassed all other presidents in using polls for politicized purposes.

Will Congress Mimic the President?

Why Congress has trailed presidents in adopting polls is the theme of another study, but part of the answer may be that members of Congress genuinely believe that a representative poll is no substitute for person-to-person contact or deliberative interaction such as a constituent who takes the time to write a letter. When I asked one senator how he gauged public opinion, the senator eagerly showed me his office's tabulations of incoming mail. When I mentioned to him that these numbers are unrepresentative of his constituents, he answered:

The mail is representative of elites who care. I use mail, telephone contacts, and question and answer sessions with my constituents as the primary means to measure public opinion. I rarely use opinion polls. I don't want to be making decisions based on polls. Also, polls are expensive.[49]

Similarly, a former senator's chief of staff confirmed that his former boss infrequently used polls:

Two years before an election, maybe we'll do a poll to ask about popularity, our opponent or a few issues. But by and large, we do not use polls to find out what the state is thinking. We talk to key people, we ask people, we count the letters, and we discount the letters we get out of state.[50]

A letter from another senator substantiates the point that members of Congress trail presidents in their trust of polls as accurate devices for gauging attitudes. When asked how he measured public opinion of his constituents, the senator replied, "First of all, I gauge public opinion through direct contact with constituents during my frequent travels back to the state. Also,

---

[48] For discussions about presidential symbolism and communication, see Barbara Hinckley, *The Symbolic Presidency: How Presidents Portray Themselves*. New York: Routledge, 1990, and Samuel L. Popkin, *The Reasoning Voter: Communication and Persuasion in Presidential Campaigns*. Chicago: University of Chicago Press, 1991.

[49] Interview with Senator Charles Grassley, August 3, 1994.

[50] Interview with Rob McDonald, former chief of staff to former Senator John Danforth, August 3, 1994.

reading my mail and keeping track of phone calls are important." When asked if he tabulated the mail and telephone calls, or if he disregarded these methods because of potential biases in favor of "issue publics," the senator answered as follows: "I do tabulate letters and phone calls. Obviously these are an important factor in gauging public opinion, but I also realize that certain organized phone and letter campaigns, while significant in volume, sometimes do not represent a majority of my constituents." He continued:

Do you ever conduct public opinion polls of Iowans to help ascertain public opinion on certain issues? Sometimes I have included surveys (unscientific) in some mailing back to the state, asking constituents to let me know their feeling on a particular issue. Moreover, during election cycles my campaign organization does conduct some polling.

If so, what do polls enable you to do that other methods of gauging public opinion cannot do? Polls, because they are scientific, can give me an accurate reflection of public opinion on a given issue on a given day. Again, however, they are only one tool among many that I use to gauge public opinion. Polls cannot always tell you the strength of feeling or the priority that constituents place on certain issues.[51]

Finally, an adviser to another senator remarked that her boss receives a weekly "Voice of the People" memo, outlining tabulations of phone calls and letters.[52] Note in all of these responses a repeated downplaying of polls. To be a polling president is to be an engaged chief executive pursuing a strategy of gaining public approval. To be a member of Congress extensively conducting private polls, is, I suspect, tantamount to being negligent in not communicating personally with one's constituents.

Unanswered questions remain concerning how technology has affected the trajectory of presidential polling. It took until 1969 for the presidency to organize a tightly run polling operation. Why did it take so long, considering the legislative presidency and growth of the presidential branch had already been established?[53] Why did Johnson's advisers allow for the use of nonrepresentative polling techniques? Why were computer simulation experiments quickly abandoned without exploring their merits in greater depth?

The answers to these questions may be found in institutional intransigence and personalities. Some of the players who helped institutionalize presidential polling did not reflect on the theories underlying their mode of operation. Rather, they sought to advance these theories by increasing the amount of what they were doing (for example, Harris' providing more examples that religion is a crucial factor, Haldeman's seeking numerous ways to coopt media pollsters). Each administration developed an internal polling strategy.

---

[51] Letter from Senator Tom Harkin, September 22, 1994.
[52] Conversation with Valerie West, aide to Senator Gordon Smith, June 21, 2000.
[53] See Milkis, *The President and the Parties*; Stephen J. Wayne, *The Legislative Presidency*. New York: Harper & Row, 1978; and Nelson W. Polsby, *Consequences of Party Reform*. New York: Oxford University Press, 1983.

Over time, the same people often read and wrote different polls. What resulted was a dearth of reevaluation apropos polling within many presidents'
terms.[54]

A former senior policy adviser to Vice President Gore asked me how I
thought White House officials envisioned polls. I asked her if she wanted
to ask me how I thought polls were used. She remained adamant in her
wording and then answered her own question. "Polls," she said, "provide
an illusion of certainty. Outside of the academy, there are few people who
understand social science and research methods. Provide a table, a graph,
and a chi-square, and you've got the whole room thinking you're a genius."[55]

Presidents and their advisers appreciate not just poll data, but the pollsters
who amass the data. The opinions of the people are tabulated, interpreted,
and misinterpreted by presidential advisers. The processes by which White
House advisers listen to *vox populi* have altered the nature of the presidency, parties, Congress, the media, and representative democracy. To think
otherwise would be to ignore the evolution of presidential polling.

[54] For more discussion about the inability of institutions to adapt to changing environments,
see Mary Douglas, *How Institutions Think*. Syracuse, NY: Syracuse University Press, 1986.
[55] Conversation with Elaine Kamarck, August 1994, Washington, DC.

Bibliography

"1-800-TROUBLE," *The New York Times*, Editorial, June 13, 1992, A22.

"A New Situation," Forward, *Public Opinion Quarterly* 1 (1937): 3.

"A Third Pollster in the White House," *Newsweek*, July 5, 1982, 17.

Abrams, Mark. *Social Surveys and Social Action*. London: William Heinemann, 1951.

Achen, Christopher H. "Mass Political Attitudes and the Survey Response," *American Political Science Review* 69 (1975): 1218–1231.

———. "Measuring Representation: Perils of the Correlation Coefficient," *American Journal of Political Science* 4 (1977): 805–815.

"A Good Word for Polls," *The Washington Post*, Editorial, December 10, 1993, A30.

Albig, William. "Two Decades of Opinion Study: 1936–1956," *Public Opinion Quarterly* 21 (1956): 14–22.

———. *Public Opinion*. New York: McGraw Hill, 1939.

Allen, Craig. *Eisenhower and the Mass Media: Peace, Prosperity & Prime-Time TV*. Chapel Hill: University of North Carolina Press, 1993.

Allport, Gordon W. "Attitudes." In *A Handbook of Social Psychology*, edited by Carl Murchison. Worcester, MA: Clark University Press, 1935.

Alpert, Harry. "Opinion and Attitude Surveys in the U.S. Government," *Public Opinion Quarterly* 16 (1952): 33–41.

———. "Public Opinion Research as Science," *Public Opinion Quarterly* 20 (1956): 494–500.

Altschuler, Bruce E. *Keeping a Finger on the Public Pulse: Private Polling and Presidential Elections*. Westport, CT: Greenwood Press, 1982.

———. *LBJ and the Polls*. Gainesville: University of Florida Press, 1990.

Ambrose, Stephen E. *Eisenhower: Soldier and President*. New York: Simon and Schuster, 1990.

Archival Data, Dwight David Eisenhower Library.

Archival Data, Franklin Delano Roosevelt Library.

Archival Data, George H.W. Bush Library.

Archival Data, Gerald R. Ford Library.

Archival Data, Jimmy Carter Library.

Archival Data, John Fitzgerald Kennedy Library.

Archival Data, Lyndon Baines Johnson Library.

Archival Data, Richard M. Nixon Project, National Archives.

Arterton, F. Christopher. *Teledemocracy: Can Technology Protect Democracy?* Washington, DC: Sage Publications, 1987.

Ayers, B. Drummond, Jr. "G.O.P. Keeps Tabs on Nation's Mood," *The New York Times*, November 16, 1981, A20.

Baker, Russell. "Polls Aren't Perfect, But They Beat Chicken Entrails," *Wisconsin State Journal*, November 8, 1991.

Barber, Benjamin R. *Strong Democracy: Participatory Politics for a New Age.* Berkeley: University of California Press, 1984.

Barber, James David. *The Pulse of Politics: Electing Presidents in the Media Age.* New Brunswick, NJ: Transaction Publishers, 1992.

Barclay, Thomas S. "The Publicity Division of the Democratic Party, 1929–30," *American Political Science Review* 25 (1931): 68–72.

Barnes, James A. "The Endless Campaign," *National Journal* (February 20, 1993): 460–462.

———. "Polls Apart," *National Journal*, July 10, 1993, 1750–1754.

Barone, Michael. "The Power of the Presidents' Pollsters," *Public Opinion* 11 (September/October 1988): 2–57.

Bauer, Wilhelm. "Public Opinion." In *Encyclopaedia of the Social Sciences, Vol. XI*, edited by Edwin R.A. Seligman. New York: Macmillan, pp. 669–674.

Beal, Richard S., and Ronald H. Hinckley. "Presidential Decision Making and Opinion Polls," *Annals of the American Academy of the Political and Social Sciences* 472 (1984): 72–84.

Berelson, Bernard. "The Study of Public Opinion." In *The State of the Social Sciences*, edited by Leonard D. White. Chicago: University of Chicago Press, 1956, pp. 299–318.

Bernays, Edward L. *Propaganda*. New York: Liveright, 1928.

———. "Attitude Polls – Servants or Masters?" *Public Opinion Quarterly* 9 (1945): 264–268.

Bernstein, Irving. *Guns or Butter: The Presidency of Lyndon Johnson.* New York: Oxford University Press, 1996.

Binkley, Wilfred E. *American Political Parties: Their Natural History.* New York: Knopf, 1947.

Bloom, Allan, ed. *Confronting the Constitution.* Washington, DC: AEI Press, 1990.

Blumer, Herbert. "Public Opinion and Public Opinion Polling," *American Sociology Review* 13 (1948): 542–554.

Bonafede, Dom. "Carter and the Polls – If You Live By Them, You May Die By Them," *National Journal* 10 (August 19, 1978): 1312–1313.

———. "As Pollster to the President, Wirthlin Is Where the Action Is," *National Journal* 13 (December 12, 1981): 2184–2188.

Bonaparte, Charles J. "Government by Public Opinion," *Forum* 40 (1908): 384–390.

Bond, Jon, and Richard Fleisher. *The President in the Legislative Arena.* Chicago: University of Chicago Press, 1990.

Bornet, Vaughn Davis. *The Presidency of Lyndon Baines Johnson.* Lawrence: University Press of Kansas, 1983.

Bourdieu, Pierre. "Public Opinion Does Not Exist." In *Communication and Class Struggle*, edited by Armand Mattelart and Seth Siegelaub. New York: International General, 1979, pp. 124–130.

Bowles, Nigel. *The White House and Capitol Hill: The Politics of Presidential Persuasion*. Oxford: Clarendon Press, 1987.

Brace, Paul, and Barbara Hinckley. *Follow the Leader: Opinion Polls and the Modern Presidents*. New York: Basic Books, 1992.

Bradburn, Norman M., and Seymour Sudman. *Polls and Surveys: Understanding What They Tell Us*. San Francisco: Jossey-Bass, 1988.

Brady, Henry E., and Richard Johnston. "What's the Primary Message: Horserace or Issue Journalism?" In *Media and Momentum: The New Hampshire Primary and Nomination Politics*, edited by Gary R. Orren and Nelson W. Polsby. Chatham, NJ: Chatham House, 1987, pp. 127–188.

Branch, Taylor. *Pillar of Fire: America in the King Years 1963–65*. New York: Simon and Schuster, 1998.

Branyan, Robert L., and Lawrence H. Larsen. *The Eisenhower Administration 1953–1961: A Documentary History*. New York: Random House, 1971.

Brezovšek, Marjan. "Changing Attitudes Towards Political Representation," *Javnost, The Public* 4 (1997): 105–118.

Broder, David S. *The Party's Over: The Failure of Politics in America*. New York: Harper & Row, 1972.

Brody, Richard A. *Assessing the President: The Media, Elite Opinion, and Public Support*. Stanford, CA: Stanford University Press, 1991.

Brooks, Robert C. *Political Parties and Electoral Problems, Third Edition*. New York: Harper & Brothers, 1933.

Bruce, John M., John A. Clark, and John A. Kessel. "Advocacy Politics in Presidential Parties," *American Political Science Review* 85 (1991): 1089–1105.

Bryce, James. *The American Commonwealth, Vol. II*. New York and London: Macmillan, [1889] 1981.

Bulmer, Martin, Kevin Bales, and Katheryn Kish Sklar. *The Social Survey in Historical Perspective 1880–1940*. Cambridge: Cambridge University Press, 1990.

Bulmer, Martin. "The Methodology of Early Social Indicator Research: William Fielding Ogburn and 'Recent Social Trends', 1933," *Social Indicators Research* 13 (1983): 109–130.

Burdick, Eugene. *The 480*. New York: Dell, 1964.

Burke, Edmund. "Speech to the Electors of Bristol (3 November 1774)," *The Works of the Right Honorable Edmund Burke*. Boston: Little, Brown, and Company, 1889.

Burner, David. *Herbert Hoover: A Public Life*. New York: Knopf, 1979.

Burnham, Walter Dean. *The Current Crisis in American Politics*. New York: Oxford University Press, 1982.

Burns, James MacGregor. *Roosevelt: The Lion and the Fox*, New York: Harvest, 1956.

———. *The Deadlock of Democracy: Four-Party Politics in America*. Englewood Cliffs, NJ: Prentice Hall, 1963.

———. *Leadership*. New York: Harper & Row, 1978.

———. *The Power to Lead: The Crisis of the American Presidency*. New York: Simon and Schuster, 1984.

———. *Presidential Government: The Crucible of Leadership*. Boston: Houghton Mifflin, 1966.

Caesar, James. *Presidential Selection: Theory and Development*. Princeton, NJ: Princeton University Press, 1979.

Cameron, Charles M. *Veto Bargaining: Presidents and the Politics of Negative Power*. New York: Cambridge University Press, 2000.

Campbell, Colin, and Bert A. Rockman, eds. *The Clinton Presidency: First Appraisals*. Chatham, NJ: Chatham House, 1996.

Cantril, Albert. *The Opinion Connection: Polling, Politics, and the Press*. Washington, DC: Congressional Quarterly Press, 1991.

Cantril, Hadley. *Gauging Public Opinion*. Princeton, NJ: Princeton University Press, 1947.

_____. "Straw Votes This Year Show Contrary Winds," *The New York Times*, October 25, 1936, A3.

_____. *The Human Dimension: Experiences in Policy Research*. New Brunswick, NJ: Rutgers University Press, 1967.

Carlson, Peter. "Hocus Focus," *The Washington Post Magazine*, February 14, 1993, 15–30.

Carney, James. "Playing by the Numbers," *Time*, April 11, 1994, 40.

Caro, Robert A. "Annals of Politics: The Johnson Years: The Old and the New, II – Whirlwind," *The New Yorker*, January 22, 1990, 58.

"Carter's Outside Insiders," *Business Week*, June 27, 1977, 94.

"Carter's Pollster," *Time*, August 6, 1979, 14.

Casey, Ralph D. "Republican Propaganda in the 1936 Campaign," *Public Opinion Quarterly* 1 (1937): 27–44.

Chubb, John E., and Paul E. Petersen, eds. *The New Direction in American Politics*. Washington, DC: The Brookings Institute, 1985.

Citizens and Politics: A View from Main Street America. Prepared for the Kettering Foundation by The Harwood Group, 1991.

_____. "Poll Takers Say It Was the Economy, Stupid, but Future Is Less Clear," *The New York Times*, May 24, 1993, A12.

Collier, Kenneth E. *Between the Branches: The White House Office of Legislative Affairs*. Pittsburgh: University of Pittsburgh Press, 1997.

Congressional Quarterly, Congress and the Nation, Vol. II, 1965–1968. Washington, DC: CQ Press, 1969.

Connelly, Gordon M. "Now Let's Look at the Real Problem: Validity," *Public Opinion Quarterly* 9 (1945): 51–60.

Converse, Jean. *History of Survey Research in the United States*. Berkeley: University of California Press, 1987.

Converse, Philip E. "The Nature of Belief Systems in Mass Publics." In *Ideology and Discontent*, edited by David E. Apter. New York: Free Press, 1964, pp. 206–261.

_____. "Public Opinion and Voting Behavior." In *Handbook of Political Science: Nongovernmental Politics, Vol. 4*, edited by Fred I. Greenstein and Nelson W. Polsby. Reading, MA: Addison-Wesley, 1975, pp. 75–169.

_____. "Changing Conception of Public Opinion in the Political Process," *Public Opinion Quarterly* 51 (1987): S12–S24.

Converse, Philip, and Michael W. Traugott. "Assessing the Accuracy of Polls and Surveys," *Science* 234 (November 28, 1986): 1094–1098.

Cornwell, Elmer E., Jr. "Wilson, Creel, and the Presidency," *Public Opinion Quarterly* 23 (1959): 189–202.

———. *Presidential Leadership of Public Opinion*. Bloomington: Indiana University Press, 1965.

———. "Coolidge and Presidential Leadership," *Public Opinion Quarterly* 21 (1957): 265–278.

Corwin, Edward S. *The President: Office and Powers, Fourth Edition*. New York: New York University Press, 1957.

Council of American Survey Research Organizations (CASRO), *Code of Standards for Survey Research*, 1995.

Crespi, Irving. *Public Opinion, Polls and Democracy*. Boulder, CO: Westview Press, 1989.

Cronin, Thomas E. *The State of the Presidency, Second Edition*. Boston: Little Brown, 1980.

———. *Direct Democracy: The Politics of Initiative, Referendum, and Recall*. Cambridge, MA: Harvard University Press, 1989.

———. "How Much is His Fault?" *The New York Times Magazine*, October 16, 1994, 56.

Crossley, Archibald M. "Early Days of Public Opinion Research," *Public Opinion Quarterly* 21 (1957): 159–164.

———. "Straw Polls in 1936," *Public Opinion Quarterly* 1 (1937): 24–35.

Dallek, Robert. *Franklin D. Roosevelt and American Foreign Policy, 1932–1945*. New York: Oxford University Press, 1979.

———. *Flawed Giant: Lyndon Johnson and His Times 1961–1973*. New York: Oxford University Press, 1998.

Delaire, Alexis. "Observation in Social Science," translated from the *Revue des Deux Mondes* (with some abridgment) by J. Fitzgerald. *Popular Science Monthly* (1877), 1–13.

Delli Carpini, Michael X., and Bruce Williams, "The Method is the Message: Focus Groups as a Method of Social, Psychological, and Political Inquiry." In *Research in Micropolitics: New Directions in Political Psychology*, edited by Michael X. Delli Carpini, Leonie Huddy, and Robert Y. Shapiro. Greenwich, CT: JAI Press, 1994, pp. 57–84.

"Democracy's Emil Hurja," *Time*, March 2, 1936, 16–18, 27.

de Tocqueville, Alexis. *Democracy in America*, edited by J.P. Mayer. New York: Perennial Library, [1850] 1988.

Diamond, Sigmund. "Some Early Uses of the Questionnaire: Views on Education and Immigration," *Public Opinion Quarterly* 27 (1963): 528–542.

Dionne, E.J., Jr. "The Business of Pollsters," *The New York Times*, June 29, 1980, Sec. 3, 1.

———. *Why Americans Hate Politics*. New York: Simon and Schuster, 1991.

Dorsett, Lyle W. *FDR and the City Bosses*. Port Washington, NY: Kennikat Press, 1977.

Douglas, Mary. *How Institutions Think*. Syracuse, NY: Syracuse University Press, 1986.

Downs, Anthony. *An Economic Theory of Democracy*. New York: Harper, 1957.

Doyle, William. *Inside the Oval Office: White House Tapes from FDR to Clinton*. New York: Kodansha International, 1999.

"Dr. Gallup Chided by Digest Editor," *The New York Times*, July 19, 1936, A21.

Drew, Elizabeth. "A Reporter at Large: In Search of Definition," *The New Yorker*, August 27, 1979, 45–73.

———. *On The Edge: The Clinton Presidency*. New York: Simon and Schuster, 1994.

Dryzek, John S. "The Mismeasure of Political Man," *Journal of Politics* 50 (1988): 705–725.

Duverger, Maurice. *Political Parties: Their Organization and Activity in the Modern State*, translated by Barbara and Robert North. London: Meuthen & Co, 1961.

Edwards, George C., III. "Frustration and Folly: Bill Clinton and the Public Presidency." In *The Clinton Presidency: First Appraisals*, edited by Colin Campbell and Bert A. Rockman. Chatham, NJ: Chatham House, 1996, pp. 234–261.

Edwards, George C., and Stephen J. Wayne. *Presidential Leadership: Politics and Policy Marking, Third Edition*. New York: St. Martin's Press, 1994.

Edwards, Lynda. "The Focusing of the President," *The Village Voice*, June 23, 1992, 25–29.

Eisinger, Robert M. "Pollster and Public Relations Advisor: Hadley Cantril and the Birth of Presidential Polling," Paper presented to the Annual Meeting of the American Association of Public Opinion Research (AAPOR), Danvers, MA, 1994.

Eldersfeld, Samuel J. *Political Parties: A Behavioral Analysis*. Chicago: Rand McNally, 1964.

"Electronic Democracy: The PEN is Mighty," *The Economist*, February 1, 1992, 96.

Euchner, Charles C. "Public Support and Opinion." In *The Presidents and the Public*. Washington, DC: CQ Press, 1990, pp. 75–90.

Evans, Jr., Rowland, and Robert D. Novak. *Nixon in the White House: The Frustration of Power*. New York: Random House, 1971.

"Face Off: A Conversation with the President's Pollsters Patrick Caddell and Richard Wirthlin," *Public Opinion*, December–January 1981, 2.

Fausold, Martin L. *The Presidency of Herbert C. Hoover*. Lawrence: University of Kansas Press, 1985.

Fenno, Richard F., Jr. *Homestyle: House Members in Their Districts*. Boston: Little Brown, 1978.

Fisher, Louis. *The Politics of Shared Power: Congress and the Executive, 4th ed.* College Station: Texas A&M University Press, 1998.

Fishkin, James S. *Voice of the People*. New Haven, CT: Yale University Press, 1995.

———. *Democracy and Deliberation*. New Haven, CT: Yale University Press, 1991.

Ford, Gerald R. "Imperiled, Not Imperial," *Time*, November 10, 1980, 31.

Foster, H. Schuyler, Jr., and Carl J. Friedrich. "Letters to the Editor as a Means of Measuring the Effectiveness of Propaganda," *American Political Science Review* 31 (1937): 71–79.

Franklin, Fabian. "Refiguring the Digest Poll," *The New York Times*, October 28, 1936, 24.

Frisch, Morton J., ed. *Selected Writings and Speeches of Alexander Hamilton*. Washington, DC: American Enterprise Institute, 1985.

Gallup, George. "Government and the Sampling Referendum," *Journal of the American Statistical Association* 33 (1939): 131–142.

———. "Polls and the Political Process: Past, Present, and Future," *Public Opinion Quarterly* 29 (1945): 544–549.

———. "The Changing Climate for Public Opinion Research," *Public Opinion Quarterly* 21 (1957): 23–32.

Gallup, George, and Saul Forbes Rae. *The Pulse of Democracy: The Public-Opinion Poll and How It Works*. New York: Simon and Schuster, 1940.

Geer, John G. *From Tea Leaves to Opinion Polls: A Theory of Democratic Leadership*. New York: Columbia University Press, 1996.

George, Alexander L. "Assessing Presidential Character," *World Politics* 26 (1974): 234–282.

Gerber, Robin. "You Can't Lead by Following," *The Washington Post*, December 18, 1994, C7.

Gergen, David, and William Schambra. "Pollsters and Polling," *Wilson Quarterly* 3 (1979): 61–72.

Germond, Jack, and Jules Witcover. "Politicians, Press Become Captives of Opinion Polls," *The Baltimore Sun*, March 26, 1994, 2A.

Ginsberg, Benjamin. *The Captive Public: How Mass Opinion Promotes State Power*. New York: Basic Books, 1986.

Ginsberg, Benjamin, and Martin Shefter. *Politics by Other Means: The Declining Importance of Elections in America*. New York: Basic Books, 1990.

Glickman, Harvey. "Viewing Public Opinion in Politics: A Common Sense Approach," *Public Opinion Quarterly* 23 (1960): 495–504.

Goldman, Eric F. *The Tragedy of Lyndon Johnson*. New York: Knopf, 1969.

Goodwin, Doris Kearns. *No Ordinary Time: Franklin and Eleanor Roosevelt: The Home Front in World War II*. New York: Simon and Schuster, 1994.

Graham, Tom. Telephone conversation, October 25, 1991.

Grassley, Charles. Personal interview with the author, August 3, 1994.

Greenberg, Stanley. Comments made at the American Association of Public Opinion Research 1992 Annual Meeting, St. Charles, IL.

———. Telephone conversation, June 6, 2000.

Greenstein, Fred I. *The Hidden-Hand Presidency: Eisenhower As Leader*. New York: Basic Books, 1982.

———, ed. *Leadership and the Modern Presidency*. Cambridge, MA: Harvard University Press, 1988.

Gregg, Gary L., II. *The Presidential Republic: Executive Management and Deliberative Democracy*. Lanham, MD: Rowman & Littlefield, 1997.

Halberstam, David. *The Fifties*. New York: Villard, 1993.

Haldeman, H.R. *The Haldeman Diaries*. CD-ROM. New York: Sony, 1994.

Hamby, Alonzo L. *Man of the People: A Life of Harry S. Truman*. New York: Oxford University Press, 1995.

Hamby, Alonzo L. *Beyond the New Deal: Harry S. Truman and American Liberalism*. New York: Columbia University Press, 1973.

Hamilton, Alexander. *Selected Writings and Speeches of Alexander Hamilton*, edited by Morton J. Frisch. Washington, DC: American Enterprise Institute, 1985.

———. *The Federalist*, edited by Jacob E. Cooke. Middletown, CT: Wesleyan University Press, 1982.

Hansen, Morris H., and William G. Madow. "Some Important Events in the Historical Development of Sample Surveys." In *On the History of Statistics and Probability*, edited by D.B. Owen. New York: Marcel Dekker, 1976, pp. 75–102.

Hardy, Thomas. "What Matters? Candidates Know Because Their Pollsters Tell Them So," *Chicago Tribune*, August 3, 1990, Sec. 2, 11.

———. "Governor Hopefuls Use Polls to Cash in with Contributors," *Chicago Tribune*, June 26, 1989, Sec. 2, 7.

Hargrove, Erwin C. "Presidential Personality and Leadership Style." In *Researching the Presidency: Vital Questions, New Approaches*, edited by George C. Edwards, John H. Kessel, and Bert A. Rockman. Pittsburgh: University of Pittsburgh Press, 1993, pp. 69–109.

Harkin, Tom. Letter to the author, September 22, 1994.

Harris, John F. "A Clouded Mirror: Bill Clinton, Polls, and the Politics of Survival." In *The Post-Modern Presidency: Bill Clinton's Legacy in U.S. Politics*, edited by Steven E. Schier. Pittsburgh: University of Pittsburgh Press, 2000, pp. 87–105.

Harris, Louis. "Polls and Politics in the U.S.," *Public Opinion Quarterly* 27 (1963): 3–8.

———. *The Anguish of Change*. New York: Norton, 1973.

Harris, Paul. "What's Behind the 'Digest' Poll?" *The American Criterion* 1 (January 1936): 4–7.

Harrison, Shelby M. *Community Action through Surveys*. New York: Russell Sage Foundation, 1916.

Hart, Clyde W., and Don Cahalan. "The Development of AAPOR," *Public Opinion Quarterly* 21 (1957): 165–173.

Hauser, Philip M., and Morris H. Hansen. "On Sampling of Market Surveys," *Journal of Marketing* 9 (1944): 26–31.

Hawver, Carl. "The Congressman and His Public Opinion Poll," *Public Opinion Quarterly* 18 (1954): 123–129.

Heith, Diane J. "Staffing the White House Public Opinion Apparatus: 1969–1988," *Public Opinion Quarterly* 62 (1988): 165–189.

Herbst, Susan. *Numbered Voices: How Opinion Polling Has Shaped American Politics*. Chicago: University of Chicago Press, 1993.

Herbst, Susan. *Politics at the Margins*. New York: Cambridge University Press, 1994.

Herrnson, Paul S. *Playing Hardball: Campaigning for the U.S. Congress*. Upper Saddle River, NJ: Prentice Hall, 2001.

Hursh-Cesar, Gerald. Personal conversation with the author, April 4, 1995.

Hertsgaard, Mark. *On Bended Knee: The Press and the Reagan Presidency*. New York: Farrar Straus Giroux, 1988.

Hilderbrand, Robert C. *Power and the People: Executive Management of Public Opinion in Foreign Affairs, 1897–1921*. Chapel Hill: University of North Carolina Press, 1981.

Hinckley, Barbara. *The Symbolic Presidency: How Presidents Portray Themselves*. New York: Routledge, 1990.

Historical Statistics of the United States: Colonial Times to 1970, Part 2. Washington, DC: U.S. Bureau of the Census, Series Y 308–317.

Hitchens, Christopher. "Voting in the Passive Voice: What Polling Has Done to American Democracy," *Harper's*, April 1992, 45–52.

Hoff, Joan. *Nixon Reconsidered*. New York: Basic Books, 1994.

Hoffman, Karen. "The President as Representative: The Founders' Intent." M.A. thesis, unpublished, University of Chicago, 1992.

Hofstadter, Richard. *The Idea of the Party System*. Berkeley: University of California Press, 1969.

Holli, Melvin G. "Emil E. Hurja: Michigan's Presidential Pollster," *Michigan Historical Review* 21 (1995): 125–138.

Honan, William H. "Johnson May Not Have Poll Fever, But He Has a 'Good Case of the Poll Sniffles,'" *The New York Times Magazine*, August 21, 1966, 34–69.

Honomichl, Jack J. "How Reagan Took America's Pulse," *Advertising Age*, January 23, 1989, 1.

Hoover, Herbert C. *Memoirs, Vol. III: The Great Depression*. New York: Macmillan, 1952.

———. *Public Papers of the Presidents of the United States, Herbert Hoover*. Washington, DC: Government Printing Office, 1974–1977.

———. *The State Papers and Other Public Writings of Herbert Hoover, Vol. 1*, edited by William Starr Myers. Garden City, NY: Doubleday, Duran & Co., 1934.

Hudson, Frederic. *Journalism in the United States*. New York: Harper & Brothers, 1972.

Huntington, Samuel P. "The Democratic Distemper," *The Public Interest* 41 (1975): 9–38.

Hurwitz, Jon. "Presidential Leadership and Public Followership." In *Manipulation Public Opinion: Essays on Public Opinion as a Dependent Variable*, edited by Michael Margolis and Gary A. Mauser. Pacific Grove: Brooks/Cole, 1989, pp. 222–249.

Iyengar, Shanto. *Is Anyone Responsible?: How Television Frames Political Issues*. Chicago: University of Chicago Press, 1991.

Jacobs, Lawrence R. *The Health of Nations: Public Opinion and the Making of American and British Health Policy*. Ithaca, NY: Cornell University Press, 1993.

Jacobs, Lawrence R., and Robert Y. Shapiro. "Presidential Power: Dilemmas of Democracy," Paper prepared for the 1998 Annual Meeting of the American Political Science Association, Boston, MA, September 3–6, 1998.

———. "Presidential Manipulation of Polls and Public Opinion: The Nixon Administration and the Pollsters," *Political Science Quarterly* 110 (Winter 1995–1996) [http://epn.org/psnixo.html].

———. "The Rise of Presidential Polling: The Nixon White House in Historical Perspective," *Public Opinion Quarterly* 59 (1995): 163–195.

———. "Disorganized Democracy: The Institutionalization of Polling and Public Opinion Analysis during the Kennedy, Johnson, and Nixon Presidencies," Paper prepared for presentation at the Annual Meeting of the American Political Science Association, New York, NY, September 1–4, 1994.

———. "Issues, Candidate Image, and Priming: The Use of Private Polls in Kennedy's 1960 Presidential Campaign," *American Political Science Review* 88 (1994): 527–540.

———. "Leadership in a Liberal Democracy: Johnson's Private Polls and Public Announcements," Paper prepared for delivery at the Midwest Political Science Association, Chicago, IL, April 15–17, 1993.

———. *Politicians Don't Pander: Political Manipulation and the Loss of Democratic Responsiveness*. Chicago: University of Chicago Press, 2000.

Jacobs, Lawrence R. "The Recoil Effect: Public Opinion and Policymaking in the U.S. and Britain," *Comparative Politics* 24 (1992): 199–217.

Jamieson, Kathleen Hall. *Packaging the Presidency*. New York: Oxford University Press, 1984.

Javitz, Jacob K. "How I Used A Poll in Campaigning for Congress," *Public Opinion Quarterly* 11 (1947): 222–226.

Jenkins, Roy. *Truman*. New York: Harper & Row, 1986.

Jensen, Richard. "Democracy by the Numbers," *Public Opinion* (Spring 1980): 53–59.

_____. "American Election Analysis: A Case History of Methodological Innovation and Diffusion." In *Politics and the Social Sciences*, edited by Seymour Martin Lipset. New York: Oxford University Press, 1969, pp. 226–243.

_____. "History and the Political Scientist." In *Politics and the Social Sciences*, edited by Seymour Martin Lipset. New York: Oxford University Press, 1969, pp. 1–28.

_____. *The Winning of the Midwest: Social and Political Conflict, 1888–1896*. Chicago: University of Chicago Press, 1971.

Johnson, Lyndon Baines. *The Vantage Point: Perspectives of the Presidency 1963–1969*. New York: Holt, Rinehart and Winston, 1971.

Jones, Charles O. *The Presidency in a Separated System*. Washington, DC: The Brookings Institute, 1994.

_____. *The Trusteeship Presidency: Jimmy Carter and the United States Congress*. Baton Rouge: Louisiana State University Press, 1988.

Joslin, Theodore G. *Hoover Off the Record*. New York: Doubleday, 1934.

Kaiser, Robert G. "White House Pulse-Taking Pollster," *The Washington Post*, February 24, 1982, A1.

Kalb, Marvin. "Too Much Talk and Not Enough Action," *Washington Journalism Review* (September 1992): 33–34.

Karl, Barry D. "Presidential Planning and Social Science Research: Mr. Hoover's Experts," *Perspectives in American History* 3 (1969): 364–371.

Kamarck, Elaine. Conversation with the author, August 1994.

Kearns, Doris. *Lyndon Johnson and the American Dream*. New York: Harper & Row, 1976.

Kelley, Stanley Jr. *Public Relations and Political Power*. Baltimore, MD: Johns Hopkins University Press, 1956.

Kennedy, John F. "A Force That Has Changed the Political Scene," *TV Guide* (November 14, 1959): 6–7.

Kent, Frank R. "Charley Michelson," *Scribners* 88 (1930): 290–296.

Kernell, Samuel. *Going Public: New Strategies of Presidential Leadership*. Washington, DC: CQ Press, 1986.

Key, V.O., Jr. *Public Opinion and American Democracy*. New York: Knopf, 1964.

_____. "Public Opinion and the Decay of Democracy," *Virginia Quarterly Review* 37 (1961): 481–494.

_____. *Politics, Parties and Pressure Groups, Fourth Edition*. New York: Crowell, 1958.

Kinder, Donald. "Presidents, Prosperity, and Public Opinion," *Public Opinion Quarterly* 45 (1981): 1–21.

King, Anthony, ed. *Both Ends of the Avenue: The Presidency, the Executive Branch, and Congress in the 1980s*. Washington, DC: American Enterprise Institute, 1983.

Kolbert, Elizabeth. "Test-Marketing A President: How Focus Groups Pervade Campaign Politics," *The New York Times Magazine*, August 30, 1992, 18–72.

Kruskal, William, and Frederick Mosteller. "Representative Sampling, IV: The History of the Concept in Statistics, 1895–1939," *International Statistical Review* 48 (1980): 169–195.

Kutler, Stanley I. *The Wars of Watergate: The Last Crisis of Richard Nixon*. New York: Knopf, 1990.

Kuttner, Robert. *The Life of the Party: Democratic Prospects in 1988 and Beyond*. New York: Penguin Books, 1988.

LaCerra, Charles. *Franklin Delano Roosevelt and Tammany Hall of New York*. New York: University Press of America, 1997.

Lambert, Gerard. *All Out of Step*. New York: Doubleday, 1956.

Lanouette, William J. "When a Presidential Candidate Moves, a Pollster May Be Pulling the Strings," *National Journal* 11 (December 15, 1979): 2092.

Lasswell, Harold D. *Democracy Through Public Opinion*. Menasha, WI: George Banta, 1941.

———. "The Impact of Public Opinion Research On Our Society," *Public Opinion Quarterly* 21 (1957): 32–38.

Lazarsfeld, Paul F. "Notes on the History of Quantification in Sociology – Trends, Sources and Problems," *Isis* 52 (1961): 277–333.

———. "Public Opinion and the Classical Tradition," *Public Opinion Quarterly* 21 (1957): 39–53.

Leach, William. *Land of Desire: Merchants, Power, and the Rise of a New American Culture*. New York: Pantheon, 1993.

Lécuyer, Bernard-Pierre. "Probability in Vital and Social Statistics: Quetelet, Farr and the Bertillons." In *The Probabilistic Revolution, Vol. I: Ideas in History*, edited by Lorenz Krüger, Lorraine J. Daston, and Michael Heidelberger. Cambridge, MA: MIT Press, 1987, pp. 317–335.

Lehman, Herbert H. "A Public Opinion Sustaining Democracy," *Public Opinion Quarterly*, Special Supplement, Public Opinion in a Democracy, January, 5–7, 1938.

Lengle, James I. *Representation and Presidential Primaries: The Democratic Party in the Post-Reform Era*. Westport, CT: Greenwood Press, 1981.

Leonard, Thomas C. *News for All: America's Coming of Age with the Press*. New York: Oxford University Press, 1995.

Levy, Fabian F. "Forecasting the Election," Letter to the Editor, *The New York Times*, October 16, 1936, 24.

Liebovich, Louis W. *The Press and the Modern Presidency: Myths and Mindsets from Kennedy to Clinton*. Westport, CT: Praeger, 1998.

Likert, Rensis. "Opinion Studies and Government Policy," *Proceedings of the American Philosophical Society* 92 (1948): 341–350.

Link, Arthur S., ed. *The Papers of Woodrow Wilson, Vol. 18: 1908–1909*. Princeton, NJ: Princeton University Press, 1974.

Lippmann, Walter. *Public Opinion*. New York: Free Press, 1965.

———. "The Peculiar Weakness of Mr. Hoover," *Harper's Magazine*, June 1930, 1–7.

Lipset, Seymour Martin, and William Schneider. *The Confidence Gap: Business, Labor, and Government in the Public Mind*. New York: Free Press, 1983.

———. "Manipulating 'Public Opinion'?: Polls for the White House, and the Rest of Us," *Encounter* 49 (November 1977): 24–34.

"Live Press Conferences," *Chicago Tribune*, Editorial, January 2, 1961, A20.

Lowell, A. Lawrence. *Public Opinion and Popular Government*. New York: Longmans Green, [1913] 1926.

Lowi, Theodore J. *The Personal President: Power Invested, Promise Unfilled*. Ithaca, NY: Cornell University Press, 1985.

Lyons, Gene M. *The Uneasy Partnership: Social Science and the Federal Government in the Twentieth Century*. New York: Russell Sage, 1969.

MacKensie, Donald A. *Statistics in Britain 1865–1930: The Social Construction of Scientific Knowledge*. Edinburgh: Edinburgh University Press, 1981.

Macmahon, Arthur W. "Second Session of the Seventy-first Congress," *American Political Science Review* 24 (1930): 913–946.

Macneil, Robert. "The Flickering Images That May Drive Presidents," *Media Studies Journal* 8 (Spring 1994): 145–153.

Madigan, Charles M. "Glut of Polls Muddies Campaign: Numbers May Be Receiving More Attention Than Issues," *Chicago Tribune*, October 2, 1992, A1.

Magruder, Jeb. *An American Life: One Man's Road to Watergate*. New York: Atheneum, 1974.

Mankiewicz, Herman J. "The Virtuous Press Agent," *The New York Times*, April 6, 1924, Sec. 3, 2.

Mansfield, Harvey C., Jr. "Social Science and the Constitution." In *Confronting the Constitution*, edited by Allan Bloom. Washington, DC: AEI Press, 1990, pp. 411–436.

McCoy, Donald R. *The Presidency of Harry S. Truman*. Lawrence: University Press of Kansas, 1984.

McCullough, David. *Truman*. New York: Simon and Schuster, 1992.

McDonald, Rob. Interview with the author, August 3, 1994.

Mayhew, David. *Congress: The Electoral Connection*. New Haven, CT: Yale University Press, 1974.

Mendelsohn, Harold A., and Irving Crespi. *Polls, Television, and the New Politics*. Scranton, PA: Chandler Publishing, 1970.

Michels, Robert. *Political Parties: A Sociological Study of the Oligarchical Tendencies of Modern Democracy*, translated by Eden and Cedar Paul. New York: Free Press, [1911] 1968.

Michelson, Charles. *The Ghost Talks*. New York: Putnam, 1944.

Milkis, Sidney M. *The President and the Parties*. New York: Oxford University Press, 1993.

Miller, Merle. *Plain Speaking: An Oral Biography of Harry S. Truman*. New York: Berkley, 1974.

Miller, Peter V. "The Industry of Public Opinion." In *Public Opinion and the Communication of Consent*, edited by Theodore L. Glasser and Charles T. Salmon. New York: Guilford, 1995, pp. 105–131.

Mills, Stephen. *The New Machine Men: Polls and Persuasion in Australian Politics*. Ringwood, VIC, Australia: Penguin Books, 1986.

Moe, Terry M. "Presidents, Institutions, and Theory." In *Researching the Presidency: Vital Questions, New Approaches*, edited by George C. Edwards, III, John H. Kessel, and Bert A. Rockman. Pittsburgh: University of Pittsburgh Press, 1993, pp. 337–385.

———. "The Politicized Presidency." In *The New Direction in American Politics*, edited by John E. Chubb and Paul E. Petersen. Washington, DC: Brookings Institute, 1985, pp. 235–271.

Mohr, Charles. "A Young Pollster Plays a Key Role for Carter," *The New York Times*, August 1, 1976, A28.

Moore, David W. *The Superpollsters: How They Measure and Manipulate Public Opinion in America*. New York: Four Walls Eight Windows, 1992.

Morris, Dick. *Behind the Oval Office: Winning the Presidency in the Nineties*. New York: Random House, 1997.

Mueller, John E. *War, Presidents and Public Opinion*. Lanham, MD: University Press of America, 1985.

Murray, Shoon Kathleen. "The Reagan Administration's Use of Private Polls: Impact on Policy," Paper prepared for the Annual Meeting of the American Political Science Association, San Francisco, August 30–September 2, 2001.

Myers, Walter. "FDR vs. The Democratic Party," *Esquire*, March 1959, No. 59.

Nathan, Richard P. *The Administrative Presidency*. New York: John Wiley & Sons, 1983.

———. *The Plot That Failed: Nixon and the Administrative Presidency*. New York: John Wiley & Sons, 1975.

Nelson, Michael, ed. *The Presidency and the Political System*. Washington, DC: CQ Press, 1988.

Neuman, W. Russell. *The Paradox of Mass Publics*. Cambridge, MA: Harvard University Press, 1986.

Neustadt, Richard E. *Presidential Power and the Modern Presidents*. New York: Free Press, 1990.

———. "Approaches to Staffing the Presidency,"*American Political Science Review* 54 (1963): 855–864.

Nevins, Allan, ed. *Interpretations, 1931–1932*. New York: Macmillan, 1932.

New York Times Archival Material.

Nisbet, Robert. "Public Opinion Versus Popular Opinion," *The Public Interest* 41 (1975): 166–192.

Nixon, Richard M. *RN: The Memoirs of Richard Nixon, Vol. I*. New York: Warner Books, 1979.

———. *RN: The Memoirs of Richard Nixon*. New York: Grosset & Dunlap, 1978.

Noelle-Neumann, Elisabeth. "Political Opinion Polling in Germany." In *Political Opinion Polling: An International Review*, edited by Robert M. Worcester. New York: St. Martin's Press, 1983, pp. 44–60.

———. *The Spiral of Silence: Our Social Skin, Third Edition*. Chicago: University of Chicago Press, 1998.

Noonan, Peggy. *What I Saw at the Revolution: A Political Life in the Reagan Era*. New York: Random House, 1990.

Oberschall, Anthony. *Empirical Social Research in Germany 1848–1914*. Paris: Mouton & Co, 1965.

O'Neill, Harry. Personal conversation with the author, May 19, 1995.

"Omnipotence of Press-Agents," *The New York Times*, March 14, 1932, A16.

Page, Benjamin, and Robert Y. Shapiro. *The Rational Public: Fifty Years of Trends in Public Opinion*. Chicago: University of Chicago Press, 1991.

Parten, Mildrid. *Polls, Surveys, and Samples*. New York: Harper & Brothers, 1950.

Patterson, Thomas E. *Out of Order*. New York: Knopf, 1993.

Payne, Stanley LeBaron. *The Art of Asking Questions.* Princeton, NJ: Princeton University Press, 1951.

Perry, James M. "Clinton Relies Heavily on White House Pollster To Take Words Right Out of the Public's Mouth," *Wall Street Journal,* March 23, 1994, A16.

Peterson, Mark A. *Legislating Together: The White House and Capitol Hill from Eisenhower to Reagan.* Cambridge, MA: Harvard University Press, 1991.

Pierce, William. *Congressional Record,* 77th Congress, 1st session, 1941, Vol. 87.

Pious, Richard M. *The American Presidency.* New York: Basic Books, 1979.

Pollard, James. *The Presidents and the Press.* New York: Macmillan, 1947.

Polsby, Nelson W. *Consequences of Party Reform.* New York: Oxford University Press, 1983.

————. "Some Landmarks in Modern Presidential-Congressional Relations." In *Both Ends of the Avenue: The Presidency, the Executive Branch, and Congress in the 1980s,* edited by Anthony King. Washington: American Enterprise Institute, 1983, pp. 1–25.

————. 1980. "The News Media as an Alternative to Party in the Presidential Selection Process." In *Political Parties in the Eighties,* edited by Robert A. Goldwin. Washington, DC: American Enterprise Institute, 1983, pp. 50–66.

Pool, Ithiel de Sola, and Robert P. Abelson. "The Simulmatics Project," *Public Opinion Quarterly* 25 (1961): 167–183.

Pool, Ithiel de Sola, Robert P. Abelson, and Samuel L. Popkin. *Candidates, Issues, and Strategies: A Computer Simulation of the 1960 Presidential Election,* Cambridge, MA: MIT Press, 1964.

Pool, Ithiel de Sola. *Technologies Without Boundaries: On Telecommunications in a Global Age,* edited by Eli M. Noam. Cambridge, MA: Harvard University Press, 1990.

Popkin Samuel. *The Reasoning Voter: Communication and Persuasion in Presidential Campaigns.* Chicago: University of Chicago Press, 1991.

Porter, Theodore M. *The Rise of Statistical Thinking 1820–1900.* Princeton, NJ: Princeton University Press, 1986.

Porter, Theodore M. "Lawless Society: Social Science and the Reinterpretation of Statistics in Germany, 1850–1880." In *The Probabilistic Revolution, Vol. I: Ideas in History,* edited by Lorenz Krüger, Lorraine J. Daston, and Michael Heidelberger. Cambridge, MA: MIT Press, 1987, pp. 351–375.

Powell, Jody. "Meeting the Press," *Public Opinion* (December–January 1982), 11.

President's Research Committee on Social Trends. *Recent Social Trends in the United States.* New York: McGraw Hill, 1933.

Pringle, Henry F. "The Mass Psychologist," *American Mercury,* February 1930, 155–162.

————. "Who's On the Payroll," *American Magazine,* November 1934, 18–19.

"Public Opinion Polls Vital to Democracy," *Marketing News,* August 1, 1986, 154.

Ranney, John C. "Do Polls Serve Democracy?," *Public Opinion Quarterly* 10 (1946): 346–360.

Reedy, George E. *Lyndon B. Johnson: A Memoir.* New York: Andrews & McKeel, 1982.

————. *The Twilight of the Presidency.* New York: New American Library/World Publishing, 1970.

Reeves, Richard. *President Kennedy: Profile of Power*. New York: Simon and Schuster, 1993.

Robinson, Claude E. *Straw Votes: A Study of Political Prediction*. New York: Columbia University Press, 1932.

Robinson, Daniel J. *The Measure of Democracy: Polling, Market Research, and Public Life, 1930–1945*. Toronto: University of Toronto Press, 1999.

Rogers, Lindsay. *The Pollsters: Public Opinion, Politics, and Democratic Leadership*. New York: Knopf, 1949.

Romano, Lois. "Wirthlin, The Optimist," *The Washington Post*, January 15, 1984, C12.

Roosevelt, Theodore. *Theodore Roosevelt: An Autobiography*. New York: Charles Scribner's Sons, 1923.

Roll, Charles W., and Albert H. Cantril. *Polls: Their Use and Misuse in Politics*. New York: Basic Books, 1972.

"Roosevelt, Farley, & Co." *Time*, March 2, 1936, 16–18.

Roper, Elmo. "Sampling Public Opinion," *Journal of the American Statistical Association* 35 (1940): 325–334.

_____. "So the Blind Shall not Lead," *Fortune*, February 1942, 102.

_____. "The Client over the Years," *Public Opinion Quarterly* 21 (1957): 28–32.

Rosenman, Samuel I., ed. *The Public Papers and Addresses of Franklin D. Roosevelt*, Vols. I–XIII. New York: Macmillan, 1938–1950.

Sabato, Larry J. *The Rise of Political Consultants: New Ways of Winning Elections*. New York: Basic Books, 1981.

Safire, William. *Before the Fall: An Insider View of the Pre-Watergate White House*. Garden City, NY: Doubleday, 1975.

Salinger, Pierre. *With Kennedy*. New York: Doubleday, 1966.

Savage, Sean J. *Roosevelt: The Party Leader 1932–1945*. Lexington: University Press of Kentucky, 1991.

Scheele, Harry Z. "Executive-Legislative Relations: Eisenhower and Halleck." In *Reexamining the Eisenhower Presidency*, edited by Shirley Anne Warshaw. Westport, CT: Greenwood Press, 1993, pp. 133–152.

Schier, Steven E., ed. *The Post-Modern Presidency: Bill Clinton's Legacy in U.S. Politics*. Pittsburgh: University of Pittsburgh Press, 2000.

Schlesinger, Arthur M., Jr. *A Thousand Days: John F. Kennedy in the White House*. Boston: Houghton Mifflin, 1965.

_____. *The Age of Roosevelt, the Crisis of the Old Order, 1919–1933*. Boston: Houghton Mifflin, 1956.

_____. *The Imperial Presidency*. Boston: Houghton Mifflin, 1989.

Schlesinger, Arthur M., Jr., and Alfred de Grazia. *Congress and the Presidency: Their Role in Modern Times*. Washington, DC: American Enterprise Institute, 1974.

Schudson, Michael. *Discovering the News: A Social History of American Newspapers*. New York: Basic Books, 1978.

Schwarz, Jordan A. *The Interregnum of Despair: Hoover, Congress, and the Depression*. Urbana: University of Illinois Press, 1970.

Sege, Irene. "Weld Says He Polled While Cutting," *The Boston Globe*, February 25, 1991, 19.

Shafer, Byron E. *Bifurcated Politics: Evolution and Reform in the National Party Convention*. Cambridge, MA: Harvard University Press, 1988.

Shafritz, Jay M. *HarperCollins Dictionary of American Government and Politics.* New York: Harper Perennial, 1992.

Sheatsley, Paul B. "The Public Relations of the Polls," *International Journal of Opinion and Attitude Research* 2 (1948–1949): 453–468.

Sheatsley, Paul B., and Warren J. Mitovsky, eds. *A Meeting Place: The History of the American Association for Public Opinion Research.* Ann Arbor, MI: AAPOR, 1992.

Shull, Steven A., ed. *Presidential Policymaking: An End-of-Century Assessment.* Armonk, NY: M.E. Sharpe, 1999.

Shull, Stephen A. *Presidential-Congressional Relations: Policy and Time Approaches.* Ann Arbor: University of Michigan Press, 1997.

Shull, Steven A., and Thomas C. Shaw. *Explaining Congressional-Presidential Relations.* Albany, NY: SUNY Press, 1999.

Sidey, Hugh. *John F. Kennedy, President.* New York: Atheneum, 1964.

Smith, Hedrick. *The Power Game: How Washington Works.* New York: Ballantine, 1988.

Smith, Sally Bedell. *In All His Glory: William S. Paley: The Legendary Tycoon and His Brilliant Circle.* New York: Simon and Schuster, 1991.

Smith, Tom W. "The First Straw: A Study of the Origins of Election Polls," *Public Opinion Quarterly* 54 (1990): 21–36.

"Social Fact Finding," *The New York Times*, December 22, 1929, 4E.

Sorensen, Theodore C. *Decision-Making in the White House: The Olive Branch or The Arrows.* New York: Columbia University Press, 1964.

———. *Kennedy.* New York: Harper & Row, 1965.

Sparrow, Carroll Mason. "Measurement and Social Science." In *Voyages and Cargoes, University of Virginia Studies, Vol. III.* Richmond: Dietz Press; Charlottesville: University of Virginia, 1947, pp. 150–179.

Stanley, Harold W., and Richard G. Niemi. *Vital Statistics on American Politics 1999–2000.* Washington, DC: CQ Press, 2000.

State Department Hearings. 85th Congress, H1612-1, June 21–July 11, 1957.

Steele, Richard W. "The Pulse of the People: Franklin D. Roosevelt and the Gauging of American Public Opinion," *Journal of Contemporary History* 9 (1974): 195–216.

Steeper, Fred. Comments made at the American Association of Public Opinion Research 1992 Annual Meeting, St. Charles, IL.

Stephanopoulos, George. *All Too Human: A Political Education.* Boston: Little Brown, 1999.

Sudman, Seymour. "The Presidents and the Polls," *Public Opinion Quarterly* 46 (1982): 301–310.

Sugrue, Thomas. "Farley's Guess Man," *American Magazine*, May 1936, 22–23, 87–91.

Sundquist, James L. "Party Decay and the Capacity to Govern." In *The Future of American Political Parties: The Challenge to Governance*, edited by Joel Fleishman. Englewood Cliffs, NJ: Prentice Hall, 1982, pp. 42–69.

Sussman, Leila A. "Mass Political Letter Writing in America: The Growth of an Institution," *Public Opinion Quarterly* 23 (1959): 203–212.

———. "FDR and the White House Mail," *Public Opinion Quarterly* 20 (1956): 5–15.

T.R.B. "Washington Notes," *New Republic*, October 14, 1931, 219.

Taylor, Carl C. *The Social Survey, Its History and Methods*, Social Science Series 3 (20). Columbia: University of Missouri, 1919.

Teeter, Robert M. Letter to the author, June 20, 1996.

"The Deliberative Opinion Poll: A Dialogue," *The Public Perspective*, May/ June 1992, 29–34.

"The Discussion Goes On," *Public Opinion Quarterly* 9 (1945): 403–410.

_____. "Studying the Presidency: Where and How Do We go From Here?," *Presidential Studies Quarterly* 7 (1977): 169–175.

Thurber, James A., ed. *Rivals for Power: Presidential-Congressional Relations*. Washington, DC: CQ Press, 1996.

Thurstone, L.L. "The Measurement of Social Attitudes," *Journal of Abnormal and Social Psychology* 26 (1932): 249–269.

Tönnies, Ferdinand. *Community and Society (Gemeinschaft and Gesellschaft)*, translated and edited by Charles P. Loomis. East Lansing: Michigan State Press, [1887] 1957.

"Transcript of President's Address to Country on Energy Problems," *The New York Times,* July 16, 1979, A10.

Trefousse, Hans L. *Lincoln's Decision for Emancipation*. Philadelphia: J.B. Lippincott, 1975.

Truman, David B. *The Governmental Process: Political Interests and Public Opinion*. New York: Knopf, 1951.

Truman, David. "Public Opinion Research as a Tool of Public Administration," *Public Administration Review* (Winter 1945), 62–72.

Truman, Harry S. *Memoirs by Harry S. Truman, Volume Two: Years of Trial and Hope*. New York: Doubleday, 1956.

_____. *Public Papers of the Presidents of the United States*. Washington, DC: General Services Administration, 1956.

Tucker, Ray. "Chart and Graph Man," *Collier's*, January 12, 1935, 28–29.

Tulis, Jeffrey K. *The Rhetorical Presidency*. Princeton, NJ: Princeton University Press, 1987.

Tye, Larry. *The Father of Spin: Edward L. Bernays and the Birth of Public Relations*. New York: Crown, 1998.

Uslaner, Eric M. *The Decline of Comity in Congress*. Ann Arbor: University of Michigan Press, 1993.

Van Riper, Paul P. *History of the United States Civil Service*. New York: Row, Peters, 1958.

Walsh, Kenneth T. "Bush's Cautious Alter Ego: Pollster Bob Teeter Is an Outsider with an Insider's Influence," *U.S. News and World Report*, March 26, 1990, 26–27.

Walsh, Timothy, and Dwight M. Miller, eds. *Herbert Hoover and Franklin D. Roosevelt: A Documentary History*. Westport, CT: Greenwood Press, 1998.

Ward, Lester Frank. *Dynamic Sociology, Vols. I and II*. New York: Johnson Reprint, 1968. *Dynamic Sociology, or Applied Social Science, as based upon Statical Sociology and the less Complex Sciences, in two volumes*. New York: Appleton, 1883.

Warshaw, Shirley Anne, ed. *Reexamining the Eisenhower Presidency*. Westport, CT: Greenwood Press, 1993.

Watson, James E. *As I Knew Them: Memoirs of James Watson, Former United States Senator from Indiana*. Indianapolis: Bobbs-Merrill, 1936.
Wattenberg, Martin P. *The Decline of American Political Parties 1952–1992*. Cambridge, MA: Harvard University Press, 1994.
Wayne, Stephen J. *The Legislative Presidency*. New York: Harper & Row, 1978.
Weed, Clyde P. *The Nemesis of Reform: The Republican Party During the New Deal*. New York: Columbia University Press, 1994.
West, Valerie. Conversation with the author, June 21, 2000.
Wheeler, Michael. *Lies, Damn Lies, and Statistics: The Manipulation of Public Opinion in America*. New York: Liveright, 1976.
White, Graham J. *FDR and the Press*. Chicago: University of Chicago Press, 1979.
White, William Allen. *A Puritan in Babylon: The Story of Calvin Coolidge*. New York: Macmillan, 1958.
Wilcox, Walter F. "An Attempt to Measure Public Opinion about Repealing the Eighteenth Century Amendment," *Journal of the American Statistical Association* 26 (1931 New Series): 243–261.
Will, George F. "Bush: Read My Polls," *Newsweek*, May 7, 1991, 76.
_____. *Restoration: Congress, Term Limits, and the Recovery of Deliberative Democracy*. New York: Free Press, 1992.
_____. "Initiate the Populists' Voguish Darling," *The Washington Post*, July 28, 1977, A23.
Wilson, James Q. *Political Organizations*. New York: Basic Books, 1973.
Wilson, Joan Hoff. *Herbert Hoover: Forgotten Progressive*. Boston: Little Brown, 1975.
Wilson, Woodrow. *Constitutional Government in the United States*. New York: Columbia University Press, 1908.
_____. *The Papers of Woodrow Wilson, Vol. 18: 1908–1909*, edited by Arthur S. Link. Princeton, NJ: Princeton University Press, 1974.
Winfield, Betty Houchin. *FDR and the News Media*. New York: Columbia University Press, 1994.
Woodward, Bob. *The Agenda: Inside the Clinton White House*. New York: Simon and Schuster, 1994.
Yankelovich, Daniel. *Coming to Public Judgment: Making Democracy Work in a Complex World*. Syracuse, NY: Syracuse University Press, 1991.
Zeigler, Harmon. *Interest Groups in American Society*. Englewood Cliffs, NJ: Prentice Hall, 1964.
Zeisel, Hans. "Lawmaking and Public Opinion Research: The President and Pat Caddell," *American Bar Foundation Research Journal* 8 (1980): 133.
Zobrist, Benedict K. Letter to the author, November 7, 1991.

Index

AAPOR (American Association of Public Opinion Research), 143–4
Abelson, Robert, 88, 89 fn. 48, 89 fn. 50, 159
Abrams, Mark, 137, 137 fn. 4
Adams, Sherman, 51, 51 fn. 32, 84, 114–15, 114 fn. 34–5
Agnew, Spiro, 4, 102
Akerson, George, 39, 107
Albig, William, 12 fn. 28, 35 fn. 1
Allen, Craig, 47 fn. 46, 113, 113 fn. 31, 114 fn. 25, 116
Allport, Gordon, 140, 140 fn. 14
Altschuler, Bruce E., 24 fn. 12, 98 fn. 75, 122, 122 fn. 52
Anthony, Edward, 76, 76 fn. 10
Arterton, F. Christopher, 33 fn. 40
Ash, Roy L., 61
Atwater, Lee, 174

Bailey, Douglas, 150
Bailey, John, 90
Baker, James, 163 fn. 50, 165, 167, 167 fn. 65, 171
Balsdon, Kathleen, 132
Bankhead, William B., 80 fn. 21
Barber, James David, 30, 30 fn. 33, 110, 110 fn. 22, 143 fn. 24
Barkley, Alben, 80
Barnes, James A., 179 fn. 20–1, 181 fn. 26, 181 fn. 28
Barone, Michael, 24 fn. 12

Bass, Perkins, 51 fn. 54
BBDO (Batten, Barton, Durstein, and Osborn), 13, 113, 113 fn. 32
Beal, Richard S., 24 fn. 12, 162
Behavioral Research Associates, 69
Belknap, George, 88–9, 88 fn. 47, 89 fn. 49, 89 fn. 51
Benham, Thomas, 62, 62 fn. 41, 100–1, 101 fn. 84
Berelson, Bernard, 15, 15 fn. 35
Bernays, Edward, 17–18, 17 fn. 40–1, 106–7, 106 fn. 7–8
Bernstein, Irving, 57 fn. 22
Biden, Joseph, 160
Binkley, Wilfred E., 35–6, 35 fn. 2, 75 fn. 3
Boggs, Danny, 167, 167 fn. 64
Bond, Jon R., 28 fn. 24
Booth, Charles, 137
Bornet, Vaughn Davis, 121 fn. 50
Branch, Taylor, 57 fn. 22, 121 fn. 50
Branyan, Robert L., 46, 47 fn. 47
Brezovšek, Marjan, 29 fn. 28
Bricker, John, 47, 53
Brinkley, David, 53
Broder, David S., 8–9, 9 fn. 19, 90, 90 fn. 52
Brokaw, Tom, 169
Brooks, Charles, 46
Brooks, Robert C., 14, 14 fn. 30
Brown, George, 153
Brown, Trude, 65

Bruner, Jerome, 43
Bryant, Farris, 55
Bryce, James, 22, 22 fn. 4, 31, 31
    fn. 35–7, 52 fn. 1
Brzezinski, Zbigniew, 157
Buchanan, Pat, 104 fn. 93, 165
Bull, Stephen, 63 fn. 46
Bulmer, Martin, 19 fn. 49, 138 fn. 5,
    139 fn. 9
Burdick, Eugene, 89 fn. 48
Burke, Edmund, 33
Burner, David, 75 fn. 1, 76 fn. 6, 107
    fn. 13
Burns, James MacGregor, 26, 26 fn. 18,
    27 fn. 21, 54, 79 fn. 18–19, 80
    fn. 21, 81 fn. 23, 142, 143 fn. 23,
    158
Busby, Horace, 60 fn. 31, 92 fn. 60
Bush, George H.W., 5, 33, 173–80, 174
    fn. 2, 175 fn. 5, 177 fn. 11, 177
    fn. 13, 177 fn. 15
Bush, Nancy Ferguson, 98 fn. 76

Caddell, Patrick, 4, 10, 33, 69, 156–62,
    157 fn. 25–6, 158 fn. 28–30,
    159 fn. 33, 161 fn. 42, 169, 186
Caesar, James, 8, 8 fn. 17
Calkins, John T., 154 fn. 21
Callaway, Bo, 148 fn. 4, 153 fn. 19
Cambridge Opinion Studies, 101
Cambridge Survey Research, 159, 161,
    169
Cameron, Charles M., 28 fn. 24
Campbell, Alan "Scotty," 161, 161
    fn. 40
Campbell, John, 66, 66 fn. 61
Cantril, Albert, 23 fn. 11, 60, 126,
    126 fn. 70
Cantril, Hadley, 3, 8, 20, 29, 42–5,
    42 fn. 26–7, 43 fn. 31, 43 fn. 34, 45
    fn. 37, 48, 69, 72, 84, 100, 111–12,
    111 fn. 25, 112 fn. 27, 120, 126,
    141–5, 141 fn. 17, 148, 181
Capehart, Homer, 47
Card, Andrew, 177
Caro, Robert A., 90, 90 fn. 53
Carswell, G. Harrold, 62
Carter, Clifton, 90

Carter, Hugh, 160, 160 fn. 38–9
Carter, Jimmy, 4, 10, 33, 69, 150–1,
    153, 153 fn. 18, 155–61, 157 fn. 25,
    158 fn. 28–30, 159 fn. 31, 159
    fn. 33–4, 160 fn. 36, 161 fn. 42,
    170–1
Casey, Bob, 177
Casey, Ralph D., 111 fn. 23
Cater, Douglass, 60 fn. 31, 92 fn. 60
Chanock, Foster, 4, 153–5, 154 fn. 20
Chapin, Dwight L., 63 fn. 46, 127–8,
    127 fn. 73, 131, 131 fn. 87, 133
    fn. 96
Cheney, Richard, 4, 148–9, 148 fn. 4–5,
    149 fn. 6, 153–5, 153 fn. 19,
    154 fn. 22, 171
Chew, Daniel, 160, 160 fn. 39
Chew, David, 163–6, 163 fn. 50–1,
    164 fn. 52–3, 166 fn. 62, 168 fn. 68
Childs, Harwood, 22–3, 22 fn. 7
Chiles, Lawton, 152
Chotiner, Murray, 62–3, 63 fn. 44
Clark, Ed, 90
Clawsen, Kenneth, 132
Clements, Earle, 90 fn. 54
Clinton, William J., 5, 33, 146 fn. 31,
    173, 177, 179–81, 185, 187
Cohen, Jeffrey, 24
Cole, Ken, 66
Collier, Ken, 24
Colson, Charles, 2–3, 2 fn. 8, 3 fn. 9,
    62–3, 62 fn. 43, 63 fn. 47, 67,
    67 fn. 62–3, 127–8, 127 fn. 73,
    129 fn. 79, 129 fn. 83, 131–2
Combest, Larry, 178 fn. 16
Committee on Public Information,
    16–17, 36
Converse, Jean M., 20, 20 fn. 52, 48
    fn. 49, 106, 139 fn. 9, 141
    fn. 15–17
Coolidge, Calvin, 16–17, 107–8
Corbett, Robert J., 51 fn. 54
Corcoran, Tommy, 80
Cornwell, Jr., Elmer E., 16–17, 16
    fn. 36–7, 17 fn. 38–40, 23 fn. 12,
    107 fn. 11
Corwin, Edward S., 27 fn. 21
Coughlin, Lawrence, 178 fn. 16

Cox, Oscar, 43, 43 fn. 30
Creel Committee; *see* Committee on Public Information
Creel, George, 16
CREEP (Committee for the Re-Election of the President), 101–2
Crespi, Irving, 123, 123 fn. 56
Cronin, Thomas E., 27 fn. 21, 33 fn. 40
Crossley, Archibald, 11–13, 11 fn. 26, 12 fn. 28, 13 fn. 29, 15, 142 fn. 22
Curtis, Charles, 77
Curtis Publishing Company, 13

Dallek, Robert, 44 fn. 36, 57–8, 57 fn. 22, 58 fn. 24, 121 fn. 50, 127 fn. 72
Daniels, Mitchell, 167, 167 fn. 64
Danner, Fred W., 115–16, 116 fn. 39
Dawson, Rhett, 168, 168 fn. 67
Deardourff, John, 150
Deaver, Michael, 163 fn. 50, 165, 165 fn. 57, 167 fn. 65, 171
Decision/Making/Information (DMI), 101, 162, 168–9, 169 fn. 71
Delli Carpini, Michael X., 150 fn. 9
Democratic National Committee (DNC), 3, 6, 18, 29–30, 55, 68, 79–84, 79 fn. 18, 88–9, 97–8, 98 fn. 76, 121–4, 129, 182
Dent, Harry, 64–5, 65 fn. 55–6, 99 fn. 77, 99 fn. 79–80, 104 fn. 93, 127 fn. 73
Derge, David R., 69, 71, 99, 100, 129, 133
Dewey, Thomas, 14, 72, 85, 112 fn. 27, 116 fn. 40, 142, 144–5
Dionne, Jr., E. J., 170 fn. 76
Dirksen, Everett, 57–8
Disher, David, 177
Dole, Robert, 63, 174
Dorsett, Lyle W., 79–80, 79 fn. 18, 80 fn. 21
Douglas, Chuck, 178
Douglas, Mary, 190 fn. 54
Doyle, William, 72–3, 73 fn. 76
Dreis, Thelma A., 141 fn. 16
Dryzek, John S., 23 fn. 10

Duval, Michael, 150, 150 fn. 7, 154 fn. 20
Duverger, Maurice, 29 fn. 28

Early, Stephen, 142
Edwards, III, George C., 24, 173, 173 fn. 1, 183, 183 fn. 34
Ehrlichman, John D., 66, 66 fn. 61, 69–70, 70 fn. 73
Eisenhower, Dwight D., 3, 35, 46–7, 84–5, 104–5, 105 fn. 1, 112–14, 116, 134, 145, 186
Eizenstat, Stuart, 157, 157 fn. 26–7, 160, 160 fn. 36, 171
Eldersfeld, Samuel J., 29 fn. 28
Elliot, Roland, 187 fn. 46
Ellsworth, Clayton S., 20 fn. 52
Euchner, Charles C., 24 fn. 12, 41 fn. 24
Evans, Jr., Roland, 2 fn. 5, 65, 65 fn. 54

Fahrenkopf, Frank, 163, 163 fn. 50, 165
Farley, James, 81–2, 81 fn. 23, 84, 144
Faulsold, Martin L., 19 fn. 51, 75–6, 75 fn. 3–4, 76 fn. 6
Fess, Simeon, 39
Field, Harry, 143
Field, Mervin, 129–30
Fisher, Louis, 184 fn. 38
Fisher, R. A., 137 fn. 4
Fishkin, James S., 185 fn. 42
Fleisher, Richard, 28 fn. 24
Flynn, Edward J., 81 fn. 23
Fong, Hiram, 146
Ford, Gerald, 4, 33, 147–55, 147 fn. 1, 148 fn. 5, 150 fn. 7, 152 fn. 14, 170–1, 180
Ford, Jack, 149
Forster, Rudolph, 108
Foster, H. Schuler, 49–50
Franklin, Fabian, 141 fn. 17
Free, Lloyd, 93
Friedersdorf, Max, 165
Fuller, Craig, 174

Gallup, George, 12–15, 12 fn. 27–28, 14 fn. 31, 22–3, 22 fn. 6, 43, 72, 84, 114–15, 115 fn. 37, 123–4, 141–3, 141 fn. 17, 142 fn. 20, 145

Gallup, Jr., George, 123, 130, 134
Gallup: organization, 123, 154, 159,
    168; polls, 42, 45 fn. 38, 73 fn. 75,
    84–5, 106 fn. 1, 110, 114–15,
    114 fn. 33, 130–1, 141–4,
    141 fn. 17
Galton, Francis, 137 fn. 4
Garment, Leonard, 61
Garner, John, 78 fn. 15, 111
George, Walter, 80
Gerard, James W., 79
Gergen, David, 24 fn. 12, 150
Gibson, Hugh, 75
Gimpel, Jim, 7 fn. 15
Ginsberg, Benjamin, 22–3, 22 fn. 8,
    184–5
Gleason, Jack, 67 fn. 62
Goldman, Eric F., 90, 90 fn. 53
Goldstein, Ed, 175
Goldwater, Barry, 90–1, 94, 125, 146
Gore, Albert, 190
Gore, Tipper, 171
Gorman, Teresa A., 175 fn. 5
Grady, Bob, 175 fn. 6
Granquist, Wayne, 161, 161 fn. 40
Grassley, Charles, 7 fn. 15, 128 fn. 16,
    188 fn. 49
Grazia, Alfred de, 35–6, 35 fn. 3,
    36 fn. 3
Greenberg, Stan, 146 fn. 31, 171,
    171 fn. 79, 180–1, 181 fn. 27, 186,
    186 fn. 43
Greener, Bill, 166
Gregg, II, Gary L., 183 fn. 32
Griscom, Tommy, 169, 169 fn. 72
Gwinn, Ralph W., 51 fn. 54

Hagerty, James, 51, 51 fn. 54, 113,
    115–16, 115 fn. 37, 116 fn. 40
Haig, Alexander, 66, 174
Halberstam, David, 113 fn. 32
Haldeman, H.R., 2–3, 2 fn. 4, 2 fn. 6–7,
    3 fn. 9, 52, 62–7, 62 fn. 42–3, 63
    fn. 44, 63 fn. 46, 63 fn. 48–50,
    64 fn. 53, 66 fn. 58, 66 fn. 60,
    67 fn. 63, 69, 69 fn. 72, 71–2,
    99 fn. 77, 100–3, 100 fn. 81,
    101 fn. 84, 101 fn. 86, 127–34,

    128 fn. 77, 129 fn. 79–80, 129
    fn. 83, 130 fn. 84–5, 131 fn. 87–8,
    132 fn. 93, 133 fn. 97, 134, 134
    fn. 98, 147 fn. 2, 153–5, 167, 171,
    175, 187–9
Hall, Leonard W., 113 fn. 32
Halleck, Charles, 46
Hamby, Alonzo, 46, 46 fn. 43–4
Hamilton, Alexander, 22, 22 fn. 3,
    183
Harding, Warren, 16
Harkin, Tom, 189 fn. 51
Harlow, Bryce, 51, 64
Harper, Edwin, 128 fn. 78, 167,
    167 fn. 64
Harris, John F., 186 fn. 44
Harris, Jr., Hubert, 160, 160 fn. 35
Harris, Louis, 4, 9, 52, 55–7, 56
    fn. 16, 57 fn. 20, 69, 72, 86–8, 94,
    100, 118–23, 118 fn. 43, 127–30,
    128 fn. 78, 134, 145, 148, 159,
    168, 175, 175 fn. 7, 181, 186–7,
    189
Harris, Paul, 141 fn. 17
Harris polls, 55, 106 fn. 1, 127–9, 154
Harrison, Gail, 159, 159 fn. 34
Harrison, Pat, 80
Harrison, Shelby M., 139–40, 139 fn. 9,
    140 fn. 10
Hart, Gary, 156
Hartmann, Robert, 148 fn. 4, 149–50
Hawver, Carl, 6, 6 fn. 14
Haynesworth, Clement F., 62
Hearst, William Randolph, 78 fn. 15,
    111
Heith, Diane, 170–1, 170 fn. 75,
    171 fn. 78
Heller, Francis, 46 fn. 44
Henderson, John Earl, 51 fn. 54
Hennegan, Bob, 81 fn. 23
Herbst, Susan, 6–7, 6 fn. 14, 7 fn. 16,
    184–5, 185 fn. 39
Herrnson, Paul S., 29 fn. 30
Higby, Larry, 2–3, 2 fn. 6–7, 3 fn. 9,
    62–3, 62 fn. 43, 63 fn. 49–50,
    66–7, 66 fn. 58, 67 fn. 63, 69
    fn. 72, 101, 101 fn. 86, 129–30,
    129 fn. 81, 130 fn. 84, 132

Hilderbrand, Robert C., 108, 108 fn. 16
Hill, William H., 77
Hinckley, Barbara, 188 fn. 48
Hinckley, Ronald H., 24 fn. 12, 169
Hitchens, Christopher, 23, 23 fn. 10,
    184–5, 185 fn. 40
Hitler, Adolph, 111 fn. 25
Hoar, George, 36 fn. 3
Hoff Wilson, Joan, 1, 61 fn. 35–7,
    76 fn. 1, 107 fn. 13
Hoffman, Karen, 183 fn. 32
Hofstadter, Richard, 30 fn. 32
Holland, Ken, 160
Holli, Melvin G., 83 fn. 28, fn. 30
Honan, William H., 91 fn. 58, 95, 95
    fn. 66
Hoover, Herbert, 18–19, 19 fn. 45–7,
    20, 32, 35–40, 37 fn. 6, 37 fn. 8,
    39 fn. 20, 40, 40 fn. 20, 44, 46, 71,
    73–9, 75 fn. 3, 75 fn. 5, 104–10,
    107 fn. 12, 133, 134
Hoover, J. Edgar, 3
Hosmer, Craig, 51 fn. 54
Houchin Winfield, Betty, 42 fn. 27, 110,
    110 fn. 22
Houser, J. David, 77
Howard, Richard, 132
Howe, Louis, 79–80
Huddleston, George, 80
Hudson, Frederic, 30 fn. 32
Humphrey, Hubert, 54, 61, 68 fn. 67,
    94, 121, 121 fn. 50, 126 fn. 69, 131
Huntsman, Jon, 66, 66 fn. 60
Hurja, Emil, 81–4, 83 fn. 31, 143–4
Hursh-Cesar, Gerald, 126 fn. 69
Hurwitz, Jon, 26–7, 26 fn. 19, 27 fn. 20
Hutcheson, Rick, 158–9, 158 fn. 28,
    159 fn. 34

Ickes, Harold, 80, 82

Jackson, Andrew, 35–6
Jackson, C. D., 51
Jackson, Henry "Scoop," 6
Jacobs, Lawrence, 2 fn. 4, 23–4, 24
    fn. 13, 36 fn. 4, 43, 43 fn. 33, 53,
    53 fn. 5, 62 fn. 41–2, 67 fn. 62, 69
    fn. 70, 95–6, 95 fn. 68, 96 fn. 68,

99 fn. 78, 100 fn. 83, 122, 122
    fn. 51, 127 fn. 75, 134 fn. 98, 171,
    171 fn. 80, 179, 185 fn. 41
Jacobsen, Jack, 95 fn. 68, 122 fn. 51
Jamieson, Kathleen Hall, 113 fn. 30
Javits, Jacob, 153
Jenner, William, 47
Jenkins, Roy, 46 fn. 43, 46 fn. 45
Jenkins, Walter, 93
Jennings, Peter, 169
Jensen, Adolph, 139 fn. 8
Jensen, Richard, 106, 106 fn. 6, 140
    fn. 14
Johnson, Lyndon B., 4, 52–3, 57–60, 57
    fn. 21, 58 fn. 24, 60 fn. 30, 90–2,
    92 fn. 59, 92 fn. 61, 94–8, 95
    fn. 67–8, 98 fn. 75–6, 121–7, 121
    fn. 50, 122 fn. 52–3, 122 fn. 55,
    123 fn. 57–8, 124 fn. 61, 145,
    185–6, 188
Jones, Charles O., 26–8, 26 fn. 16, 27
    fn. 22, 183–4, 183 fn. 33, 184 fn. 37
Jones, James, 93, 93 fn. 63, 125, 125
    fn. 67
Jones, Jerry, 148 fn. 4, 154, 154 fn. 21–2
Jorden, William J., 124
Joslin, Theodore G., 38, 38 fn. 11, 40
    fn. 20, 107, 109–10, 110 fn. 20

Kaiser, Robert G., 170 fn. 76
Kalb, Marvin, 9, 9 fn. 20
Kamarck, Elaine, 190 fn. 55
Karl, Barry, 19 fn. 49
Katzenbach, Nicholas deB., 93–4
Kaufman, Ron, 175 fn. 6, 177 fn. 15
Kearns Goodwin, Doris, 42 fn. 26, 42
    fn. 28, 57, 57 fn. 22–3, 90 fn. 52
Keating, Kenneth, 51 fn. 54
Kelley, Jr., Stanley, 113 fn. 32, 145 fn. 29
Kellogg, Paul, 139, 139 fn. 9
Kemp, Jack, 174
Kennedy, Edward, 68 fn. 67
Kennedy, John F., 4, 6, 8–9, 52–7, 56
    fn. 15–16, 72, 74, 87–9, 96,
    117–20, 117 fn. 41–2, 134, 145,
    159
Kennedy, Robert, 88–9, 88 fn. 47, 89
    fn. 49

Kent, Frank R., 18 fn. 42–4
Kernell, Samuel, 26–8, 26 fn. 19, 71
Key, Jr., V. O., 1, 10 fn. 23, 111 fn. 23, 136 fn. 1
Kiaer, A. N., 139 fn. 8
King, John W., 96
Kissinger, Henry, 69
Klingon, Alfred, 169 fn. 73
Klink, Ron, 184
Knowland, William, 47
Knox, Victor, 49–50
Kraft, John, 90, 90 fn. 54
Kraft, Tim, 158
Kramer, Orin, 157, 157 fn. 27
Krim, Arthur, 90–1, 93, 93 fn. 62, 98
Kruskal, William, 139 fn. 8
Kutler, Stanley I., 61, 61 fn. 37–8, 62 fn. 40

LaCerra, Charles, 79
Lacey, William, 168 fn. 68
Lambert, Gerard, 3 fn. 10, 8, 43, 45, 142
Lambie Jr., James M., 115, 115 fn. 38
Landon, Alfred, 13–14, 141
Lanouette, William J., 170 fn. 76
Langer, William, 47
Larmon, Sigurd "Sig," 84–5, 114, 114 fn. 33–5, 120, 186
Larsen, Lawrence H., 46–7, 47 fn. 47
Lasswell, Harold D., 16 fn. 35
Latham, Henry J., 51 fn. 54
Latta, M. C., 108
Lawrence, David, 80 fn. 21, 110
Laxalt, Paul, 165
Lazarsfeld, Paul, 60, 89, 137, 137 fn. 2–3, 150
Leach, William, 106 fn. 7
Lee, Richard C., 4, 86
Lehman, Herbert H., 11, 11 fn. 24, 12 fn. 28
Lengle, James I., 8 fn. 17
Leonard, Thomas C., 30 fn. 32
LePlay, Frederic, 137
Levy, Fabian, 141 fn. 17
Lewinsky, Monica, 179
Lichenstein, Chuck, 151, 151 fn. 11

Liebovich, Louis W., 119–21, 119 fn. 46, 120 fn. 48, 121 fn. 50
Likert, Rensis, 20, 143
Lincoln, Abraham, 108, 158
Lindsay, John, 68 fn. 67
Lippmann, Walter, 7, 7 fn. 16, 80, 80 fn. 21, 110, 121
Lipscomb, Glenard, 49–50
Lipset, Seymour Martin, 106 fn. 6
Literary Digest poll, the, 13–14, 20, 45, 77, 84, 141
Lowell, A. Lawrence, 28–9, 29 fn. 26–8
Lowi, Theodore J., 26, 26 fn. 17, 28 fn. 25, 171, 171 fn. 77, 184, 184 fn. 37
Lubin, Isador, 43
Luce, Henry, 110
Lynch, Dottie, 161
Lyons, Gene M., 19 fn. 49

MacArthur, Douglas, 85, 112
MacGregor, Clark, 63 fn. 48
Mack, Norman, 79
MacKensie, Donald A., 137 fn. 4
MacLafferty, James, 38–40, 38 fn. 13, 39 fn. 14–19, 75 fn. 3, 110, 175
Macmahon, Arthur W., 37 fn. 7
Magruder, Jeb, 63–4, 64 fn. 52, 101, 101 fn. 86, 104 fn. 93, 127 fn. 73, 129
Mankiewicz, Herman J., 106 fn. 9
Market Opinion Research (MOR), 101–3, 148, 152–4, 152 fn. 13, 174–6
Marsh, 149
Martin, Charles H., 80
Martin, Joseph, 47
Martin, Thomas, 51 fn. 54
Martinez, Bob, 176
Matalin, Mary, 174, 174 fn. 4, 178
Mayhew, David R., 5, 5 fn. 12
McCarthy, Eugene, 96–7, 125
McCarthy, Joseph, 47
McClure, Frederick, 177
McCooey, John H., 80
McCoy, Donald R., 107 fn. 13
McDaniel, Rod, 168–9, 168 fn. 69, 169 fn. 70
McDonald, Robert, 7 fn. 14, 188 fn. 50

McEwan, Bob, 177
McFarlane, Bud, 163, 165
McGovern-Fraser Commission, 9, 151
McGovern, George, 68 fn. 67, 102, 129, 156
McGregor, J. Harry, 51 fn. 54
McIntyre, Thomas J., 96
McKee, Joseph V., 80 fn. 21
McKinley, William, 36, 108
McKinney, Cynthia, 184
Mead, Emily, 175 fn. 5
Meese, Edwin, 163 fn. 50, 167 fn. 65, 171
Michels, Robert, 29 fn. 28
Michelson, Charles, 18, 107
Milchuk, Jr., Leonard C., 187, 187 fn. 47
Milkis, Sidney M., 24, 29, 29 fn. 31, 41 fn. 24, 79 fn. 18, 81, 81 fn. 23, 182, 182 fn. 29–30, 189 fn. 53
Miller, Warren, 60, 60 fn. 33
Miller, William E., 94
Mills, Stephen, 89 fn. 48
Mitchell, John, 101, 101 fn. 86
Mitovsky, Warren J., 143 fn. 25
Mohr, Charles, 161 fn. 41
Mondale, Walter, 159, 159 fn. 34
Moore, David, 148, 156, 159 fn. 32, 160 fn. 37, 162 fn. 43, 163 fn. 47
Moore, Frank, 160, 160 fn. 36
Morgan, Jerry, 115–16
Morris, Dick, 179, 179 fn. 22–3, 181, 181 fn. 27
Morton, Rogers, 99
Mosteller, Frederick, 138 fn. 8
Moyers, Bill, 60, 60 fn. 31, 93, 95 fn. 68, 122, 122 fn. 51, 122 fn. 53
Murchison, Carl, 140 fn. 14
Murphy, Morgan F., 184
Muskie, Edmund, 68, 68 fn. 67, 125, 130
Myers, Walter, 79 fn. 20

NAACP, 37
Nader, Ralph, 68
Napolitan, Joseph, 567, 56 fn. 18, 57 fn. 20, 95–6, 96 fn. 69

Nathan, Richard P., 1
Neustadt, Richard, 25–6, 26 fn. 16, 28, 41, 41 fn. 23
Neyman, Jerzy, 139 fn. 89
Niemi, Richard G., 41 fn. 25
Niles, David, 112
Nisbet, Robert, 21
Nixon, Richard M., 1–4, 2 fn. 3, 52–3, 61–4, 61 fn. 37–8, 62 fn. 39, 67–9, 71–3, 85–7, 94, 97–103, 100 fn. 81, 118, 123, 127–34, 131 fn. 86, 147, 172, 178, 181, 185–8
Noelle-Neumann, Elisabeth, 185 fn. 42
Nofzinger, Lyn, 64, 104 fn. 93, 127–8
Norris, George, 82 fn. 27
North, Oliver, 168–9
Novak, Robert D., 2 fn. 5, 65, 65 fn. 54

Oberschall, Anthony, 137–8, 138 fn. 5
O'Brien, Lawrence, 53
Office of Public Opinion Research (OPOR), 8; *see also* Cantril, Hadley
Ogburn, William, 19
Oglesby, M. B., 165
Olvany, George, 80
O'Neill, Harry, 63, 63 fn. 45, 67–71, 67 fn. 64, 69 fn. 71, 102, 102 fn. 90, 129, 132, 181
Opinion Research Corporation (ORC), 63, 66–72, 67 fn. 63, 68 fn. 67, 100–3, 115, 124 fn. 61, 129–33, 132 fn. 94, 159, 187
Ostertag, Harold, 51 fn. 54

Panzer, Fred, 60 fn. 31, 93–4, 93 fn. 63–4, 94 fn. 65, 122–6, 122 fn. 55, 123 fn. 58, 124 fn. 60
Parker, John Jay, 37
Parten, Mildred, 138 fn. 5
Pastore, John O., 125
Patterson, Thomas E., 8, 8 fn. 18
Payne, Stanley, 14
Pearson, Karl, 137 fn. 4, 139 fn. 8
Pell, Claiborne, 98 fn. 75, 125
Penn, Mark, 181 fn. 27
Perkins, Francis, 42
Perry, James M., 180 fn. 25

Persons, Wilton B. "Jerry," 115–16, 116 fn. 39
Petersmeyer, C. Gregg, 175 fn. 6, 177
Peterson, Mark A., 27–8, 27 fn. 21, 28 fn. 23–4, 184, 184 fn. 36–7
Pfeiffer, Lloyd, 78
Phillips, Kevin, 133
Pierce, William, 7 fn. 16
Pinkerton, Jim, 175 fn. 5
Poindexter, John, 163, 168–9, 168 fn. 69, 169 fn. 70
Politz Research Inc., 47–8, 48 fn. 48
Pollard, James E., 107 fn. 11, 107 fn. 13
Polsby, Nelson W., 8 fn. 17, 189 fn. 53
Pool, Ithiel de Sola, 88–9, 89 fn. 48, 89 fn. 50, 100
Popkin, Samuel, 89, 89 fn. 48, 89 fn. 50, 159, 188 fn. 48
Porter, Roger, 175, 175 fn. 6
Powell, Jody, 157, 158–9, 158 fn. 28, 159 fn. 31, 171
President's Advisory Council on Executive Organization (PACEO), 61
President's Research Committee (PRC), 19, 19 fn. 50
Price, Ray, 187 fn. 46
Pringle, Henry F., 82 fn. 27, 106 fn. 9

Quayle, Dan, 174, 177, 177 fn. 11
Quayle, Oliver, 4, 52, 58–60, 60 fn. 29–30, 69, 72, 91–8, 93 fn. 62, 95 fn. 68, 98 fn. 75, 100, 186
Quayle polls, 58, 124–6, 124 fn. 62
Quetelet, Adolphe, 137
Quigley, James M., 51

Rabb, Maxwell, 113, 113 fn. 31
Rae, Saul Forbes, 12–13, 12 fn. 27–8, 22 fn. 6, 142, 142 fn. 20
Rafshoon, Gerald, 160, 160 fn. 35
Ranney, John C., 15, 15 fn. 33
Raskob, John J., 81
Rather, Dan, 169
Rayburn, Sam, 80 fn. 21
Read, Benjamin H., 124 fn. 62

Reagan, Ronald, 5, 33, 101, 123, 148 fn. 4, 152–3, 152 fn. 16, 155, 159, 161–72, 163 fn. 50, 166 fn. 58, 168 fn. 66–7, 178, 181, 185
Redmon, Hayes, 60, 60 fn. 31, 122–4, 122 fn. 54, 123 fn. 56, 124 fn. 62
Reed, Thomas, 99, 99 fn. 79
Reedy, George E., 105 fn. 2, 121 fn. 50
Reeves, Richard, 53–4, 53 fn. 8, 54 fn. 11
Regan, Donald, 163–4, 163 fn. 50–1, 164 fn. 52–3, 166, 166 fn. 62, 169 fn. 73, 171
Republican National Committee (RNC), 2–4, 18, 37, 39, 50, 63–4, 68, 73–5, 77–8, 85, 99–100, 99 fn. 78, 103, 104 fn. 93, 111, 113, 113 fn. 32, 145, 148 fn. 4, 151, 155, 163, 163 fn. 50, 164–6, 166 fn. 62, 174–5, 178 fn. 19
Research Committee on Social Trends; *see* President's Research Committee (PRC)
Ribicoff, Abraham, 125
Richards, Dick, 165–6
Rizzo, Frank, 132
Robertson, Pat, 174
Robinson, Claude, 114–15, 114 fn. 33
Robinson, Daniel J., 142–3, 143 fn. 23
Robinson, Joe, 37, 80
Rockefeller, Nelson, 93–4, 123, 152–3
Rodham Clinton, Hillary, 171
Rogers, Ed, 175, 175 fn. 6, 178
Rogers, Lindsay, 14, 144, 144 fn. 26
Rogich, Sig, 176–7
Roll, Charles W., 23 fn. 12
Rollins, Ed, 165
Romano, Lois, 170 fn. 76
Romney, George, 97
Roosevelt, Eleanor, 43
Roosevelt, Franklin D., 1, 3, 8, 13–14, 20, 29–30, 36, 40–2, 42 fn. 26, 44–5, 59, 71, 75, 75 fn. 2, 78–84, 80 fn. 21, 81 fn. 23, 83 fn. 31, 105, 110–11, 111 fn. 25, 120, 141–5, 158, 171–2, 182, 186
Roosevelt, Theodore, 35, 108

Roper, Elmo, 13, 13 fn. 29, 15, 115, 129
Roper organization, 129, 159
Roper polls, 129, 133
Rosenberg, Anna, 42
Rosenman, Samuel, 43, 45, 80, 111–12, 111 fn. 25, 112 fn. 27
Rumsfeld, Donald, 131, 148 fn. 4
Russell, Richard, 57–8
Ryan, Jr., Frederick, 165–6, 166 fn. 58

Sabato, Larry J., 9, 9 fn. 21, 33 fn. 38
Safire, William, 127, 127 fn. 74
Salinger, Pierre, 52, 52 fn. 2, 119
Sanford, Terry, 92
Savage, Sean J., 79–82, 79 fn. 18, 80 fn. 21, 81 fn. 22–3, 82 fn. 26
Sawyer, Ernest Walker, 77, 77 fn. 11
Schambra, William, 24 fn. 12
Scheele, Harry Z., 47 fn. 47
Schier, Steven F., 186 fn. 44
Schlesinger, Jr., Arthur M., 6 fn. 13, 35–6, 35 fn. 3, 36 fn. 3, 53–4, 53 fn. 3, 53 fn. 6–7, 54 fn. 9–10, 79 fn. 18
Schoen, Doug, 181 fn. 27
Schudson, Michael, 30, 30 fn. 32
Schwartz, Jordan A., 36, 36 fn. 5
Scrivner, Erret P., 51 fn. 54
Sears, John, 162
Shafer, Byron E., 8 fn. 17
Shafritz, 76 fn. 7
Shapiro, Robert Y., 2 fn. 4, 23, 43, 43 fn. 33, 62 fn. 41–2, 67 fn. 62, 69 fn. 70, 95 fn. 68, 96 fn. 68, 99 fn. 78, 100 fn. 83
Shaw, George Bernard, 17
Shaw, Thomas C., 27 fn. 21
Sheatsley, Paul B., 143 fn. 25
Shull, Steven A., 24, 24 fn. 14, 27 fn. 2
Sidey, Hugh, 54 fn. 12
Simmons, Steve, 161, 161 fn. 40
Simpson, Jane, 160 fn. 38
Simulmatics Corporation, the, 88–9, 89 fn. 48, 159
Sindlinger polls, 134, 154
Skinner, Sam, 176–7, 177 fn. 11
Slayden, James L., 80

Slight, Fred, 153 fn. 19
Smathers, George, 55
Smith, Al, 76, 78–80
Smith, Judy, 175 fn. 6
Smith, Sally Bedell, 150 fn. 9
Smith, Steve, 89 fn. 49
Smith, Tom W., 106, 106 fn. 4–5
Solarz, Stephen, 7 fn. 15
Sorensen, Theodore C. "Ted," 4, 53, 53 fn. 4, 118, 118 fn. 43, 121, 121 fn. 49
Sparrow, Caroll Mason, 15, 15 fn. 34
Speakes, Larry, 165
Spencer, Stuart, 149, 153 fn. 19, 165
Stanley, Harold W., 41 fn. 25
Stanton, Frank, 150
State Department polls, 3, 7, 8, 32, 48–9, 72, 145
Steele, Richard W., 24 fn. 12, 111, 111 fn. 24
Steeper, Fred, 176, 179
Stephanopoulos, George, 180, 180 fn. 24
Stevenson, Adlai, 96, 113
Stockman, David, 167, 167 fn. 64
Strachan, Gordon, 62 fn. 41, 63 fn. 47, 100 fn. 82, 129–33, 129 fn. 81, 130 fn. 84, 131 fn. 88, 131 fn. 90, 132 fn. 93, 133 fn. 96
Strauss, Lewis, 77–8
Strother, E. French, 19
Sudman, Seymour, 24 fn. 12
Sugrue, Thomas, 81 fn. 24, 82 fn. 25
Sununu, John, 175, 175 fn. 7, 178
Sussman, Leila, 3 fn. 10, 41 fn. 22, 144 fn. 27
Svahn, Jack, 165

Taft, William Howard, 35, 85
Tammany Hall, 79–80, 143
Taylor, Zachary, 35, 61
Teeter, Robert, 33, 101–3, 103 fn. 91, 133, 133 fn. 96, 148–53, 148 fn. 4–5, 149 fn. 6, 150 fn. 8–9, 152 fn. 14, 152 fn. 16, 155, 168, 174–7, 176 fn. 9, 179–81
Thaxton, Dick, 151, 151 fn. 11

Thomas, Dennis, 165
Thomas, Norman, 78
Thompson, Dorothy, 110
Thompson, William O., 19 fn. 47
Thomson, Jr., Meldrim, 152
Thurber, James A., 27 fn. 21
Thurmond, Strom, 178
Thurstone, L. L., 140, 140 fn. 11–13
Timmons, William E., 65, 65 fn. 55–6
Tocqueville, Alexis de, 22, 22 fn. 5
Tolley, Howard, 141, 141 fn. 16
Tönnies, Ferdinand, 137
Trefousse, Hans L., 108 fn. 15
Truman, David B., 10–11, 10 fn. 22
Truman, Harry S., 1, 3, 14, 45–6, 45
    fn. 41–2, 46 fn. 43–4, 72–3, 72
    fn. 75, 73 fn. 75, 112–13, 135,
    144–5, 145 fn. 28
Tucker, Ray, 83 fn. 28
Tulis, Jeffrey K., 24–5, 25 fn. 15
Tully, Grace, 45
Tydings, Millard, 80
Tye, Larry, 106 fn. 7, 107 fn. 10

United States Department of
    Agriculture (USDA), 20
Updike, Fritz S., 116, 116 fn. 40
Uslaner, Eric M., 184, 184 fn. 35

Van Riper, Paul P., 82 fn. 27
Van Shumway, Devan L., 132, 187
    fn. 47
Vardaman, James K., 80

Wagner, Robert F., 125
Walker, Frank C., 81, 81 fn. 23
Walker, Jimmy, 80
Wallace, George, 92, 97
Ward, Lester Frank, 138–9, 138 fn. 6
Warshaw, Shirley Anne, 47 fn. 47
Watson, James E., 37, 37 fn. 6
Watson, W. Marvin, 60 fn. 31, 92, 92
    fn. 59, 92 fn. 61, 93–5, 93 fn. 64,
    94 fn. 65, 95 fn. 67–8, 98 fn. 76,

122–5, 122 fn. 54, 123 fn. 57, 124
    fn. 59–61, 125 fn. 67, 175
Wattenberg, Marvin P., 8 fn. 17
Wayne, Stephen J., 6 fn. 13, 24, 24
    fn. 14, 41 fn. 24, 189 fn. 53
Weber, Max, 137
Weed, Clyde P., 19 fn. 51
West, Valerie, 189 fn. 52
Westmoreland, William C., 97
Whitaker, John D., 69–70, 70 fn. 73,
    132–33, 133 fn. 95
White, Graham J., 110, 110 fn. 22
White, William Allen, 108 fn. 17
Wilbur, Cressy L., 139 fn. 8
Wilbur, Ray, 77
Wilcox, Walter F., 141 fn. 17
Will, George F., 33 fn. 39
Williams, Bruce, 150 fn. 9
Willkie, Wendell, 110, 112 fn. 27
Wilson, Bob, 51 fn. 54
Wilson, James Q., 10 fn. 23
Wilson, Pete, 176
Wilson, Woodrow, 16–17, 20, 30–1,
    31 fn. 34, 38 fn. 12, 79–80, 108,
    158
Wirthlin, Richard, 5, 33, 148 fn. 4, 159,
    161–70, 162 fn. 44–6, 163 fn. 50,
    165, 165 fn. 54, 165 fn. 56–7, 167
    fn. 63–5, 168 fn. 66, 169 fn. 72,
    170 fn. 74, 174, 177, 180–1
Woodward, Bob, 180, 180 fn. 24
Wray, James, 174 fn. 4, 175 fn. 6, 177
Wright, Carroll D., 139 fn. 8

Yankelovich, Daniel, 153, 159, 185, 185
    fn. 42
Yeutter, Clayton, 176, 176 fn. 9
Yorty, Sam, 132
Young and Rubicam, 84, 114, 114
    fn. 33, 143

Zeigler, Harmon, 10 fn. 23
Zobrist, Benedict K., 72 fn. 75, 73 fn. 75